Amy Raphael has been writing about music for the past ten years, moving on from fanzines to join the staff of *The FACE* in 1990. After a year as Features Editor on *ELLE* magazine, she is now a freelance journalist working for the *NME*, the *Guardian*, the *Observer*, *The FACE* and *ELLE*.

Grrrls

Grrrls

Viva Rock Divas

Amy Raphael
Foreword by Deborah Harry

St. Martin's Griffin
New York

Photos: Courtney Love © Kevin Cummins; Echobelly © Kevin Cummins; Sonya Aurora Madan and Debbie Smith © Tom Sheehan; Björk © Kevin Cummins; Veruca Salt © Philin Phlash; The Raincoats © Martin Goodacre; Kim Gordon © Kevin Cummins; Sister George © MAIR; Huggy Bear © Liane Hentscher; Belly © Steve Double; Pam Hogg © Derek Ridgers; Kristin Hersh © Steve Double; Liz Phair © S. Apicella Hitchcock.

Lyrics: Courtney Love: Mother May I Music BMI; Sonya Aurora Madan: Fauve Music; Björk: Polygram Music; Nina Gordon and Louise Post: Copyright Control; Gina Birch: Rough Trade Publishing; Kim Gordon: Just Send All The Money Directly To Us Music; Ellyott Dragon: Copyright Control; Huggy Bear: Wiiija Music; Tanya Donelly: Copyright Control; Pam Hogg: Copyright Control; Kristin Hersh: Copyright Control; Liz Phair: Copyright Control.

Extract from *Meeting the Madwoman* by Linda Schierse Leonard courtesy Bantam, USA, 1994.

ISBN 0-312-14109-2

First published in Great Britain under the title *Nevermind the Bullocks: Women Rewrite Rock* by Virago Press

First St. Martin's Griffin Edition: February 1996
10 9 8 7 6 5 4 3 2 1

To Mum and Dad, for taking me to the first
Glastonbury when I was three.

In memory of my much-missed Dad.

We read so as not to feel alone.

Contents

foreword

The phone rings. Not the one across the hall but the one right next to my bed. I had to answer or be annoyed by the ringing or push the answer button. I answered.

'Hi Pam (Pam Hogg, Scottish singer-songwriter, fashion designer). How are things in the dark doll house?'

'Very good, thanks,' she says. 'I'm calling about a women-in-rock book I'm gonna be in by Amy Raphael. She wants to call you about possibly writing an intro for it.'

'Oh no, not another one,' I said.

As you can see, I agreed to do the foreword. Soon after, I received my Fed Ex package with chapters from the book and a cassette tape with selections of music by some of the female artists. I then went ahead and started reading what the girls had to say for themselves. Each life so different and similar and intriguing. And me obliged by experience to read on and into their stories and revelations and struggles. Fascinated and disgusted by similarities I've overlooked or overcome in my own stupid struggle. Don't struggle.

Ride on, rock bitches, ride on rock. I can't be responsible for this, can I? I mean I took some bits out and put some back in and maybe I didn't work hard enough . . . but I did. And so we go round to ride on rock bitches, give it back, take it out, need it some more and press on. The beautiful twins. The matching fats that suckle desire. Those two sisters who make you lose your concentration and then chase the chaser. Perpetual motion, the alchemical dream machine. And the physicist's proof – the event of the universe. Ride on rock.

My intro. My my. Here they come, the wet ones, the pools and swamps and warm currents of insistence – cold currents of existence. Surf's up. Tide is high. Out at night for your insight. Shake your tambourine. Shake your moneymaker. Shake it, baby, shake it. I like listening to and seeing live bands and going to the movies. Other than that, it's my business what I do with my time life. Let's keep some bits of mystery in our souls. Men are not women. Viva la Diva. All that image stuff becomes marketing as soon as you sign a deal. You are in showbiz; live with it or fight it, it's just not gonna go away. Once you accent a few fundamentals, you're home free. Enjoy the biz.

Enjoy yourselves.

Enjoy the book.

Deborah Harry
New York, July 1994

introduction

S exism killed her. Everybody wanted this sexy chick who sang really sexy and had a lot of energy . . . and people kept saying one of the things about her was that she was just 'one of the guys' . . . that's a real sexist bullshit trip, 'cause that was fuckin' her head around. Smart, y'know? But she got fucked around.

(Country Joe McDonald, who was romantically involved with Janis Joplin for a short time in San Francisco, talking to Deborah Landau in *Janis Joplin: Her Life and Times*)

I know it's a sexist thing to say, but women aren't as good at making music as men – like they're not as good as men at football. A girl in a dress with a guitar looks weird. Like a dog riding a bicycle. Very odd. Hard to get past it. It's okay on the radio, because you can't see them. Chrissie Hynde is an exception. Very few of them are exceptions. And if they don't have a guitar, they become the dumb girl in front of the band. I'm not a great fan of girls in pop.

(Julie Burchill, journalist and author, in response to a request to be interviewed for *Never Mind the Bollocks*, London, 2 May 1994)

I don't think about myself as being specifically a woman as far as music goes . . . My vagina doesn't come into my guitar playing or singing . . . It makes me inarticulate and angry when I have to discuss my job in terms of my gender . . . I want to get to the point where women aren't treated like . . . giraffes. It shouldn't even be interesting at this point that I'm female and I do this. It shouldn't even be a point of contention. But it is. In a way, it undermines everything Chrissie Hynde and Patti Smith did, because it isn't any easier for us.

(Tanya Donelly, singer-songwriter-guitarist with Belly, during an interview for *Never Mind the Bollocks*, Boston, 10 April 1994)

The future of rock belongs to women.

(Kurt Cobain, a few months before his suicide in April 1994)

IF BONO HAD BEEN a woman, what would have happened to U2?

Think of how many female musicians fit the description of 'rampant sex god with a huge ego' (a term U2's guitarist The Edge once jokily used to describe Bono) and, chances are, Madonna is the only one who will spring to mind. Being a rampant sex god with a huge ego and a habit of crotch-grabbing has been the key to success for countless generations of male musicians, but taking the cock out of rock doesn't emasculate it. Cock-free rock has as much balls as cock rock, it can be as sexual and as sleazy. Witness Janis Joplin in the sixties, Deborah Harry in the seventies, Madonna in the eighties or Courtney Love in the nineties.

Women have always influenced rock as the passive recipients of pop 'lurve' in lyrics – the Beatles went for simple but effective titles such as 'From Me To You' and 'I Want To Hold Your Hand'; the Rolling Stones were more sexually explicit, with singles like 'Lets Spend the Night Together'. It would, however, be a mistake to think that women performing in rock is a *new* phenomenon, although the mass media tends to treat them as such each time a new batch comes of age.

G R R R L S

Most of the women in this book arrived in the 1990s but all of them have been empowered, to varying degrees, by the enduring legacy of punk. From Courtney Love to Tanya Donelly, Huggy Bear to Echobelly, Björk to Liz Phair, punk has been the most pervasive influence, on both music and attitude. Some of the role models are obvious – Patti Smith, Deborah Harry and Chrissie Hynde – others less so – The Slits, The Raincoats, Sonic Youth's Kim Gordon.

Pre-punk, women had a much more defined and confined role in pop music. In the early 1960s, the so-called 'girl group sound' exploded in America – the Shangri-Las, the Ronettes, the Shirelles (the first all-female group to top the American charts with 'Will You Love Me Tomorrow', in 1961) and, of course, the Supremes, who had twelve number one records in America. With their love lost, love longed for, love left behind lyrics, these teenage girl groups were, on the face of it, successful. But behind them were male song-writers, managers and Svengalis who shaped and engineered their careers and who dropped them as soon as they passed their sell-by date.

In the mid-1960s, 'girl singers' began to appear in the UK: Marianne Faithfull, Dusty Springfield, Sandie Shaw, Lulu, Cilla Black. They enjoyed more independence and longevity than most of their predecessors, but they still had the male business establishment behind them. It was, by way of example, the Rolling Stones' man-ager Andrew Loog Oldham who gave Marianne Faithfull her first record contract and who co-wrote her first single, 'As Tears Go By', with Mick Jagger and Keith Richards. He has been quoted as saying: 'I saw an angel with big tits and signed her.'

By the end of the 1960s and into the 1970s, singer-songwriters like Joni Mitchell, Janis Joplin and Carly Simon were looking to their own lyric-writing skills. Unfortunately, this didn't mean they weren't manipulated. Joplin complained of journalists quizzing her more on her lifestyle than her blues singing, sarcastically asserting: 'Maybe my audiences can enjoy my music more if they think I'm destroying myself.' The contradictions of Joplin's life were encapsu-lated in her attempts to be 'one of the lads' and, simultaneously, a 'sexy chick'. Her short life in the music business remains one of the saddest to date. She died from a heroin overdose in 1970, aged 27. If Joplin was portrayed as the rock whore with a heart of gold, the altogether more 'sensitive' Joni Mitchell was incensed when her record company sold her as '99% virgin' in the advert for her 1968 début album *Songs to a Seagull.*

IF EVERY GENERATION OF female musicians includes women who in some way act as martyrs for the next, Joplin and Mitchell's experiences weren't all in vain. Seven years after the '99% virgin' advert, Patti Smith had a female manager and appeared on the front of her début album, *Horses,* looking like a tomboy in jeans, white T-shirt and tie. Smith arrived at a time when there was a drought of women rockers. As well as an unorthodox singer-songwriter, she was also a writer and poet with influences ranging from William Burroughs and Rimbaud to Sam Shepard.

In *Idle Worship* (1994), Chris Roberts's collection of stars' thoughts on being fans, Kristin Hersh empathises with and eulogises Patti Smith:

She *was* a first. I saw her as so physical . . . I guess she was just walking around being a woman. She was so jumpy and screechy, and always going from confused/delicate to confused/screaming . . . If there is a parallel between us, maybe it's that she was dismissed as 'crazy' in the man-world of rock . . . She made an incredible mark, with dignity. She's a landmark, all by herself.

Smith came out of the fledgling New York art rock scene in the mid 1970s and found herself immediately 'at home' in the new freedom offered by the decade's latest cultural phenomenon. Punk.

In 1976 punk happened in the UK. It was anti-hippie protest music fuelled by speed rather than marijuana. Its DIY ethos and anti-muso attitude allowed women a much-needed space to perform without fear of ridicule. Punk was about everyone starting from scratch and throwing away traditional rock clichés. It was lo-fi, chaotic, basic. It was exciting, unpredictable and anti-fashion.

Punk made female performers truly visible and gave them a unique forum for the first time. As Gillian G. Gaar affirms in *She's a Rebel: The History of Women in Rock & Roll* (1992): 'If feminism had inspired women to create their own opportunities, punk offered women a specific realm in which to create their own opportunities as musicians.' Using fanzines as a grassroots way of communicating, and developing small, independent labels to sign new acts, punk avoided relying on the mainstream music press and the anonymous suits running big, corporate record labels. It lasted barely two years (1976–78), but its impact on white urban teenagers was dramatic.

Poly Styrene, who fronted X-Ray Spex, presented the world with punk's first female, asexual, aggressive persona. The Slits – with Ari Up on vocals, Viv Albertine on guitar, Palmolive on drums and Tessa Pollitt on bass – made an amateurish, cacophonous sound that was, for many, the real spirit of punk. They ran into trouble with the cover of their first album, *Cut*, caking their bodies in mud and appearing naked except for loincloths. *They* said they were parodying the received images of women; for others they were simply pandering to the traditional marketing of female musicians. But, initially at least, punk operated in a hazily defined area where playing with these sorts of contradictions was part and parcel of the whole cultural dynamic. The Raincoats, who were joined by Palmolive when she left the Slits in 1978, also addressed the issue of gender and image, while making more conceptual music than many of their peers. (Two decades later they were cited as a prime influence by the likes of Kurt Cobain and Courtney Love.)

The only real punk band fronted by a woman to stay around for any length of time was Siouxsie and the Banshees. Siouxsie Sioux, like many women who joined punk bands, was a fan first – before getting up on stage and singing like a demented wild child, she was a devout Sex Pistols groupie. Siouxsie became a significant cult icon for female adolescents, responsible for launching a nation of lookalikes who dressed in black, stuck their hair up and out, painted black triangles round their eyes, didn't smile very often – and who later, at the start of the 1980s, denied being Goths.

IF SIOUXSIE WAS THE first punk rock woman to be widely cloned, Deborah (then Debbie) Harry was punk's first female pin-up. Her sexy image appealed to girls as well as boys; she was the first female musician that girls could admit to having a crush on. She exuded something previously associated only with male musicians: cool.

Harry's band, Blondie, initially fused the chaos of punk with girl group melodies, and their 1978 album *Parallel Lines* became – along with the Sex Pistols' *Never Mind the Bollocks* (1977) – an album every self-respecting punk record collector had to own.

Born in Miami, Florida in 1945, Deborah Harry moved to New York 'to be a performer'. She was briefly in a band called Wind in the Willows and (infamously) a *Playboy* bunny waitress. She bleached her hair for the first time in 1959 and the look stuck. With Blondie, which she formed with sometime lover Chris Stein in 1974, Harry became Andy Warhol's favourite pop star and a tough, glamorous singer-songwriter – sassy, sexy and in control. Her barbed lyrics were sweetened with a saccharin smile. On 'Heart of Glass' she sang: 'Once had a love and it was a gas, soon turned out to be a pain in the ass.'

Yet, despite her hand in the band's songwriting ('One Way or Another', 'Call Me', 'Dreaming', amongst others), Harry remained a pin-up. The game she played was a dangerous one: flaunting her high cheekbones, slightly tarty image and traditional, up-front sex appeal. At times it appeared to the music business that she was little more than a package perfectly suited to the male fantasy factor. She certainly used her glamour to sell her product, but when her record company used her sexuality to encourage the fantasy factor, she decided it was time to regain control. The promotional poster for her début single, 'Rip Her to Shreds', featured the provocative line: 'Wouldn't You Like to Rip Her To Shreds?' 'I was *furious* when I saw that fuckin' ad! I told them not to fuckin' put it out anymore – and. they didn't,' she told Tony Parsons in a *New Musical Express* interview in the summer of 1978.

In an extensive profile of Deborah Harry in the August 1993 issue of *Q*, Tom Hibbert writes: 'She was The New Monroe, The Punk Garbo. Now there are 488 Rock Femmes. Madonna is one of them, Wendy James is another and it's all *her* fault. Debbie Harry changed the face of civilisation and popular culture and music and everything else as we know it.' Harry is a role model *extraordinaire*. She has influenced everyone from Madonna – 'she [Madonna] mentioned I was important to her. That's very satisfying, but a check would be better' – to 1994's media-created, retro-punky New Wave Of New Wave. Justine Frischmann of Elastica told *SKY* magazine:

'*Parallel Lines* was the first record I really got into. The thing that was so appealing about her look was that she was both soft and hard. Her look is part angel, part prostitute. It comes across in her singing, too.'

Like Harry, Chrissie Hynde is a true rock 'n' roll survivor (she has also been called a female Keith Richards). She was born in Ohio but was inspired by British punk and, like Harry, Hynde was a late developer. She was already in her late twenties when the Pretenders' self-titled début album hit the top of the American album charts in 1980. Hynde's music and look was defined by a distinctly pre-punk aesthetic. And, like Harry, she had had to wait for punk to come along for her music to be taken seriously. In her chapter in this book, Veruca Salt's Nina Gordon talks about hearing the Pretenders for the first time as a teenager:

I remember being completely floored. I heard that voice, saw the picture of Chrissie Hynde with her guitar, and I learned that she had written all the songs . . . I had this moment of feeling really daunted and alienated – how did she know how to do that? But from then on there was an increased awareness that maybe this was something I could do one day.

WHILE PUNK WAS HAPPENING in 1976, an arguably more dramatic development occurred. The appearance of the 12-inch single format had an impact that is still being felt today. While British punks were burning with boredom, this extended vinyl format was firing up the transatlantic disco scene, where everyone from Evelyn 'Champagne' King to the Bee Gees was taking advantage of the six- or seven-minute dance mix. A decade later, Madonna became the ultimate 1980s disco pop superstar – a female icon whose whole creative dynamic was forged in the New York disco scene.

Madonna Louise Veronica Ciccone's timing was immaculate. She was born in 1958 in Michigan (a year before Deborah Harry became a bottle blonde) and moved to New York aged 20, hoping to become a dancer. In 1983 the dancer-turned-singer crossed over from clubs to the mainstream with the funky pop single 'Holiday'. The following year 'Borderline' and 'Lucky Star' were both Top 10 hits in the States. The album, *Like a Virgin*, went on to sell over nine million copies. Madonna's success has been phenomenal. Besides being christened with the perfect first name and being an expert in the field of three-minute pop songs, Madonna is the ultimate female rock chameleon, teasing and seducing the world with a dozen different looks while ultimately being remembered for one persona – the vulnerable vamp with naked, blonde ambition.

Madonna's ascendancy coincided with the emergence of Music Television (MTV). By the mid-1980s MTV was redefining the marketing of music. It made *image* of central importance. In America, where cable television is as common as burger joints, MTV lulled a generation into thinking that the Look was as crucial as the song. In theory it was a great way of transmitting music from around the world – across the world. Soon, however, bands were giving in to the pressure to be 'MTV-friendly', to make expensive videos which seduced the eye, often at the expense of the ear. In MTV-land, a video is ultimately more important than the song it is promoting.

MTV means dressing up; contriving an image if the Look is lacking. For women, the predominant image that endures in the mainstream pop media is that of the 'rock chick' or the 'babe'. Female musicians are still made to feel they have to pay great attention to the traditional concept of 'beauty' or 'sexiness', the standards of which are defined by the male record industry and media. In this business, the likes of L7, or even Kim Gordon, are viewed as extremists, and indeed their music and attitude are informed by contempt for the marketing values and image-making ploys of the mainstream.

MTV arrived at the start of a decade during which, as Naomi Wolf writes in *The Beauty Myth* (1990): 'eating disorders rose exponentially and cosmetic surgery became the fastest growing medical speciality'. Wolf continues to argue that women in the 1990s may be 'worse off than their unliberated grandmothers' in terms of 'how they feel about themselves physically' and argues that 'We are in the midst of a violent backlash against feminism that uses images of female beauty as a political weapon against women's advancement.'

No one used video with such ease as Madonna. She told *The FACE* in 1990: 'I've always wanted to be a movie star. Even when I was a child, I behaved as if I were one.' From the early days, Madonna realised that you had to have something more than a good record to sell and it didn't matter if your voice wasn't great. She packaged her image and presented herself to the world. Following Deborah Harry's lead, but taking the concept further than any other female artist before her, Madonna sold herself almost exclusively in terms of her sexuality. She went from a slightly pudgy, dull blonde doing a dodgy dance routine to a streamlined, pumped-up platinum blonde control freak with pointed bras and balls aplenty. And she knew *exactly* what she wanted. As Helen Fielding wrote in the *Sunday Times* in 1992, she is 'the belligerent beauty, the sexy warrior, vulnerable yet confident in her exposure, ironic, laughing at herself, playing with her power'.

Today, academics debate Madonna's place in 1990s post-feminist feminism. One of her biggest champions, Camille Paglia, American 'academic and commentator on gender', gushed in 1992's *Sex, Art, and American Culture*:

Playing with the outlaw personae of prostitute and dominatrix, Madonna has made a major contribution to the history of women today. She has rejoined and healed the split halves of women: Mary, the Blessed Virgin and holy mother, and Mary Magdalene, the harlot . . . Madonna is the true feminist . . . [she] has taught young women to be fully female and sexual while still exercising control over their lives.

LOVE OR LOATHE HER, this 'true feminist' has forced everyone from the record industry to the record-buying public to reconsider the role of female pop artists. Madonna's appearance in the mid-1980s coincided with a decade that redefined feminism – while some women camped out at Greenham Common, others invested in suits with shoulder-pads and became shameless power players. Some called this apparent loss of direction 'post-feminism'. Susan Faludi and others use the term 'backlash'.

In *Backlash: The Undeclared War Against Women* (1992), Faludi, an American journalist and Pulitzer Prize winner, argues that over the last ten years an 'undeclared war' has been waged against women's rights. She says that women remain unhappy not because feminism has let them down, but because it hasn't gone far enough. Faludi's arguments are convincing – she shuns any thought of a conspiracy theory and uses specific details from history to show patterns of backlashes against women. She draws from popular culture to illustrate her points, showing how Hollywood played upon the New Right's idea of single women having sacrificed 'fulfilling' family values for 'hollow' independence.

'Feminism' has become a word with which many women and men are uncomfortable. It has become the new 'F' word and, in media terms, it simply isn't sexy. The 'New Wave' of feminists – notably the all-American team of Naomi Wolf, Katie Roiphe and Camille Paglia – have tried, to differing degrees, to make feminism sexy again. Yet, despite widespread media attention, it's hard to know how many young people have actually gone out to buy their books and even harder to gauge how many have actually read them.

During an interview for *The FACE* at the end of 1992, Courtney Love drew my attention to Paglia – 'I'm beginning to see why she's dangerous as well as original'. Describing Faludi's *Backlash*, Love said: 'It made me cry, it's so fuckin' true. You must read it; it's your responsibility as a journalist.' Love was impressed by the book's anger and historical perspective. Faludi points out, for example, how Rebecca West's 1913 observation still holds true: 'I myself have never been able to find out precisely what feminism is: I only know that people call me a feminist whenever I express sentiments that differentiate me from a doormat.'

For young women (and men) in the 1990s who are still striving for change and for parity between the sexes, feminism has become a more mischievous and slippery concept, part of a wider cultural agenda that questions all received notions of gender and politics and what constitutes popular culture. Madonna's inexorable ascendancy has helped shape this agenda, but it has also posed more questions than it has answered and has proved problematical for many feminists, who have noted how her ideas of 'control' and personal empowerment blur so easily into egocentrism and self-obsession.

In *Black Looks: Race and Representation* (1992), American feminist theorist and cultural critic bell hooks deconstructs Madonna as a cultural icon. Examining Madonna's commodification of black culture for purely 'selfish' reasons, hooks writes: 'the image Madonna most exploits is that of the quintessential "white girl". To maintain that image she must always position herself as an outsider in relation to black culture. It is that position of outsider that enables her to colonize and appropriate black experience for her own ends even as she attempts to mask her acts of racist aggression as affirmation.' hooks criticises Madonna for failing to 'articulate the cultural debt she owes black females', pointing out that Madonna's career was made easier by predecessors like Tina Turner, whose 'public image of aggressive sexual agency . . . belied the degree to which she was sexually abused and exploited privately'. (The question of race and gender politics in, for instance, rap music, raises enough questions for a whole other book.)

IF, DESPITE HER CONTRADICTIONS, Madonna remains the most potent mainstream female role model of the 1990s, many of the women in this book drew their inspiration from more contemporary female – and male – sources. Kurt Cobain recognised the feminine in himself more than any other nineties male rock artist and was, for many of us, a more subversive role model than Camille Paglia could ever hope to be. Equally important for most of the female musicians in this book, he identified the nihilistic apathy of a generation when, in 1991, he wrote about the futility of life in 'Smells Like Teen Spirit' ('I'm worse at what I do best and for this gift I feel blessed, I found it hard, it was hard to find, oh well, whatever, nevermind').

When Cobain put a gun to his head in April 1994, he became the ultimate symbol of angst for today's disaffected twentynothings. Cobain's suicide was reported and pondered upon in the UK; in the US it not only created hysteria, but was also seen as an acknowledgement of the hopelessness that had infected a whole stratum of 'youth culture'. With a single bullet, Cobain defined a generation – making the extent of their alienation apparent in a way that even his most intense songs had not.

That generation championed grunge. And grunge empowered women in much the same way as punk had. As the Slits and the Raincoats had done in the late 1970s, American bands like Hole, L7 and Babes in Toyland got up on stage and created a defiant noise that said: fuck anyone who doesn't like it. Direct sexual confrontation became the norm. L7 are all-female speed metalheads with an ear for an anthemic pop song: they pulled their pants down while performing live on *The Word*, and shamelessly threw a used tampon into the audience at Reading Festival. Their song 'Fast & Frightening' paid tribute to someone with 'so much clit she don't need balls'.

For a brief moment at least, gender roles were reversed. Kurt Cobain reacted against the hegemony of the male rock image by trying on his wife Courtney Love's dresses, by clumsily applying her eyeliner and lipstick to soften his angular face and give it a sinister prettiness. Cobain was the neurotic boy outsider who tended to be quiet, unassuming, even passive, while Love, initially dismissed by the media as someone who should be 'seen and not heard', voiced her opinion at every opportunity. He played the introvert Angry Young Man to her confessional Angry Young Woman. Love challenges all the received wisdoms about women in rock by taking on the verbal (and occasionally physical) aggressive male role, and alternating it with the female tradition of confessing. She often finds herself in trouble for motor-mouthing about heroin (ab)use and bitching about fellow musicians.

Grunge in part substituted cock rock with frock rock. In Nirvana's wake, male American punk rock bands like the Afghan Whigs and the Lemonheads relinquished macho roles and were photographed on music and style magazine covers wearing dresses. Frock rock worked for male musicians; for women punk rockers image was more problematic. Courtney Love and Babes in Toyland frontwoman Kat Bjelland are great on/off friends who wear babydoll, lacy, ripped dresses; slashes of loud red lipstick; platinum hair with roots visible. Love describes her dress code as the 'Kinderwhore' look. It's child-woman, a fucked-up Lolita, innocence disturbed. It is a potent, on-the-edge image which toys with vulnerability and power. It hints, disturbingly, at a 'rape victim' look, although both women would insist that they are ultimately in control. Courtney and Kat's image is less about artifice than, say, Madonna's; they are wilfully expressing themselves by whatever means necessary. Their music – fast, furious, emotional and full of frustration – says much more than this image provocation can.

The antithesis of Kinderwhore is the sassy tomboy image, and although female musicians who shun traditional glamour are not always accepted by the press and music business, the Patti Smith tomgirl look works for some. Justine Frischmann of Elastica wears Doc Martens half-way up her calfs, spray-on blue jeans and T-shirts. Her face is androgynous; she could pass for a pretty boy. Frischmann gets away with it – her individual look is the hook. Echobelly's Sonya Aurora Madan was called a 'dyke' (albeit jokingly) by a male friend as soon as she cut off her long, fluffy locks. When making the video for 'Insomniac', she planned to wear a wig and sparkly, glammy dress for the opening few shots, but the director and record company were so taken by her 'in drag' instead of her usual 'tomboy' clothes they used the image throughout.

If women like Courtney Love and Sonya Aurora Madan are reconstructing fem-rock, there is a group of female musicians who hijacked the punk manifesto and took it a step further. In the early 1990s, some female musicians were so frustrated with the lack of space reserved for them in the music press and mainstream media, and with the misogyny which often lurked in pieces that were written, that they stopped stomping around their suburban bedrooms and unleashed their anger on the world. They simply felt their voices *had* to be heard, their stories chronicled.

RIOT GRRRL WAS PUNK with politics – it didn't matter how badly you played so long as you had something to say. It began in America in 1991, in Olympia, Washington on the West Coast and in Washington, DC on the East. It caught on in the UK in 1992, and bands like Huggy Bear, Linus, Mambo Taxi, Skinned Teen and the Voodoo Queens looked to their American counterparts (Bikini Kill, 7 Year Bitch, Bratmobile, Heavens To Betsy, God Is My Co-Pilot) for inspiration, using fanzines and meetings to communicate.

The 'zines were cheap to make and buy; the meetings were reminiscent of the feminist consciousness-raising meetings of the 1970s. Riot Grrrls could identify with each other at gigs; at the end of 1992 and into 1993, women (sorry, grrrls) would write words like 'slut' on their exposed tummies in black pen or kohl, pre-empting what some men (and women) might think of them. They claimed that their acts of sexual confrontation challenged sexism and simultaneously questioned what was 'politically correct'.

Like the original punks, Riot Grrrls were bored. They were particularly bored with the status quo and wanted to be involved in something creative which they could completely control. They rioted against the parameters of boy rock (punk and indie); they drew attention to the overwhelming maleness of the moshers and stagedivers who dominate the front of the stage at gigs. Courtney Love was into Riot Grrrl for a while and accepted her role as icon until she got irritated by their 'brattiness'. Once brutally fingered by rowdy beerboys while crowd-surfing during a Hole gig at a north London venue, Love quickly accepted an invitation to play at one of Huggy Bear's women-only evenings.

The on-off collaboration – a gig at west London's Subterania – was only partly successful. There were rumours before Huggy Bear played that some Riot Grrrls had been distraught at the presence of male bouncers and had quizzed each of them about his sexual history. It felt odd standing in a room full of women, with some moshing by the stage and others calmly watching. Other single-gender nights at smaller venues created a more intimate atmosphere for female bonding.

Gigs were important; 'zines were vital. Riot Grrrls felt able to open up, to write honestly about their experiences of being in a band, of sex and sexual harassment, of personal politics and revolution. In a 1993 issue of *Leeds & Bradford Riot Grrrls* (contactable via a PO box to 'avoid harassment'), one writer asks:

Why is there something odd and unnatural about women who want to try to do something with their lives? Why are women such fucking appendages in everything? . . . Feminism isn't over, it didn't fail, but something new must happen – Riot Grrrl . . . Next time a guy feels your ass, patronises you, slags off your body – generally treats you like shit – forget the moral highground, forget he's been instilled with patriarchy and is a victim too, forget rationale and debate. Just deck the bastard.

It is easy to criticise Riot Grrrl for being a movement with a manifesto aimed at a limited group of women and even fewer men. It is easy to say that they sometimes refused to explain themselves and in doing so alienated people; that they suffered from taking themselves far too seriously and were way too pretentious. It's easy to scorn the punk fuck-you-we-can-do-it-without-your-patronising-help posturing when you've forgotten what it's like to be a teenager. And anyway, Riot Grrrl was extremist because, like punk before it, it *had* to be.

But Riot Grrrl – which I have talked about in the past tense not because the trend has passed but because as a movement it has moved on and fragmented – undeniably gave women more confidence to make music. It also created vital space for Queercore. A lesbian and gay movement which evolved from hardcore punk 'homocore' in the US, Queercore arrived in the UK in 1993, when bands like Sister George formed to offer gay indie/punk rockers an alternative to the Pet Shop Boys and Erasure.

RIOT GRRRL'S NATURAL SUCCESSOR should have been Queercore, but instead a media-inspired antidote arrived: the New Wave of New Wave. What the original New Wave was to punk, NWONW was to Riot Grrrl. If Riot Grrrl interrogated everyone's sexual politics, the NWONW – or New Rage/New Art Riot/New Brit pop/New anything – took people's apathy firmly in its grubby hands. Suddenly born-again all-male punk bands were sticking two fingers up at Tory rule, spitting on political atrophy and reclaiming rock from the Americans. S*M*A*S*H wrote a song called 'Kill Somebody', calling for the execution of John Major. Bands like Blur and Oasis made Brit pop hip again.

The music press gave the NWONW space in its pages because it was *their* invention. 'I've heard that it was concocted by a handful of male journalists during a pub discussion,' says Echobelly's Sonya Aurora Madan. 'We were initially roped into this celebration of macho posturing because I wore a T-shirt with a Union Jack on it. (It's called irony, boys.)'

NWONW didn't challenge in the way Riot Grrrl did. It didn't threaten guys; it catered instead to lad fantasy, to slam dancing, po-going and gobbing. Riot Grrrl may have paved the way – compare the anger, the passion, the political/musical mix – but NWONW was its less prissy, more traditional and familiar older brother.

Although it is slowly changing, the music industry is still male dominated and the music press has some way to go in its championing of female musicians. *NME* may be proud of its handful of teenage grrrl journalists, but from the start of 1985 until the end of April 1994, less than 15 per cent of its weekly covers featured female musicians or even mixed-gender bands. Of its 95 issues up to and including August 1994, *Q* magazine has put 13 female musicians on its cover; of its 50 issues, the younger music magazine *Select* could only find three such covers. Two of those (Elastica's Justine Frischmann dressed as a guy with a cigar in her mouth and Björk) are from 1994.

It is, of course, difficult to tell how these statistics relate directly to the number of good female musicians around. But when women *are* given space, it still tends towards the tokenistic. The May 1994 issue of *Q* had three female musicians on its cover. Björk, Polly Harvey and Tori Amos looked demure in white outfits under the headline: 'Hips. Tits. Lips. Power.' (The slogan was one of the catchphrases of summer 1992, when you couldn't move at the English rock festivals for T-shirts advertising Silverfish's song). They seemed a bizarre combination: Björk as the quirky torch singer/dance diva with the Voice; Polly Harvey as a dark, publicity-shy curiosity who could be a Patti Smith for the nineties; Tori Amos as the daffy, kooky character with Kate Bush vocals. They have little in common musically; what linked them, for the purposes of the story, was not so much their bolshie independence as their feminine 'eccentricity'.

In the feature, Tori Amos says: 'We have tits. We have three holes. That's what we have in common.' True. But she was overlooking something as unmistakable as shared body bits; what really links female musicians is not the fact that they play the same instruments, make similar-sounding music or share a passion for certain bands. From Courtney Love to Kylie Minogue, they have shared the same experience. They are not men.

THE FACT IS THAT gender will remain an issue as long as the music industry is dominated by men, and female musicians remain an exception to the rule. While the infrastructure of rock is essentially male, from A&R to producers, from record company executives to journalists, female musicians may be successful – but in a man's world and on a man's terms.

The reality is that the world of rock music intimidates women on the most basic levels and this has held true from generation to generation. Most female wannabe musicians are intimidated by the idea of even walking into a guitar shop, never mind sitting down and trying out the latest model surrounded by a bunch of music lads. Women are seen as being somehow estranged from their instruments – how can they hump their own gear around if they are physically inferior? And in the late 1960s, Karen Carpenter not only suffered from anorexia (the disease wasn't recognised for a long time because she was thought to be taking a 'healthy interest' in her image) but was prevented from taking her drums on the road because they hid her fragile form on stage.

What's so disquieting about rock is that it presents (and prides itself) upon its liberalism, its daring and its ability to be subversive. Yet its liberalism hides a deep-rooted conservatism. If rock clichés traditionally number sex and drugs, there's a third equally important image: the groupie. The pervading picture of women's role in rock is as groupie and muse. Women approach music in a different way to men; they are more interested in personalities and their interest in music often centres around being a fan and idolising male bands, while the boys bond and train-spot, believing that a precise knowledge of a band's or artist's history leads to an infinitely greater enjoyment of their product.

While female groupies have been elevated to mythic status, they are also a reality. More so than in any other artistic genre, boys who are sad, spotty and socially handicapped can get up on stage and become sex gods who are suddenly wanted for illicit sex. Pamela Des Barres came clean in her book *I'm with the Band: Confessions of a Groupie*: 'I wanted to express myself creatively. I didn't know what to do or how to do it. The nearest thing was to be with the people who created the music.'

If a fundamental male fantasy is to be surrounded by screaming, adoring women, women don't tend to need their ego massaged in such a way. Compare Jimi Hendrix's take on groupiedom – 'I only remember a city by its chicks' – to Janis Joplin's: 'On stage, I make love to 25,000 different people, then I go home alone.' Female musicians just don't get the same buzz from the idea of sexually conquering each member of their audience. In a feature on male groupies in the *Guardian* in December 1993, journalist Miranda Sawyer has a simple answer: 'Men make crap groupies.' She continues by suggesting that perhaps it's a fundamental difference between the sexes that is the problem: 'It's not that women don't get the offers, it's that when they do, they are the wrong kind for women.'

WHEN WOMEN DO ATTAIN positions of power in the music business, they respond in varying ways. Not all are interested in promoting their gender or 'fighting the cause'. In a recent *New York Times* interview Chrissie Hynde bristled at the idea of being a feminist role model: 'I never said I'm a feminist, and I don't have any answers. As long as we're getting paid and can vote, what's the problem? . . . I work with men because they're single-minded, straightforward and they can rock. Most women can't.' But for every Chrissie Hynde, there's someone who, through experience, has changed their viewpoint. Guitar pop 'babe' Juliana Hatfield has, on several occasions, flippantly said that women are biologically ill-equipped to play guitar – but after Veruca Salt opened for her in Chicago in February 1994, Hatfield stood in front of the 2,000-capacity audience and said: 'I know I went on record saying women can't play guitar. Veruca Salt proved me wrong.'

Sarah Cracknell, singer with quirky popsters Saint Etienne, told *Vox* in April 1994 how bored she had become with being labelled a blonde bimbo who doesn't 'even sing on the records': 'People within the music business, particularly the older men, don't take me seriously . . . If I'd lost as much weight as people had told me, I'd be completely emaciated. It's such an insult to my intelligence that they think I believe what they're saying.' American feminist rock critic Ann Powers points out that because pop music is about fantasy, it is also about objectification. Everything within the pop arena is made into a symbol which can be consumed – women are no exception.

Powers, who is part of the New York-based coalition Strong Women in Music (SWIM), feels that this time round, women-in-rock are here to stay:

What I see happening in America is women getting more involved at all levels of the music business – as video makers, managers, record company executives. Bands like Luscious Jackson have a female manager and Tamra Davis has directed their videos. The road informs one of the most basic elements of what rock 'n' roll is – the ongoing party from hotel room to hotel room with the groupies in tow. With bands like The Breeders constantly touring, we're seeing these seismic shifts – the boys' club that is the road is being undermined, and that will have a knock-on effect.

Along with some record business friends, Powers formed SWIM to help create a vital all-female support system within the music industry. 'As much as I want to get excited,' she says, 'I don't want to declare a revolution. Not just yet.'

Change is slow. During a women-in-music seminar in New York in April 1994, Monica Lynch, president of US rap label Tommy Boy, recounted one of her first experiences of a record company event. 'I could hear some guy asking about me: "Who's that fat-assed redhead? Is she here to suck dick?"' From an extreme example to everyday occurrences, attitudes remain essentially conservative. Diane Graham, one of two female MDs running major record labels in the UK (the other being Warner's Moira Bellas), has been in the music business for twenty-two years. She has, she says, witnessed a more positive approach to women in management and 'more senior positions' over the past ten years. 'But it is still, as in all industries, an old boys' club.'

WHAT LINKS THE WOMEN in *Grrrls* is their comparative success in dealing with the male-dominated infrastructure. This book is about women rising to the challenge, getting a record deal, filling gigs and selling records without selling out. It is about her-story rather than just his. It is about letting female musicians speak for themselves, in a monologue which they were able to see and discuss at every stage – because usually an interview is always conducted on the journalist/writer's terms. *Grrrls* is about giving a new generation of female musicians space because their voices need to be heard. It is an aural testament to their single-mindedness and determination as well as an insight into their music. It is about recognising that the price of silence is too high.

Rock needs to be constantly challenged by women. It is essential that it doesn't ever become antiseptic, clinical and fake, and implode. With the 1990s hot-pot of sexual confusion, women are able to construct their own images in a way they couldn't before. Men are still in control of the music industry, but women are becoming more acceptable. Real progress will come only when women have power at all levels of the record industry; when Arista's MD Diane Graham is no longer in a minority; when more women are writing about music; when female musicians are no longer a cyclical phenomenon; and when Madonna doesn't have to fight for 'male' power and independence to be 'free' to establish herself in her field.

The women in *Grrrls* are very conscious of pinpointing problems and doing something about them. They may not all consider themselves feminists, but they are all startlingly aware of their gender. They may want to be seen as musicians first and women second, but they accept that there is some way to go – and talking helps. As each generation becomes more media-wise, female musicians are fighting for a space that is getting bigger all the time. Most are aware of the sex = rock equation (try and sell music without it) but each of them deals with it increasingly on her own terms.

As is obvious from their monologues, these women are not in the habit of whinging, but of taking control of their careers. U2's Bono Vox said in 1992: 'Being a rock star is like having a sex change. People stare at you, follow you down the street shouting comments, they hustle you and touch you up. I now know what it must feel like to be a woman.' Try empathising with a female musician, Mr Vox – can you imagine what it's like to be sexually assaulted at a gig à la Courtney Love?

The musicians in this book may still be babes in boyland, but they're learning fast. They've looked to and taken from the female musicians before them and are now doing what they can to make it easier for the next generations of women-in-rock. Women in dresses playing guitars don't look like 'dogs riding bicycles' (not from where I'm standing), nor should they be seen as awkward or peculiar, 'like giraffes'. Janis Joplin was one 'strong, groovy woman'. She will never be alone. Grrrls: Viva Rock Divas – women are rewriting rock. Hips. Tits. Lips. Power.

Amy Raphael
London, August 1994

Grrrls

Courtney Love in her London hotel room, 27 August 1994

courtney love

Hole

I want to be the girl with the most cake
I love him so much it just turns to hate
I fake it so real I am beyond fake
Some day you will ache like I ache.

('Doll Parts' from *Live Through This*)

We just happen to piss off all different kinds of people; especially Courtney does. She's a totally threatening woman. She 's totally smart and she's threatening. She speaks her mind, she tells too much of the truth. Even liberals don't like smart women. (Kurt Cobain, New York, July 1993)

The Underworld, London, November 1992: Hole play one of their early British dates. They are punky, loud, shambolic. Courtney Love is a brash, spunky American in a babydoll dress screeching songs from Hole's year-old début album, *Pretty on the Inside*. When she crowd-surfs, rowdy beerboys pull and tear at her clothes and, she says afterwards, physically assault her.

London, December 1992: Hole are to release a new single, 'My Beautiful Son'. I request an interview with the band for *The FACE*. One dull afternoon, there is a call at work. It's for me. It's Courtney Love. She's in a hotel room in Seattle. I think of the woman crowd-surfing at the Underworld. Of the woman who used to earn a living as a stripper and who appeared in Alex Cox's spaghetti western spoof, *Straight to Hell*. Of the woman whose husband is Kurt Cobain. Whose child is rumoured to be addicted to methadone as a result of her parents' drug habits. Of the recent *Vanity Fair* investigative piece which made on-heroin-during-pregnancy allegations and which published a photo of Courtney heavy with child, cigarette airbrushed from raised hand. Of the fury which erupted from the Love–Cobain household in the feature's wake.

On the phone, Courtney is guarded, fragile and anxious but not aggressive. She wants to know why I want to talk to her. Am I a Nirvana fan? She quizzes me on feminism, scolds me for not having read Susan Faludi's *Backlash*. She explains how she's just about to change hair colour because she doesn't want to be considered a blonde bimbo. We talk about music – Echo and the Bunnymen, Joy Division, PJ Harvey, Led Zeppelin. She is quick as a razor, opinionated, funny.

Christmas Week, 1992: I fly to Seattle. Each night, Courtney is going to turn up at this grungey gig, that Sub Pop party. Sometimes Kurt is going to be there too. Patty Schemel (Hole's drummer) and Eric Erlandson (guitarist) entertain me. Courtney finally turns up on the third night. Her charisma swaggers before her. Her lips are a wide slash of red lipstick, her hair an orangey colour. She is tired (from looking after their baby daughter Frances Bean) but charming. She has insisted from the start that this will be an interview with the band, but once she starts talking there are few gaps to fill. Conversation swings from frustration – 'I'm famous for really crass, gross things. People think I live in a different dimension, so I can't hear them talking about me. I hear that I wasn't wearing underwear, that blood was running down my leg' – to music – 'When you hear a great song, it touches your life. It affects you, it's like a scent, it reminds you of something. You fuck to it, you feel blue to it, you feel great to it.'

Courtney explains how she took the name for her band from Euripedes' *Medea*. There's a line in the classic Greek play where Medea talks of a hole piercing through her soul. With a shrug, Courtney says simply: 'It's about the abyss that's inside.'

Watching Courtney talk is like being party to an intimate and almost out-of-control floor show. At one point she grabs a copy of Janis Joplin's biography and says: 'This is the sort of biography I want written about me. I'll read out the first sentence, OK: "I was stark naked, stoned out of my mind on heroin and the girl lying between my legs was Janis Joplin" . . . why has no one written the same about Jim Morrison?' Seconds later she seizes a copy of a magazine with

Madonna on the cover, shrieks – 'Oh my God! She could have been our boss!' – and explains how Madonna phoned her up to talk about signing Hole to her label, Maverick. Courtney turned down the offer; Madonna later claimed she'd never heard of her.

The day after *The FACE* interview, Courtney dyes her hair blonde again. 'I don't see why I have to take on a frumpy housewife look just because I'm married and have a baby.'

London, January 1993: A fax arrives at *The FACE*. Courtney is grateful not to have been stitched up in the feature. She writes about being 'so freaked out by the evil media' and about how, during a recent MTV interview, Madonna 'spoke freely of pursuing my band'. She adds, 'I am just glad she cleared up the fact that I exist and my reality is apparently on terra firma somewhere.'

The Grand, London, July 1993: Hole surprise the curious, voyeuristic members of the audience by playing a passionate, inspired set. The shambolic punk has developed into a hard-edged, punky pop which is disturbingly poignant. Courtney's lyrics are shamelessly vitriolic, her nasal vocals fuelled by anger. Tonight she is confident and in control, happily heckling with the audience between songs.

New York, July 1993: Nirvana do press for their new album, *In Utero*. At a photo shoot for *The FACE*, Kurt and Courtney goof around with Frances Bean. Kurt, dressed up in a Tigger suit, pushes his daughter round the studio in her pram. She gurgles and smiles gleefully. Courtney puts on an Echo and the Bunnymen CD and eulogises the band she occasionally used to watch rehearse when she lived in Liverpool and hung out with the likes of Julian Cope. When she lies down on a sofa to read a book, Kurt charges at her with the pram, stops short, bends over and kisses her. They are apparently oblivious to the people around them.

London, 8 April 1994: I am supposed to be interviewing Courtney in Wolverhampton for this book, but the Hole tour has been cancelled due to Kurt OD-ing in Rome the previous month. A friend phones in the early evening. He's just heard a news flash on the radio: an unidentified white male in his twenties has been found in Kurt Cobain and Courtney Love's Seattle home, a single bullet wound to the head. Rock 'n' roll suicide.

Reading Festival, 26 August 1994: Hole play their first British

3

gig since Kurt's death. It is also bass player Melissa Auf Der Maur's first appearance; she replaces the late Kristen Pfaff, who died a few months earlier of a heroin overdose. The audience is a strange, edgy mix of fans and voyeurs. The event is surreal: the audience chant her name and finally Courtney stumbles on stage, shining in a gold dress. Most of the audience squint and stare and have probably never heard Hole's startling second album, *Live Through This*; some sing along to the words very seriously. She is trying not to be, but Courtney is on the defensive big time: 'Oh yeah, I'm so goddam brave,' she scowls. 'Let's just pretend it didn't happen. Oh yeah.' And, almost under her breath: 'This is like a hobby for me.'

Backstage, Courtney rumours escalate throughout the day.

A London hotel, 27 August 1994: Courtney hasn't talked on tape for over five months. She says she's not in the mood and never will be. After two hours of non-stop chat, she apologises for being 'such a bad interview today' and continues: 'I'm not used to it. I kind of like life without interviews. I mean really, you wouldn't think so.' Her conversation veers from animated anecdotes to music to expressions of anger and loss. She is hard, controlling, emotional, occasionally tearful. She lights one cigarette from another. Room service bring her packets of Silk Cut, cups of tea and scones. Her suite is littered with books, magazines, clothes, jewellery, photos, cigarette butts.

Her (female) tour manager sits in for part of the interview to stop Courtney talking about Kurt. If Courtney didn't talk about Kurt, she'd almost be autistic. She tells of her shopping trip the previous day; she bought some T-shirts from Sign of the Times, including one with 'My Drug Shame' written on it. 'I can't wear it,' she says, laughing. 'It wouldn't even be ironic on me.' She explains how 'Teenage Whore', a furious, thrashing song on *Pretty on the Inside*, has a line in it – 'I'd give good money not to be ignored' – which she now sings as 'just to be ignored'.

She slams the press for their constant interference and their 'fucking up on the wrong person'. She surprises me with her knowledge. 'Virago are publishing the English edition of this book? Isn't that actual word Roman for "insane bitch"? A madwoman. A shrew. Shakespeare used it a lot and then in different versions, it was edited out.'

At 2.30 a.m. a photographer arrives to do a photo shoot of the band for the record company. Courtney changes into a gym skirt, laddered stockings and high heels. She applies a slash of red lipstick and turns on the charisma.

London, 11 September 1994: The phone rings at midday. It's four in the morning Seattle time. Hole have just finished a mini-tour supporting Nine Inch Nails and Courtney wants to talk about the experience. (The gigs are reported in the press as being a chaotic, distressing and emotionally-charged spectacle.) She feels our first interview was a little frivolous. She talks with disgust about 'old school' backstage attitudes on the Nine Inch Nails tour, about groupies and blow-jobs, roadies and backstage passes. We discuss how, in the past, artists and writers had muses and now rock bands have groupies. She reads from a pop psychology book she has just bought called *Meeting the Madwoman* which includes a chapter on 'the Muse'.

Her mood is intense and joky, serious and self-analytical. At one point she says: 'Imagine if you didn't have to worry about money or men. In the same week. Pretty goddam nice week. The kind of week you'd want to go: "Hey, you know what? I'm gonna stay in bed and do drugs, I'm so damn happy. I don't have to entertain this man, I don't have to be his muse. He's mine, I'm his. The end."' She worries about Frances needing a father, talks about how she cut herself when she was institutionalised for three years ('I would just bleed a little and the blood would let something go') then says, 'You put me in a movie with De Niro – fuck you, I'll win an Oscar.'

Three hours later, it's light in Seattle. Courtney sounds weary and her voice is fading. Unwilling to sleep – she has nightmares which Valium can't stop – Courtney says she's going to get a cup of tea and maybe write a little. She'll go to bed a little later, she promises. She has to get her head together for the local show Hole are playing that night.

Interview One: London, 27 August 1994
I always wanted to play music. When I was little, little, I wanted to be a movie star. I can't explain it. I'm not gonna try and rationalise it. When Tatum O'Neal got an Oscar, I was fucking jealous.

Should've been me! I was trying out for voiceovers; I did all the radio jingle ads in the north-west. I was nine. I noticed anyone in my nine-year-old age group who was getting press – which was like Tatum O'Neal and some Europop winner. It was really important. I know! I'm pathetic! I was precocious, then it turned into pretentious, so . . . to be honest, I was practically autistic. I didn't talk. Till I met fags. Then when I met fags, I got really bitchy and made up for it in spades. I got loud. They got me in touch with my inner-bitch. Thank God.

It was basic Freudian narcissism to put a picture of myself on the back of *Live Through This* – I did it because we were living in a teepee and I always smelt like piss and that day I went to school wearing sandals. My ride down the hippie lane was pretty gross. That's who I was and if you look carefully at that picture, it looks like someone who doesn't talk a lot. It's kind of a clue to who I am. Cryptic. It is also atypical of the rock star image: look at me as a child, my inner child, I'm trying to fix it. Ha.

I didn't leave home, I was put in a boarding-school at six/seven. I was basically in boarding-school or communal living from that time on. I didn't have a home – and I don't care. I'm not like: 'Poor me.' I don't care.

Reading Festival wasn't weird for me, not at all. The vibe to me was like goddess worship on the verge of stoning me to death. It was really freaky and I ignored it. I don't know what they wanted, but I ignored it. In fact, I know what they wanted, and I wasn't gonna give them that. It was strange. Usually every fucking time I play, someone says, 'Show us your tits.' I was so ready for them, I had on my Wonderbra. We just went and played a tight set. The British doing their goddess rites. Hey, aren't you the ones that used to paint yourself blue? I carry too much Irish/Welsh blood to put up with British mass hysteria – I know how to calm it down. Stiff upper fucking lip.

What did they want? A fucking cover of 'Teen Spirit'? I don't understand it. Were people curious as a freak thing? I think they wanted me to cry, and I won't.

My personal world is my personal world. It's like when I wrote *Live Through This*, I didn't write one word that had anything to do with my inner life. That's my gift, my gimmick. If it's not worth anything, then it's fine. I'm not gonna acknowledge the press in a song. Kurt wrote 'Rape Me' (on *In Utero*) about fame, but it had many other dimensions and secrets; he was such a mason. Such a Rosicrucian. He loved Umberto Eco, as I do.

I grew up on your propaganda. I lived in Liverpool, I understand it. I read *Jackie* most of my life. I used to have to hide my English magazines behind the couch so Kurt didn't read them. He didn't understand that most kids don't really believe it. A propaganda press is always a sign of impending fascism. You've had a fucking Tory government for seventeen years, which makes Republicans look liberal. We don't have people walking around in America wanting socialism in the numbers you do over here now, and there's a reason for it. But to give in to that demand would be admitting that you have Third-World-sized problems – the British would rather sit there with their British pride, have their water poisoned and die.

You asked if Reading was chic or weird? In relation to Kurt's death and my band, what was it like? Were people like: 'How could she play?' Some thought I was brave? That's spooky. It's not right. I wouldn't reference Kurt in front of 30,000 people here, whereas in America I would. It's warmer. I'm used to them, they're used to me. I like them. They respect me. It's not like they're looking for holes. You have to be watertight with the British to stop them from being invasive – 'fuck her, she's not brave at all, blah blah'. 'She's cold.' 'How can you play five months after your husband died?' Well – and I hate to sound so reactionary, 'cause I really don't go round saying 'sexist' at everything and a lot of things apply to boys just as much to me – but I really truly believe that's sexist. That music is a lot more vital when you're a boy. But if it wasn't for my baby and my music, I wouldn't even be here on this planet. I'd be gone – fast. I know it's a cheap way out to some people, but life is in essence vile.

I played spontaneously at a Lemonheads show and it felt really good . . . being in a band is not really my hobby. All the stuff that has happened to me, if I were a guy, it wouldn't be seen like: 'Oh, she's back to her hobby now.' It keeps me here, essentially. So, I got this really great vibe off the audience at the Lemonheads show and it was a real cathartic experience. My presence seemed to help them

COURTNEY LOVE

and it helped me. I could just walk on stage and say, 'Hi, I'm here and I'm healthy, wearing lipstick.' They get something out of it, swallow something that's stuck in their throat, whatever it is.

I have written for ever. Written poetry in every coffee diner in America. In 1987 my diaries changed and they got cool. Before then they were really humiliating and embarrassing, but I can't bring myself to burn them. I'd fixate on someone, write about him for about six months and project all this beatific passion on to him. Then I'd go off him and be repulsed by the very idea. And I'd still have to look at these repulsive images which could be applicable to any one of a number of guys.

I always have a lot of lyrics to choose from. Although for the most part Ian McCulloch's lyrics were great, and I learned a *lot* from watching him perform, the same lyrics were more upstanding when I was younger than they are now. Some are really dumb now, 'cause they're so ambiguous. Whereas someone like Leonard Cohen or even Bob Dylan – on a song like 'Desolation Row' Dylan's really inspired and he thinks he's the shit, which is kinda what it takes. Then you look at Led Zeppelin – and I even loved Robert Plant – and the lyrics all suck, back to front, but the music is so great, it's like Beethoven rock, really bad elfin Dungeons & Dragons lyrics. Even a genius song like 'Tangerine' is . . . if you think of a medieval maiden smoking pot . . . snore. Also AC/DC, Fleetwood Mac (the California version) are some perverted fetish of mine. I love Aerosmith and the first Cheap Trick record. And the Go-Go's and Big Black. I had a big 4AD fetish in 1983 . . . the Cocteau Twins' 'Pearly Dew Drops'.

I load up on lyrics and I always pretended that there's this divine spark, but it doesn't always work like that. I'm lazy; an idea will come, I won't write it down and then I forget it. Kurt was really quick – he was the quickest of anyone I've gone out with, which I think is why I married him. We'd both get it at the same time and we'd have screaming matches. Ultimately, *In Utero* [Nirvana's third and final album] is my title, but I could never have used it, it wouldn't have been ironic at all, I'd have been stoned for it. He was really a great songwriter as well as a number of other huge plusses.

One of the most famous things that happens to everyone is

mis-hearing a lyric. That's where some of the best stuff comes from. I used to think that Kurt was singing 'heavy metal, heavy metal' in 'Teen Spirit' – which I thought was genius, this great song where he was making fun of heavy metal. Everyone had a different theory about what he was singing in the end. I thought it was really cool. I get inspired to write songs from just watching TV and reading. I have so many books – 10,000 of them. I buy so many. Downstairs [at home] I've got every fucking anthology advice book there is, every poetry book that comes out – plagiarised like hell! Come across a good idea and paraphrase it. I try to make it more thematic – I have some discipline.

Songs need to have a secret, cryptic, thematic thing about them, otherwise they are just messy and all over the place. I listened to the songs that Justine [Frischmann, of Elastica] gave me and you can tell that it's a real British product, because they're very much about *something in particular*. The more loose, older Ian McCulloch lyrics are not about anything; the first PIL lyrics were really great and were about something.

One thing I haven't conquered is the usage of the word 'love'. Every song Billy Pumpkin writes is about love. Every goddam song. I can't say it out loud in a song. I think it's really challenging that he can do that. It's so weird that people's personas are so opposite; like I'm so 'Fuck you! Kiss my ass', and in my personal life I'm such a big pussy, I'm so passive. Like: 'Can I cook you breakfast? Do you need your morning blow-job?' I'm such a good wife. It must be some whacky rebellion against my mother's militant 70s persona. I wanted to be a 'good wife' in the most Brady Bunch way. It was really great as well.

Billy Pumpkin shouts 'Love! Love! Love!' on stage and off stage he's another mysogynistic bastard, bless his heart. And Kurt's thing was: 'You have to come to me. Fuck you, fuck with me. C'mon, I dare you.' He needed to say, 'Fuck you' in real life. He would never have dug too deep inside of himself. Some people can be amorphous like that. All of Kurt's insane eroticism, he'd never ever use it, though he was getting there. There are a lot of sexual metaphors on *In Utero*, and he was getting so close to the flame. Maybe *too* close.

Evan [Dando] destroys this theory, however, 'cause he's just the same on stage as off: goofy, lovable, he steals girlfriends without

9

trying (so it seems). He's a great friend. And Kurt liked him. He likened him to a golden retriever. So he liked him as much as a total cat person can like a dog person. But in general it's a good theory.

I don't like not being given credit for being cryptic or intelligent enough. I guess it's part of what I asked for. Songwriting is cathartic – I hate to admit it. It's a purge . . . I'm probably completely evil. Or something. Some sort of civil war inside. That's how I do it. I write the most honest things. You can't be too honest. I'm not psychic but my lyrics are. I can't really explain it. Sometimes it's like automatic fucking writing, it really is. It just comes out. The title of the record [*Live Through This*] is not that great – but it came from such a bruise, from such an honest place. Since my persona is so demonised and so huge and so not what I am about, I can practically do anything I want behind that persona, artistically. That's kind of a gift and a positive thing.

On *Live Through This*, I felt all this pressure to write about certain subjects, but I didn't. They are too much mine. I subvert them and turn them out in different ways – but I wasn't going to reference the media on *Live Through This*, and on the next record I'm not going to reference Kurt, except in ways known only to me. I can't afford to. It's not anyone's business, but inside, inside my life. I rely a lot on sexual metaphors – food as sex, music as sex, fucked up weird insane sexual vistas that haunt me and make me feel as though I were going insane sometimes.

I keep my diaries; I keep them well stocked, I do a lot of reading. I have been really afraid of writing for a while and I've only just started up again. I didn't want to write or play at all. I couldn't. I did write after, in April, with Kat [Bjelland]. We got together and we played all the time; she was the only person I could really play with except for Kurt. After all these years Kat and I still have our chemistry. It's fucking magic. At a certain point [in Seattle] I let all these kids in and we went up to the greenhouse and sang. One kid had a guitar and we sang all three Nírvana records, straight. Fifty kids as loud as we could. That was really good.

You know, I get asked about lyrics all the time, but not about the fact that I put a lot of fucking thought into using an AC30 head like John Lennon did. I put as much thought into the way we sound as Pavement or Sonic Youth do. Eric [Erlandson] and I are both obsessed by drum sounds, miking techniques. I'm crazed about snare sounds. I hate prominent hi-hats. One reason I love 'Cannonball' [by the Breeders] is the space and originality. She [frontwoman Kim Deal] is so martian and so pure. But no one ever asks about the music. It's like my persona – boom! Knocks everything else out. We'd be a really fine, quality band if people could just get over the bullshit. That's the reason I've been able to keep a drummer like Patty or get a bass player like Kristen Pfaff. Or the bass player we have now [Melissa Auf Der Maur] who's not as good yet; she's a fledgling but she has the same potential and the same snotty self-belief. And I have finally found someone who I think I can write with. Plus she can sing really well. And she has the same large ego which is able to ignore the fact that my persona is going to fuck up everything for her. If she can ignore it, it will go away. Eventually!

I just set up a show in LA – I want Elastica and Veruca Salt to play with my band. I want to fly Elastica out; I really want it to work for them on Geffen. They are real good and so lucky to be a *band*. We are a band but not perceived as such as yet. But it will come. Patty is the first woman to ever appear on the cover of *Drum World* magazine. Which is great. Had this been four years ago, three bands that have nothing to do with each other would have been thrown together on a bill – but now there's a lot more variety and the bands are all so different. An LA show with Elastica would be really cool. In the eighties the circuit used to be chick night and we'd all get stuck playing together, all of us muttering filthy things about bustiers. It was a pain in the ass and really gross. I think it's been resolved to a certain degree, and even if it hasn't been resolved in the majority of minds, pretending it has and taking the high road is the best way to do things.

Why do women see me as a role model? There haven't been too many of us. There was our first group: Exene [Cervenka], Debbie [Harry] and Patti [Smith]. Then there was a huge amount of years! Then there was a second group which was Jennifer [Finch] and Donita [Sparks], me, Kim Gordon and Kim Deal, Kat [Bjelland], Kathleen [Hanna, of Bikini Kill] and her little pack of oestrogen

11

COURTNEY LOVE

terrorists (Riot Grrrls) . . . well, oestrogen lemmings. Jenny Toomi of Tsunuami saying things like: 'women shouldn't sing loud or scream because it's physiologically not female.' ARRRRGHHH! Thank God that period is over. (No menstrual pun intended.) There's also Polly Harvey. I can't count Liz Phair, I just can't. She reminds me of a potato. I don't hate her at all, I just need a bit of angst, I guess . . . it's my problem, not hers. It isn't about being competitive in the slightest . . . Liz, have a horrible day just *once*, and *then* write a song.

There are really retarded and gross reasons for making me a role model. It's a fucking stupid thing to say, but I work in the hospital, I wanna be the best surgeon and I'm gonna go out with surgeons sometimes. I'll probably marry one. I might date an ambulance driver, but I work in the goddam hospital and it's gonna happen. I refuse to be a nurse.

I'll hail my mother as an icon. I can't stand her, but I was really sheltered that way. I thought the war had been fought and was won. I really did. Rock is still a lot like the National Football League, but that's the challenge! The challenge is so exciting. It keeps me alive in every way. I can escape in that challenge. Debbie Harry wasn't an icon. I love her, but she didn't count to me 'cause she didn't play an instrument; you had to play. Dolly Parton was, believe it or not. I had this record with 'Joleen' on it and 'Coat of Many Colours'. She wrote eight million hits. She also covered Leadbelly's 'In The Pines', which is my life's most important song. I love Joni Mitchell; I grew up on that music, so I naturally rebelled against it, but thankfully my mother had a Leonard Cohen record and a lot of Dylan too. She apparently slept with Dylan once, but she won't talk about it. My mother was a bit of a groupie, and she once told me her secret desire was to be a drummer. There are pictures of her in the sixties with long hair down to her ass, and she's wearing hot pants and a fur coat and sandals. She was kind of hot; she had big tits and rich parents who weren't her real parents but were rich. She only ever gave me one piece of advice in my entire life: 'Don't wear tight sweaters, they make you look cheap.' Um . . . Thanks.

I never thought I was fat. I saw a cover of *Flipside* US fanzine and I realised that my body took up the whole goddam magazine cover and that we'd be really limited and only sell 6,000 records. We just would, it's a fact and not a nice one. So I lost 40 pounds. End of story. It happened. I'm not bitter about it, I'm not mad at anyone about it. It shouldn't be that way, but it is. I lost the weight mid-indie career, in 1989 – I had already gone two tours. And suddenly we got good reviews. Funny that. In the smaller parts of the community, it's like: 'I've got pictures of Courtney looking really fat'. I got offered real jobs after, at trendy clothing stores and coffee bars. Before, the only job I could get was stripping.

And now I affect fashion and I like it. It's funny. But it's all happening around the time that I'm going to be 30 – so I'm afraid that I'm peaking. I go round the stores thinking: OK, I've affected this to a large degree and I'm gonna take the onus of it on, but what happens when my own clothes aren't cool any more? Will I have to change what I've been wearing for eighteen years? I've been wearing the same thing, and looking in The Gap or Kookaï and seeing all the gym slips and school uniform scares me; like what am I gonna wear next? Next I guess I'll be a woman and wear woman clothes. I like it, it's fun. I just wish I wasn't such a big deal.

When Madonna affected fashion, it sold records. I'm glad that most people sense that what I wear is about comfort as well as being a little ironic. I guess I never thought about it in a semantic sense. I didn't have more than a desire to be in a good punk rock new wave band. And then, when we started little indie bands, we certainly did not affect semantics or the fashion climate. It's kind of funny to be discussing it in retrospect. If you're gonna offer me a jeans ad campaign – your dumb jeans that I would never ever be caught dead wearing, not even when I was 10 – what you want from me is to say it's OK to wear them. Drew [Barrymore] can do that, she's more of an amorphous actress person. If I were to do it, which I'm not, I'd ask for a major amount of money, *which I think I should get*! That's how it worked in the eighties, so it should work that way now.

If people are so unimaginative fashion-wise that I have to come up with it for them, then I'll do it for them, fine. I'm giving you something more so you'll go and listen to my record. I'm fighting a war with this 'image' (which was not pre-planned. I wear the same clothes daily). And I'm not giving you disco. I'm not safe. I'm giving

---

13

COURTNEY LOVE

something hard, and I have to do some damage, 'cause that's what I'm here for. And if I don't, there's no point. No point in living.

Madonna is a great inspiration to a lot of people and she definitely deserves respect on a certain level, but her music has always sucked; even though we can probably find singles that we liked. I'm sorry she's upset that I don't like her. I don't dislike her. I *respect* her. But I can't stand her *art*. That's it. It's a low blow, I'm sorry. Most people (obviously) can, and think her lyrics are deeeep. So she shouldn't take it personal. It's just my dumb opinion as a snotty new waver.

My references are very white and very rock. I'm not going to apologise for it. When I was in New York, I always wondered why I didn't like discos – all my fag friends moved there and they had a great time and they had dance music and I hated it. When I moved to Minneapolis in 1987, everyone was into Sonic Youth and Pussy Galore. I totally rebelled; I hated them all for being trendies. I couldn't stand the Butthole Surfers and I was still listening to my REM records and my Bangles first record, alongside Bauhaus, Joy Division, The Smiths and Echo and the Bunnymen, who were *super* uncool – a position I enjoy taking: super uncool is *fun*. Even though everyone had liked them and they were some of the best bands ever to come out of England. I think I saw the Bunnymen more times than any other band except Nirvana. Fourteen times or something. Me and Kat and Lori [Babes in Toyland] would go out to 1st Avenue (Minneapolis) on Wednesdays, where they'd play Jesus and Mary Chain and we'd dance our asses off all night. We'd do the Deathrock Siouxsie Dance. Spooooky.

I was just reading a piece in *Psychology* magazine about women who can't say no. That's me. I did say 'no' to somebody once and he threw me out of his car. In the middle of the desert, in this town called Boring Oregan. Boring Oregan! I've been afraid of men in that respect since then and probably before – they are menacing to me and scare me. I used to prefer to lay there and just ignore it than say 'no'. Kurt left me a great legacy. A certain self-esteem about saying 'no'. I don't ever have to be a slut again. It's a great relief to me. Nor do I have to go out of my way for a bastard. Bastards of the world, I love you all, but you have to chase *me*. Fuck it if I will ever give you control – you've got to earn it. It may sound pretentious, but it gets me through.

If you can take on duties, you should take as much responsibility as you can. I feel a little insecure that this might be my last lifetime in my cycle of life and I can just take care of all of it. But I'm way too selfish. This might be my next-to-last lifetime and my next one might be really horrible. I look up and I think all I want is to be a fucking rock star. I don't want any of this enlightenment shit. But with what's happened, it's the only thing other than my daughter and work that keeps me from leaving. Discipline and faith fill my hole. I went away to this monastery and got my buddhism going again – I started chanting about nine years ago. It's a private thing. A two-hour chant makes you feel a lot better to say the least. I called this woman up who deals with the Namgyal, Tibetan monks and asked for them to be sent over to my house in Seattle from New York. The monks might calm the goddam place down. These monks are great. They were on the Lollapalooza tour [1992] and Kurt loved them so much – he'd play them every morning.

There was a piece in *USA Today* recently with Richard Gere and Tina Turner and me! The poster child for Buddhism. I thought that was really funny. I am really bored of people being so agnostic. I've never been agnostic; to me it's like throwing your life away. I respect someone with personal faith more than someone who doesn't believe in anything. This is turning into one big agnostic era, which is horrible and is going to usher in religious fundamentalism. Every year (actress) Uma Thurman's dad – he's one of the most learned Professors amongst Tibetan Buddhists – does a sabbatical there. I have always wanted to go to India. I may go with him next fall.

At the end of this American tour, I am going to Donegal, to scatter some of Kurt at the Cobain Nub. My intro into Liverpool (Jung's 'pool of life') was through County Meath. I find it funny that Julian Cope is finally in his full neolithic period – stories in the stones. The Irish tourist board calls them 'tombs', but they are decidedly neolithic fertility mounds. I sat in one at the vernal equinox and watched the beam of light hit the basin stone. Cope portrays me (in

COURTNEY LOVE

his recent autobiography) as a demon 15-year-old, which I was, but I was straight off the mounds. Cycles are funny . . . The night before I met him in Ireland, I had slept under an Irish moon between Knowth and Dowth, with wild cygnets screaming in the Slane River nearby, stars in the stones and all that. After I scatter Kurt's ashes, I'm getting a flat in Ireland and working. Hopefully Marianne Faithfull will befriend me and guide me to some Goddess.

People come up to me and say, 'I remember you. You were on that plane ride from San Francisco to LA and you were giving pills out to everyone with cool hair!' I couldn't remember it, but I knew it was true. I've been around so much. This one guy came up and said, 'Don't you remember me?' No. 'We fucked.' Maybe he was making it up. At least he was cute. The eighties: a blur.

Drugs in Seattle are fucking problematic and I'm not gonna back down from that. People think I'm being self-righteous and sanctimonious and conservative and Nancy Reagan, but I'm telling you, living with somebody and being prone to drug behaviour myself, accessibility is nine-tenths of the law. If I know I can get heroin from the guy downstairs, I'll probably get it. No not probably, but *will*. If I have to go all the way down to the ghetto and I might get stabbed and it might be shitty rat poison, I'm not gonna do it. End of story. I don't care what anyone says, that's the truth. When we moved into town [Seattle], I remember thinking, 'I'm glad to be in this really nice house, but we're going to be so close to the hill where the drug dealers hang out. Me and Kurt could walk there.'
    The house had such good karma and balance . . . It was the same with Kristin [Pfaff]; she lived on the hill. Seattle is the worst; everyone's a fucking junkie. Everyone knows about abscesses and what veins to use and how when you run out of veins in this part of your arm, you use this vein there. Fucking chic 16-year-olds are in my park showing me their tracks. I'm kicking them – 'Get your fucking ass home to your mom.' I never used to know this stuff. It's ugly and I hate it.
    By the time Frances grows up, it's not gonna be chic any more.

I pray. Religion, fucking discipline, certain traditions will be cool. Her generation will have something that mine doesn't. My generation . . . I'm so busted. I'm reading this book called *Generation Ecch!* and the first line of it is: 'Since when is the possibility of being less affluent than our parents a problem on the order of world hunger, the federal deficit and Courtney Love?' Talk about weirdly iconoclastic. Yuccch. You know, it's like I'm so busted reading it. I am so part of this generation where you refer to [famous] people by their first name. I hope the next generation will be better, it'll have more respect for the traditional . . . The little glimpses I got of growing up, the traditional things were those which stuck with me most, for some stupid reason. When I returned to the States after attending two British schools, they had to push me forward three grades. They didn't even do long division in fourth grade in America. I enjoyed the discipline of getting up at 6 a.m. and making my bed military style. I loved going to boarding school in a Commonwealth country. I learned. Then I got expelled.

Anyway, hopefully Frances's generation will come out better. I'm really glad she's not a son; she is more protected by being Kurt's daughter. She doesn't have to live up to something like John Lennon's son has to. It's like with JFK's son: naturally we expect him to be the next President, and so much responsibility is on him, and his daughter gets away with having babies. (A noble pursuit I might add. One of the noblest). That's why I want the monks around for my daughter.

I'm generally mostly attracted to dickheads and fuckers. People that I really *should* like, that I *wish* I could like, guys who are really good and nice don't hold my interest. It was really one of the miasma of pains for Kurt to go away [commit suicide] 'cause he was the perfect combo of fucker and not fucker. Frances Bean needs a dad. I'm not bringing one of those fuckers into my house . . . Although my standards of fucker are pretty high – they have to be really twisted bastards with IQs to burn to pull it off 'cause I'm a little twisted myself. Kurt was so pure and totally sophisticated because of it – they have to be that too or beyond twisted.

I'm used to a man, I hate not having him – it drives me crazy. But I hate sympathy. If you want to give me anything, give me some

COURTNEY LOVE

empathy. I just came here to do my little thing and get on with something that I love doing. I have this persistent idea inside my head, buzzing around, you know – fucking shave your head and don't talk for six months. Have an epiphany, a vision, a quest. In retrospect, what happened would have happened anyway. It would have happened before – I'm certainly not saying that I saved him from the gate of death. Probably anyone would have saved him from the gate of death who gave enough of a fuck and who was sophisticated enough to understand how to do it. And he certainly couldn't have found anybody to save him from dying. He didn't want to be here, unfortunately. He told me that right from the start.

I feel like not being here all the time; I've been feeling like that since I was six or seven. I remember the first time it hit me. I was on a cliff in New Zealand. But I never do anything about it because it's my responsibility not to. If I don't outgrow it in this lifetime, I'm not ever gonna outgrow it. Personally, I feel like I've done it before, I know I have. It's a failure. You have to come back and go through all this shit again and hope to God or whoever for a fortunate birth. It's a pain. Right on the verge of enlightenment – having the wisdom, the power, the money . . . it seems to take money to gain enlightenment. I know it doesn't, but it's easier. I guess if you have money, it's a giant problem out of your life.

I get mail written in blood. They write: my name, Seattle, USA. I told the Post Office to stop bringing them; I don't want them. Some teenager in Poland writing to me in blood: 'This is the blood coming out of my wrist, right now. I just thought you should know.' There is this one, she is obviously rich because the things she sends are really large. She's outta her mind, obsessed with turning me into a born-again Christian. She's from Florida, of course. She sends these gigantic glass, really well-made, grotesque Christs. They keep getting returned to sender. Really spooky. Then I get anonymous mail accusing me of keeping Kurt alive, saying: he's not dead and I'm going to kill you. Then there's the stalkers [obsessive fans] – one lives in the park next door. He has a restraining order of 500 yards and he stays just on the right side. He has mapped out exactly where he can go.

It's my house and I'm not moving. Fuck them. It's the oldest house in Seattle! It took us three goddam years to find that house and I'm not moving. I love my house and wish people would choose another spot for their pilgrimage.

I want to live in New Orleans, but not with Frances; it's bad for kids. There is definitely a leyline there. I just felt my pulse, my being. I felt on fire there, and slightly diabolical. Which is fine as long as it's chanelled, as long as I can find my muses without bleeding myself dry. I think I'll get a house there and just go for a few months a year.

Interview Two: Sunday, 11 September 1994
We've just come back from touring with Nine Inch Nails – it was great. I have always kind of liked the music; all this industrial combined with new wave, and I have always thought of Trent Reznor as a great lyricist. Our lyrics are thematically similar – on his last record there are six lines which are exactly the same as on mine. The agenda is the same, though his is more about a brutal sexuality and definitely about a very intense, very expensive stage show. A nineties Bowie equivalent. Kurt always admired him a lot. If you look at one of the first *Melody Maker* interviews after *Nevermind*, they asked him who he liked – I remember, because I gave him shit – and he said Mudhoney, Shonen Knife and Nine Inch Nails. I told Trent that Kurt really liked some of his songs. Kurt would always say, 'This song could be so great if there wasn't any synthesiser on it.' Trent laughed his head off and said, 'That's the whole fucking point! I want to use technology to make great rock music. No one has done it.' Certainly no women. If someone doesn't do it soon, I will. Just to prove a point.

It was a disturbing tour for me. It was called the Self-Destruct Tour and the imagery they are playing with, which fascinates Trent, is the imagery that's in my life. Morbidity, death and dying and all that shit. Well, get back to me when you've looked horror in the face, farmboy.

COURTNEY LOVE

There's a book out right now called *Meeting the Madwoman*, and I've just been reading the chapter on the muse. Some of it's very Jungian, but it is applicable to me on a certain level, although on another it isn't. When I was younger and listening to Leonard Cohen songs, I'd think, 'I wish that was *me*'- that fucked up Lady of Shallot/living in a swamp, making men crazy. Now that there are a lot of songs about me – my husband obviously wrote some songs about me – the muse thing is fulfilled in me. But it's sick. It doesn't mean too much any more. It's more vampiric than fulfilling, anyway.

This is how the chapter on the Muse starts, with a quote from Toni Morrison's novel, *Sula*:

In a way, her strangeness, her naïveté, her craving for the other
half of her equation was the consequence of an idle imagination.
Had she paints, or clay, or knew the discipline of the dance, or
strings; had she anything to engage her tremendous curiosity and
her gift for metaphor, she might have exchanged the restlessness
and preoccupation with whim for an activity that provided her
with all she yearned for. And like any artist with no art form, she
became dangerous.

[The author then continues:]

In my younger days, I had fantasies of being a muse. I had heard
of Madame de Staël and Alma Mahler, whose creative salons
attracted geniuses from all over Europe. More to my own liking
was Lou Andreas-Salomé, who inspired the poet Rilke and the
philosopher Nietzsche, but who also wrote herself and later
trained with Freud to be a lay analyst. How wonderful it would
be, I reflected, to inspire a great poet or artist to create a work of
beauty and spiritual meaning and in that way to contribute to the
world!

Being a Muse is appealing because it has been an acceptable
role and a feminine ideal for women in our culture throughout the
ages. At the archetypal level, as the 'eternal feminine', the Muse
inspires the spirit and leads the soul on its creative journey, as
Beatrice did for Dante. To inspire means to breathe life into, to
ignite the creative fire. Women in touch with the Muse energy
tend to be mysterious and spiritual; their inspiration comes from

love. They enjoy others' creativity and genuinely encourage it. Generous, they tend to give without expecting in return. Often they are trusting, fresh, receptive, and caring, and their simplicity opens the way for new images and ideas to develop . . . the difficulty with these women is that often they inspire others at their own expense. [See Marianne Faithfull, Anita Pallenberg, a slew of women who were victimised by not being able to have the 'Mary Shelley' outlet as I call it.] When a man wants a woman to inspire him but not to create himself, he can make her mad. [I know.] Living the role of a Muse or *femme inspiratrice* can be difficult and frustrating or a way to remain passive.

According to Jung, women who are Muses have a special capacity to reflect the 'anima' [there's a cartoon character called Anima which is based on me – how cute! She's sort of a cross between me and L7's Donita Sparks. She cuts off rapists' dicks . . . like 7–11 feminism, quite base actually, but a super heroine, anyway. Her powers, ironically, destroy her loved ones and her family, so she has to disappear] or the feminine spirit or the soul of the man.

The inspirational role of the Muse can also be misused for destructive purposes, however. The celebrated image of the beautiful Helen of Troy, whose face launched a thousand ships, is an example of the Muse misappropriated for war . . . In a commercial society ruled by greed for money, fame, success and power, the Muse can be reduced to an external means for gain and thus abused, as in the misrepresentation of the Muse as a glamour or sex object in advertisements, on billboards, and by television and Hollywood . . . The misuse of the Muse can feed the destructive side of the Madwoman: women hungry for love literally starve themselves to be the thin, glamorous model that feeds male fantasies, often suffering from anorexia or bulimia . . . some undergo psychological and physical torture – face-lifts, liposuction, even the remodelling of their bones . . . resenting such sacrifices, usually unconsciously, some women turn their anger inward in the form of various addictions such as shopping, sex, alcohol, food and codependent behaviour. [Well, it's true: reading this is like reading part of my life.]

The Muse can also be seen as any woman who tries to

embody her lover's idealised fantasies of women instead of developing herself. She may accept her husband's or boyfriend's vision of what their relationship is without ever asserting her own needs or nature. She may also be a Caged Bird [this is like *The Yellow Wallpaper*, Charlotte Perkins Gilman] caught in society's and her family's views of how a good wife or a nice girl or good mother should behave. [I don't have *that* problem at all.]

Outwardly, the Muse may be beautiful and brilliant, charming and gracious, bewitching and beguiling, sweet and demure. Despite her alluring mystique, the rage of the Madwoman simmers within, fed by her divorce from her personal energies and desires. She feels outraged and ashamed because she has betrayed herself. In *The Second Sex*, Simone de Beauvoir pointed out the seduction and bad faith to which a woman is subject when she submits to being an admired object. In a bad faith relationship, the Muse who lives an inauthentic life can be a slave. She becomes co-dependent, addicted to a dysfunctional existence in which she is cut off from her own centre of creativity.

22

Some of this bore down on me for many years. I had to take it back. To have what *they* have. Or, at least, to clear the jungle, widen the path. When I was going on 24, I thought that I was very old and that it was now or never. Let yourself bleed dry by choice, or take a hold of this damned thing and internalise it. Before I went to Alaska all I did was that. I don't even want to get into this specifically, but that's what I did. Be the crazy, mad girl that 'inspired' (heavy on the irony here readers!) these boys. And although I had my guitar sitting in the fucking corner, gathering dust and although I filled up notebook after notebook with some shit that was not so bad, I did not have the balls to get out and take the power back. I had no self-esteem whatsoever. No discipline. Just a bad reputation and a bunch of angsty diaries. *Hollywood Perfume* costs way too much.

I felt molested and stolen from constantly. It wasn't until a female friend not only wrote about me but also took some of my persona from me, that I changed my outlook. Seeing enough worth in my persona to take it from me. It was a great compliment, it was a gift. Not my soul, but my persona, that I had always felt was ugly and gross and pyschotic: this person took this and created her own world with it. It really moved me to get off my ass and do it myself. I thank her.

Being a muse is a habit, I still do it. It's not nice behaviour, but I know it when I do it. I did it this week. I feel absolutely out of control about it. It's a complex, self-defeating ritual. Very Catholic-cum-Buddhist in its intricacies. People love to talk about me and drugs; I don't have a drug problem. It's nothing compared to this. For many, many years, I have been dense and locked down and men have not been able to get me very easily. It takes a real pure motherfucker to get me . . . I trust people . . . when somebody who is a 'genius' in any way comes after me – and believe me, when you're in a band, they all come after you, and when you're me they come after you even worse. All of them. For having a great rollicking Courtney story to tell their friends. It happened before I got married. These men are attracted to me because – 'Woah! She's hot! She's like me, she can get up on stage, she's not waiting for me backstage. And . . . her publishing deal is bigger.' At the same time it threatens them completely and they *all*, I mean *all*, secretly want to destroy it and me. I have to find a way to protect myself from this power. Because truly, nothing is more exquisite and more wrong then giving up control. It's a constant temptation, a sick craving. And far beyond any narcotic. Kurt protected me. Totally. He spoiled me. I trusted him so much. I still do trust him.

You'd be surprised at some of the people hitting on me now. It's rather like – you want to go where Kurt's been? Mostly it seems to be that they want to be mothered. They think: 'Oh she's the ultimate mother.' I don't understand how they come to that conclusion, 'cause if I am, obviously I failed. These men that rock culture considers geniuses. The one that I fell for is the one that I married, and he was the pure one. We had a relationship where we would thrive back and forth creatively. The relationship only deteriorated around the idea of maternity/paternity. When I get into relationships with people and they're Daddy, I cheat on them, I want out. When I get into relationships and I'm Mummy, I have to take care of my baby. There is an inbetween. I've seen it. I love fuckers, I have always loved bastards and I always will. But how often are you going to find a bastard that's a prince? With Kurt it was inbetween: we rarely fought. We rarely had a bad mood at the same time. Our cycles

23

were different. When the occasional mood would strike in unison, it was hell on earth.

I mean, I went through a very dark period when I decided that I was going to be a movie star 'cause this musician guy I knew went out with models. He was turned off by the idea that I was in a band, but I knew that he would love me if I was a famous movie star. I put my entire energy in 1985–86 into looking ridiculous, feeling ridiculous, being an actress – how pathetic! Well, I was still a teen. And I still feel slight pressure from the 'industry' to do the jeans campaign or take the scripts on offer and be an actress. But to me those are really useless activities right now. Although acting can be cathartic, if – and only if – you lose yourself completely. This is not easy. I don't even bother to read scripts any more. When I heard my agent say on the phone in 1987: 'She's like a cross between Madonna and Bette Midler', I say, 'No! Fuck you! I'm James Dean.' And I fucked off to Minneapolis to start a punk rock band.

There is a limited group of women doing anything of value in music now. There's Polly [Harvey], Kim Deal, Kim Gordon, Kat [Bjelland] . . . A lot of us have experienced the same thing. I have this really weak inner femininity that just collapses in on itself if you say the right thing; you can say one sentence to me and if it's the right one, that's it. I'll give it up, I won't do a fucking thing for a year. I've done it. Even with Kurt. To a degree my output was considerably lower than it should have been; my record wasn't as good as it could have been. It wasn't his fault, it was because our life was more important. And I don't regret it. Not with him. Every second was worth it in every way. I now know what real love is. I know what self-respect is. I had more in those four years than most people ever have in a lifetime. I swear now that nothing will be as important again, because there is only one of him.

Reading this *Meeting the Madwoman*, I realise how lucky I am to have spent some time in Alaska and to have shut my fucking mouth while I was there. At the same time, reading this makes me feel so scared. Here again, alone again. People project the Madwoman image on to me, yeah, but I don't mind doing it, because it's a Jungian archetype. It needs to be dealt with.

GRRRLS

If you remember, during the Byron years, it was very chic to jump off London Bridge. Women did it over Byron. Some who had never met him, some who had. Look at Caroline Lamb. She was the woman who went mad because she fucked Byron, which just wasn't done in those days. I guess Italian contessas were the equivalent of B-models – Byron would always be running off with them. But he fucked around with Caroline Lamb. Her husband was this British politician and she used his money to write pamphlets about Byron, about his little weenie . . . who made her come to a ball dressed as a slave, ignored her all night, told people he had nothing to do with her and then went and fucked her.

I read this Caroline Lamb story with mortal fear. Especially before I met Kurt. I'd read it and think: Oh my God. Or the first time I saw *A Streetcar Named Desire*, I was only 16. I thought: is that going to be me? I was terrified. You're talking about Blanche Dubois, who was 54. I was doing the Muse thing already. I was involved in these men already. People were throwing poems on my doorstep already and God knows, vice versa. I was indulging in the dramatic, over-the-top behaviour that they expected of me. Love wasn't even a word I understood. All I understood was how to inspire somebody and how to be inspired by the subtlest things – a gesture, a 'sighting'. When people talk about what a big groupie I am, it's not like that; fame and power are *not* aphrodisiacs to me. Grace is. Grace, intelligence, wit and a pagan true heart. It's a really gross, old habit. This book has affected me; it's true and useful.

I just thank God that I have somehow succeeded in staying alive. Whoever is ever going to be my lover again, there is always going to be three of us in the room. There is always going to be Kurt in the room. He's not ever going away; I won't let him. But when these powerful, intriguing, dark, intense men get interested in me that are brilliant, I stay away. And I should. They will suck my blood. I will let them. I will be nothing. So it's worked out well, breaking this habit. It's not 'without you I'm nothing', but 'with you I'm nothing'. I have pretty much a whirlwind of people right now circling me like vultures. And I've got to get them out of my life. For my daughter. For my band. For my husband. For my soul. They make me wonder: am I like some weird sex freak prize? Is this my dream

25

come true? I don't think so. Maybe at the age of 15. Hey you, fuck off. Earn it.

Let's finish this chapter:

The dark muse shares and shows her vulnerability, her suffering and emotional pain and her experience with depression, mental disintegration, alcoholism, or frustrated obsessive romantic and sexual longing.

Now maybe reading through this book has made me realise that what I have contributed or what I can contribute that's positive, is to do something with this energy that has been instilled in me my whole life. By listening to Joni Mitchell and Leonard Cohen songs when I was nine or ten and thinking: 'I want to be the girl in those songs.' Not really knowing my options – not knowing that I could take that power back. Especially seeing as in this lifetime I spent many, many years just pleasing. That guy likes these clothes; I'm gonna get them. This guy wants me to be an actress; I'm gonna do that. That guy wants me to be beautiful; I'm gonna do that. This guy wants me in black, white . . . Kurt didn't have any of those agendas. Although he was a fucker, he was obviously brilliant. And obviously too good to be true.

It was really weird playing with Nine Inch Nails. It was only a few shows, but it fucked me up. It jangled me. It was like a shadow image. Because I'm singing about the same things as them only in a different way. I'm not singing about the same neo-tribal S&M or whatever, but I'm singing about ritually putting yourself in a position which is going to be your downfall. You know it's going to be your descent and you don't even care. I'm putting myself there. And yet I have duties and responsibilities that are drawing me back. One of the largest duties I have is to *report* on that madness and to try not become a victim of it in the same way as Anne Sexton or Sylvia Plath or Zelda Fitzgerald. Not that I am any of those women; they are women I can name that are obviously victims. [Or even a little of that Monroe energy; I taste a little of that and I want to come back from there alive and report on it.]

What I just quoted about 'her suffering and emotional pain and her experience with depression, mental disintegration, alcoholism or frustrated obsessive romantic and sexual longing' – reading this is really self-revelatory. I hadn't read this until just now. And it's like: Wow! Thank God I'm coming back from the front of this and reporting on it. It's like Bosnia: no one gets out of there alive. I *must* survive this. Even if it does nothing for anyone but myself, it'll save my life. If I can just manage not to become obsessive . . . but then what happens when I have been super-strong and not become obsessive? I hope to find out and never give it away for free. My marriage was my one oasis away from this kind of self-destruction.

Am I being crazy? Because I am not going to go crazy, be the Madwoman. I used to be scared that I was going to, because I'd get so obsessive, not about people but things. Goal's perfectionism. Through my Eastern beliefs, I turned this obsessive nature for a brief time into pure discipline. It was one of the purest changes I ever made. If the Madwoman rears her head again, which she does on a daily basis, she's going to go right back in the fucking closet where she came from. Fuck her. She's not going to murder me and I'm not going to fucking have her around. She's already been on these intense romantic sexual adventures, so she's not going to come back damaged because she already did it. She is not going to throw herself off fucking London Bridge. She's not going to publicly humiliate herself or anybody else. Contrary to what anyone's standards of deportment for me are at this point, I will honour my values. I've got the Madwoman under control and I don't know how I had the good grace to get that, but I did. I will die before I will go mad. This is a vow. The press, the men, the deaths, the projections – will *not* make me mad.

Transforming the Muse: How can a woman who is trapped in the role of Muse transform herself into a woman of her own, particularly when the secondary gains of the Muse are so enticing – the romance, the adoration and the glamour? [Well, can't you have it all?] How can she grow beyond a culture that glorifies beauty and youth? Once a woman has experienced the thrill of creating from her own centre, despite all the hard work this entails she will not want to be *only* a Muse to anyone.

There is nothing more true than that statement. The very first statement I opened with, the Toni Morrison quote – 'And like any artist

COURTNEY LOVE

with no art form, she became dangerous' – applies to the groupie who makes her fucking sex life into her art form. Once you have tasted the nectar of fucking them up – of doing what *they* do but better – no way will you want to go back. But it also applies to the woman who can't stand being alone without a man. The divorcees of the 70s, that Amazonian independence – do not mean that one has failed or that one has to play that one-dimensional retro archetype of 60s rock 'n' roll, all soft and old and alone. Madonna, left with nothing more to shock with, is alone and may be, I think, bitter. This 'alone' thing is bogus. The men in my field tend to cherish solitude above all else, as no one wants to be 'Yoko-ed'. Yet us alone, we are somehow failures. I think not. I work best alone.

When we played Chicago with Nine Inch Nails – there were 25,000 kids there – I jumped into the crowd. I was standing on the monitor, rocking back and forth. I jumped in because I don't care. They're rats in there. It's like clawing, biting, kissing, poking. C'mon kill me. Kill me. Love me. Fuck you. When they got me it wasn't like the Underworld [where Courtney got physically assaulted] because there were so many girls at the front. But I was definitely naked when I got back on stage. Most decidedly: nothing was on my body, nothing. It was the gold dress I wore at Reading – I spent time on that goddam dress and I'm pissed about losing it.

The first night of the small Nine Inch tour, in Cleveland, there was a death threat against me. The Chief of Police came down and told me that he didn't want me to play. I'm like: 'It's from a girl, it's bullshit.' Besides, if someone were to shoot me on stage, what a nice footnote to rock 'n' roll history. You can't tell me not to jump into the crowd; it's so deeply rooted inside me, this sickness, this disease, this obsessiveness. The only way to get rid of it is to fucking get it out.

Just having read that stuff out loud, I feel refreshed because it's like I just read my astrological chart completely accurately or something. I am terrified of what would have become of me if I had not been brave enough to just say 'Fuck it, I am terrified.' I'd be crazy. I'd be dead. If I'd been an actress, I'd be dead. And standing on a stack and saying: 'Do you want it? Do you want it? Do you want it?' and getting them in a frenzy, in a frenzy, in a frenzy, in a fucking ridiculous crowd frenzy – It's like: 'I'm fucking with you, but you are so stupid you don't even know. You are coming and waiting for me to give you an autograph.' This is so funny.

I prefer the High Road, and this was before a nine week tour of the US where the crowds were great and we oversold smaller venues (2,000 to 3,000) so as to keep the 'bad people' out. Me playing gigs is not freakish at all– only to the UK inky press. So when they see us getting album of the year in *Rolling Stone, Spin, Village Voice, New York Times* etc, they'll stop saying it. There's nothing like delivering the goods. They come out to see you fall apart, and then you deliver the goods. That's the best feeling in the world. 'Hey, you know what – kick my ass and give me diamonds.' That's what it feels like. I could kick Trent's ass through honesty. Or at least come out even. I'm pathologically competitive with men. Nine Inch Nails had the lights and the technology; I was so scared we'd eat shit, but it worked out very smoothly. Too smoothly, if you ask me. I'm glad it was only a short tour. I started ravelling, internally.

It was fun to play with some of the imagery, to pander to that audience. I got to wear black on stage, which I have never done in my life. I got to wear high spiky heels on stage, which I have also never done in my life. And then I worked my thing to death. I put my hair in ringlets every fucking night. I did my Baby-Jane-fuck-you sick thing every fucking night. In Minneapolis, I wore a dress that was so restricting and shoes that were five inches high, I could barely stage-dive. Then I got like the best write-ups: for being feminine I guess. I couldn't move well and I was restrained, which equals great review. That's pretty horrid.

Of course there are things that are always going to be mine and private. There are things that no one is ever going to understand about me that are complex. Nobody knows what I'm like in the day. No one knows what kind of discourse I actually do get into, nobody knows quite how quiet I really am on the sly. No one knows what – to quote the *New York Times* – 'feminism's last hope' – is like. Really quite traditional in terms of her relationships with men in a lot of ways. You can fuck me over and you can twist me round. You can be so sophisticated that you scare the shit out of me and you can do

29

whatever you want to me. You could fucking take my little imperial dominion full of shit and do whatever the fuck you want with it. But you will never be able to take away my creativity because that's all I've got left. I'm talking about men. Mostly.

I don't like too much small talk and I like to behave in an externally normal, wholesome manner for the most part in my daily life. Even if internally I am consumed with sick visions of violence, terror, sex, death. It's stuck deep inside. An old shrapnel wound. Just there. Just ignore it. Just use it.

I've noticed a lot of times, with a lot of my girlfriends that they'll be singularly obsessed with one man and they'll do an interview and they'll aim it at one man. I did it myself; I did it with Kurt forever. I went to Germany and every interview I did, I asked if they were interviewing Nirvana the following week – will you tell that Kurt Cobain that I have a *huge* crush on him? Everyfuckingwhere he went . . . He was like: 'Oh my God. She's crazy.' 'Oh,' I said, 'And tell him I'm pregnant . . . and my Daddy's mad about it!' Scheming females. Such bitches! Ha!

That little Nine Inch Nails tour made me feel like challenging technology on my terms – I'm a rock girl, so I'm not going to go get a fucking sampler tomorrow! But there are other formats. There are other fucking frontiers. I feel a little more ambitious about how I want the next record to sound. And thematically what I want to sing about.

I just wrote a song that wasn't about death at all. I have to write another record. I want to create a record that's really good to fuck to, like This Mortal Coil or Mazzy Star. All of that industrial music and all that sampling – I'm not going techno by any means. I've been writing like crazy. It's not because I love anybody, it's not love writing . . . I'm dealing with sex, I'm dealing with death and I'm dealing with it differently. I want to get the sound of – I know it's recorded somewhere – conception: what does it sound like when the sperm meets the egg? What is the sound of a death rattle? I want that sound. I want the sound of the agony of heroin withdrawal. I know this sounds pompous and over the top, but fuck, hey, you know what, I don't care. Previous to this night, my big goal was writing a good REM song; previous to that it was writing a good Nirvana song. It's changed me a lot. When I go see a show, I want to get turned on. I want to fucking want to fuck. I want there to be an element of sexuality about things. I like that. That's why I like rock.

I strap on that motherfucking guitar and you cannot fuck with me. That's my feeling. I just made a video for 'Doll Parts' and I was like – 'Tits, tits, more tits! Fuck it! Tits! Legs! Ass! Arms! Tits! Legs!' I want the next shot to go straight up my pussy, fuck it. When I say 'I am doll heart' I want to grab my pussy. Not in a Madonna way; it's very ironic. It's not aggressive, hey, I'm a man. I'm not a man. I couldn't stand it. I'm just the opposite. I am, I guess, a 'femmeniste'. Militant, but I recognise nature and the difference between us. I love men. They scare me. But when men learn grace, it is awesome.

I'm a crazed, obsessive, pyschotic bitch and if you fuck with me, I'll boil a rabbit. That whole chapter about *Fatal Attraction* in *Backlash* – I'm so scared that people will think I'm like that. The worst I've ever done is long letters that I never sent. Except once. That's the worst. I think Morrissey's my secret soul brother, but then so does every confused high school kid out there . . . For me, what has gone on internally has been hell. And that's where I get all my shit from. That's why I don't need anyone to die on me because I already have a back catalogue that could go on for twenty albums. It would be quite repetitive, I might add.

I feel like writing and drinking tea right now and it's also light out, so I'm going to go.

Echobelly (clockwise from top left): Andy Henderson, Alex Keyser, Glenn Johansson, Sonya Aurora Madan

sonya aurora madan & debbie smith

Echobelly

I serenade the walls
Young people have it all dear
And surely life is a gas
We never had it bad dear
Oh it was pointless from the start
Or did we cultivate the art
I swim in circles, in puddles, in trouble
And then I go

('Insomniac' from Everyone's Got One)

The first time Echobelly heard their début EP, 'Bellyache', on the radio, singer-songwriter Sonya Aurora Madan was rolling round on the floor yelping 'Oh my God!' while drummer Andy Henderson lay in the bath screaming. That was in October 1993. In less than a year, the band became cocky pop stars reaching the point of media saturation. In less than a year, 28-year-old Sonya has been hailed as a cultural icon, a Deborah Harry sing-alike, a female Morrissey, our first Asian pop star, a 'babe-to-die-for'. Morrissey turned up, without invitation, at Sonya and guitarist Glenn Johansson's west London flat for tea in early 1994. Sonya, who was in her slippers, dusting, at the time, was saucer-eyed and incredulous; six months later, she talks of him as an old and dear friend.

Echobelly were so good so soon that they made the music media gasp 'too good to be true?' and 'contrived!' When they formed in summer 1992, not even the band could have anticipated the furore which was to greet them. Those who aren't worrying about Echobelly's near-perfect guitar pop tunes can't seem to get enough of Sonya's soundbites. 'Why do I get asked such in-depth questions? Do Oasis get asked all these questions? People are trying to take bits of me all the time . . . it's doing my head in!' she said in *NME*, and in *Q*: 'I want more emphasis on being a woman in rock 'n' roll than being an Asian. I didn't go into this to represent a minority, I did it for me.'

She may not want to constantly discuss being Asian, but she has been known to wear a Union Jack T-shirt with 'My Country Too' scrawled across it, and feelings of alienation litter her lyrics. On Echobelly's début album, *Everyone's Got One* (it's an acronym), the crashing pop complements heated words about racism, sexism, abortion, drugs and tainted love. 'Give Her a Gun' incites Asian women to take control; 'Bellyache' explores how a friend went into denial after having an abortion; 'Father, Ruler, King, Computer' rails against Asian marital traditions; 'Close . . . but' deals with a couple high on drugs rather than love.

Besides having an Asian frontwoman who writes smart lyrics, gives good quotes and is a trained kick-boxer, Echobelly boasts Glenn, a Swedish guitarist who adores the Smiths, plays a mean riff and has a brief but curious history in pornographic magazines; Andy, who used to play in Bristol band Automatic Tianini with Polly Harvey until she was booted out for playing crap sax and he moved on; and Alex Keyser, who plays the moody bassist role. When Glenn broke his arm (he slipped outside a pub) in spring 1994, former Curve guitarist Debbie Smith joined the band temporarily. She never left. An Anglo-Caribbean tomboy lesbian who wears a Queer T-shirt on stage, Debbie is as much a mix of tough and pussycat as Sonya. Suffocated in her previous bands, Debbie feels that her time has come with Echobelly.

In her immaculate flat (polished floorboards, candles, carefully filed cassettes and CDs), Sonya smokes and drinks rum and Coke. Her cats – Ella who has a wonky tail and Moz, a big, sleek black tom who obsessively eats cut flowers – chase each other round and round. Charming though she is, there is an underlying feeling of controlled aggression and knowing manipulation in Sonya. If she was a guy, this would be expected. But as a woman, she has to make tough decisions about the way she plays the game – as an 'exotic Asian babe' who can get what she wants by flashing sexy smiles or as an intelligent singer-songwriter whose talent gets her places.

The rise towards the top has been demanding – in summer 1994, Echobelly not only stormed the New Music Seminar in New York but also played every British and European festival worth playing. And Sonya has had to learn to deal with 90 per cent of the attention. But, as she told the *Guardian* at the end of summer 1994: 'Being in a band, fronting it, being a strong woman and being Asian, I expect a lot of criticism and misunderstanding but at the same time I really do believe in what I'm doing. I want every prize existing, I want to be on the cover of every publication. I want to be best at what I do.' Who said anything about an ego?

Sonya Aurora Madan

I came to England from India when I was pretty young, about three years old. My parents came over a year before, leaving my older sister and me with my grandmother in Delhi. She became our surrogate mother for the year that we were separated from our parents. I never knew my grandfather; he died when my mother was a child. My grandmother had this attitude that you've really got to look after what you've got, and she was very careful with everything. That year had a lasting effect on me; I have this memory of my parents sending us a parcel and, as my mother knew my grandmother wouldn't let us play with anything expensive, she deliberately sent us these cheap plastic Woolworth's dolls. Once a month my granny would let me look at the doll in the plastic wrapper and then it would go back up on the shelf.

When we came to England, my mother came to collect us from the airport. Apparently I said to her: 'Hello, Auntie.' I'd forgotten all about her by that time, and she cried her eyes out. 'Oh, I'm not your auntie, I'm your mother.' It was a very traumatic time. But it was exciting suddenly to be the centre of attention. And it's a very egotistical thing to do what I'm doing, to be in a band, but in the back of my mind remains this almost past-life-type feeling, and it haunts me sometimes. When twilight starts to fall, I sometimes feel this real sadness, a loneliness, alienation, and it's definitely from my childhood. It's hard to explain, really.

I always felt jealous of my English friends who grew up with compatible school and home lives. I had a comfortable upbringing, though. We were reasonably well off and our parents worked very hard to look after us, but still the past is rooted in my memory. It has expressed itself in my writing, that whole alienation theme. I only started writing a few years ago and it's almost like an exorcism, to put it into words.

I went back to India for the first time about six years ago. It's an amazing country. It was the most daunting experience I've had in the past decade. I went back thinking I didn't remember anything, and when I got there it was almost like being hypnotised into a past life. I went back to the place where I was born. It was midnight when I crept inside. I was standing there in this courtyard, looking at this barn-like structure that had been my grandmother's house. It was like a manger; there was this huge cow, it was amazing . . . It was almost a spiritual experience.

I come from an Indian background, but if your parents come over when you're three years old, you end up having a reasonably westernised upbringing. And, more importantly, my parents didn't associate with many other Indian families; there wasn't this huge family structure you find with a lot of Indian and Greek families over here, none of those big family get-togethers where you celebrate your identity. We didn't really have that. My father is a bit reserved and likes his privacy. We were pretty westernised as a family, but there are still Indian elements in me which have remained. The first time I went out with an English boy, I remember feeling frustrated that he couldn't understand my identity, that he could only see the English side of me. It was almost patronising.

Every child rebels in their own way and my form of rebellious-ness . . . it's really difficult to explain. When you come here from another country, you're made to feel second class. As a child you can end up blaming your parents for your skin colour, taking out all the aggression you receive at school on them, which is really cruel, really sad, because your parents haven't done anything wrong. My own way of rebelling was refusing to speak the Hindi language, so I wouldn't learn anything except the most basic words.

I was brought up in Hillingdon, a suburb of north-west London. My father worked as a customs officer at Heathrow airport and my mother was a schoolteacher. It's a pretty nondescript suburban region. I went to a local school which was a bit rough and I got into a few battles. I've always been awkward, in the sense that I've always felt I've had an old head on a young body. I was in a gang, and as I did a lot of martial arts I was quite a tough little kid. When I was about 13, I yelled at my mates for picking on this girl. I thought I was doing a really good deed; I felt really happy for helping someone, until she turned round and started picking on me. I was so confused, I couldn't figure it out.

I tried to form my own identity when I was about 16 or 17. I was this tank girl of 17 who was ruthless and could defend herself and used all these martial arts to say: 'No one can touch me, no one can come near me.' I made a trip to a trendy hairdresser's in London, had a Mohawk done, came back home, and my father opened the door and yelled: 'You bastard.' He shut the door and wouldn't let me into the house. I was locked out for hours while my mum pleaded with him to let me in. I was really proud that I'd created that sort of angst in my father. It was almost like: 'Fuck you! This is my identity.'

It started from there and then in the sixth form at school I went overboard, had different hair every week, made my own clothes, which I used to daub with paint. I really thought I was the bee's knees, I thought I was special in some respect – a bit pathetic really, but it came from this innate need to stand out as an individual, because I didn't feel as though I fitted into anything. I wasn't like other Indian girls at school, I didn't listen to bhangra, I didn't have that sense of community, I didn't want to marry an Indian boy. I didn't fit into any category, I was an East–West casualty. I didn't think that there were other kids like me. But of course there must have been.

My parents brought us up with a combination of dictatorial tolerance and devoted love – as they had three daughters they were naturally a little more protective, but I could wear make-up, I could drink alcohol, no problem. But if I went out with a guy, all hell broke loose. My father suddenly clamped down when I was 18, and stopped me from seeing my first boyfriend. He told me I was only allowed out of the house to go to the library once a week to study. We used to have these flaming rows, because my older sister, who was a total academic, had gone to California to study astrophysics, so she was fine, she was out, and my younger sister was never a problem. All the trouble came from me. I once ran away from home for a few hours – a pathetic scene because I'd forgotten to take my slippers off, it was really quite a sitcom-type situation. My parents are both PhDs; I did a degree in psychology in London and left it at that, because unfortunately my need to do a degree was less important than my need to get out into the big wide world and discover life.

When I moved to London, I was a virgin. I was at college and there were boys. Wooah! Rock and roll! Drugs! I'm surprised I didn't go absolutely berserk. But then it was the old head on young shoulders. I didn't calm down, I just thought: 'I'm going to be a voyeur. I'm going to learn from the others.' The song 'Insomniac' is about the glorious hedonistic time that is made possible when you leave home for college. There are always a few bright sparks who have self-destructive tendencies. I didn't really see any gigs until I left home; I went to a few school parties, but I had to be in quite early. I used to listen to John Peel on Radio 1 and I remember hearing Cabaret Voltaire and other bands and thinking: 'Wow! There's another world out there.'

Most people have reference points from their older siblings' record collections, but my older sister, although she was into David Bowie, was very much out of my life at that stage as she was studying abroad. And because I didn't buy records, I wasn't really a fan of anybody. Given the opportunity I'm sure I could have been. I had limited access to pop culture. God knows why I'm doing what I'm doing, I never really grew up with a pop culture. Having said that, all suburban kids watch *Top of the Pops* and go to school, and you do get involved in the little dreams that your peers are going through. I remember Deborah Harry on *Top of the Pops* – she took off her dark glasses and she had these most amazing metallic eyes. I was fascinated by her make-up, that anyone could wear such beautiful make-up and look so glamorous. I think she had that effect on everyone. People have said my voice sounds a little like hers – including Morrissey!

As soon as I got to college, I started meeting people who had record collections. My first experience was living with these guys in Soho, and having the wildest times – it was a one-bedroom place and the guys used to sleep on the sofa, and my flatmate Maria and I used to share the double bed. It was great, it was like having a sister in bed; we'd put our teddy bears in the middle! I'd wake up in the morning and there'd be people asleep all over the living-room floor because we'd been out clubbing and they couldn't get home. It was wonderful. The guys I was living with liked the Clash and the Who, all sorts of things; I got a taste of 'cock rock'. I have to say I wasn't very discriminating, I was a total sheep, I followed what everyone else was into. I didn't know any better, and I'd go to see the bands that everybody else went to see. But music wasn't that much of a love until I met a musician at a venue in London, and he became my first proper boyfriend. He was in a band – which never made it – and he took me off to America. It was just rock 'n' roll, and I became 'number one groupie'.

It was a total change. I stopped going to college for months, but I began to understand the whole concept of pop music. I suddenly began to realise that when I was at home wandering around, I always used to love to sing. I never realised I could do something like that; I was always brought up to think I was an academic. Indian parents are quite strict in their upbringing, and unless they're very liberal, don't encourage their children to go into the arts. It's just not appreciated or understood, and when I decided that I wanted to sing properly, all hell let loose at home again. Even though I was older by that time – you're always a child to Indian parents. It was guilt-tripping all the time. My father was laying all these massive Indian guilt trips on me: 'We've looked after you, we've paid you through college . . .' I know it sounds really dull, but he broke my heart, because I had suddenly discovered what I wanted to do.

Ironically enough, my parents are now quite excited about Echobelly. They've suddenly become quite proud of me. My father said before he went to India: 'Actually Sonya, I don't mind what you do, as long as you're successful.' To me, that smacked of the whole bloody Indian attitude. I know it sounds really repulsive, but that's

SONYA AURORA MADAN & DEBBIE SMITH

the way it is. If I made a million pounds out of doing this, then fine. Sonya is a success. But if I wrote the most brilliant song and yet didn't make it, then I'd be a failure and in his eyes I would've wasted my life. Indians have this attitude towards art: they can appreciate poetry and they can quote it to each other, when they're sitting there drunk . . . Young Indians, the middle classes, often go to hotels, drink and eat a meal, and then quote poetry to each other. But at the same time, it's for others to actually write the poetry. Such hypocrisy. My mother was quite shrewd about the way I've chosen to live my life. She said: 'I'm quite happy for you not to marry an Indian boy.' After a while she was actually advocating me going out with white boys. I would like my parents' blessing, because they are two of the few people that can bring me down. We grow up Indian, Jewish, whatever, wanting to please our parents; we're brought up that way.

I never thought of being an artist, although I used to sing and make up these songs when I was a kid and get physically high off it. Maybe it was just running out of air when you're singing and you can't control your diaphragm properly! It was just such a beautiful thing to do – this is going to sound really bad – such a pure thing to use your voice as an instrument. True soul is not what people class as soul music; to me, Björk is a very soulful singer, Morrissey is a very soulful singer, as much so as Aretha Franklin. To be able to tune into yourself is a very selfish thing to do in a literal sense, but you can draw strength from it. I change when I'm on stage. I'm a totally different person. Backstage, I'm quite a shy, affable character. When I go on stage I have an ego. I will act my favourite part. I love it. I think we've got a lot going for us and that's why some people feel suspicious of it. Sometimes I'll sing and the whole experience leaves me breathless, I get off on it. And I still sing when I'm hoovering!

When I first got my cat Ella, I used to sing her to sleep, and she'd be purring away. I have a certain tone that works, because I used to use that tone when she was a kitten. There was something very comforting about my grandmother singing to me when I was a child. In India you get these amazing things called *kierthans* – groups of women who sing and dance all night. My mother would go and sometimes I'd go with her. They play tablas and you're singing folk songs with these huge voices, a few women start danc-ing, and you go off into a trance watching your aunties. It's that womanly-motherly comfort, the whole singing thing; it's almost a womb-like experience, sitting in a hall surrounded by women.

I met Glenn [Johansson] at a gig, we got on really well, started going out together and writing bits and pieces of songs. I don't think even he took me seriously at that point; I was working and living a normal life in London, then slowly but surely, it started to happen. The name 'Echobelly' existed before the band. I wanted a word that was quite female and organic and voluptuous, and Echobelly had it. It also had the meaning of being hungry for something, which I thought was quite potent. I wanted something almost birth-like. We just sat together and wrote all these names down and it stuck out. I like the idea of a word that doesn't actually mean anything by itself but which expresses succinctly what we're doing.

I had actually wanted girls in the band, or a girl, a woman, whatever, who was able to do what we wanted. As long as they could play the instrument. But we couldn't find one – not until Debbie [Smith] joined. The guys in the band are like brothers. It's a nice feeling because you do actually become a gang, a family. I'm proud of them all, as individuals, they've all got something to offer. I'm close to them. It's quite sad: you sometimes end up losing your friends, especially friends who don't understand music. The band bicker. The other day Alex [Keyser] and Andy [Henderson] had a disagreement in rehearsal, Andy lost his temper, threw a chair and it smashed a load of light bulbs. I thought: 'OK, here we go, temper tantrum,' but that's just the way he is. He's got a young heart, but he's also one of the most generous people you'll meet.

There are times when I'd like to have other women around. At one point I wanted to surround myself with a female manager, a female tour manager, but at the end of the day I think that's sexist in its own way. You choose people who are good. I find I get closer to women; with men there's usually a bit of a barrier. Men always see you as a potential sex object and there's very little you can do about it. Women can express themselves so much more honestly. I feel very comfortable sitting here talking to you, but if I was sitting here talking to a male writer it would be quite different. A lot of the men who work in the business around me come out with sexist

SONYA AURORA MADAN & DEBBIE SMITH

comments all the time. They always look at me afterwards, 'cause they know I'm going to haul them up on it. But it's the way they are, you can't change things overnight.

On the day I cut my hair off and I was wearing a man's suit, I thought I looked very nice! Someone was joking around and said: 'Oh yes, that's your new dykey look.' Which I actually found a bit cutting, because although he was joking, I knew he meant it as well. It was almost like he was saying: 'I don't find you as attractive as before.' I just thought: 'Well, fuck you. I don't need your comments anyway.' It was a prime example of judging women on what they look like. It's generally women who find skinny women attractive. Men go for curves. I'm not curvaceous, I'm like a stick. I wear children's clothes half the time! I'm not going to put on weight for anyone; I can't, I burn up the calories, that's just the way I am. I could try, I could wear sexier clothes, I could wear more make-up and in a way I suppose I have done that.

When we made the video for our second single, 'Insomniac', I got dressed up as a transvestite, to show as a quick flash at the beginning. But the record company wanted the image to be used all the way through, so I thought: 'All right, I'll play the game for a while if it keeps everyone happy.' I walked on to the video set and I had my glasses on and my jeans and a jacket, and I walked past everyone and nobody paid any attention. But when I put on the dress and some make-up and a wig, walked down the stairs, most of the men were ogling me. And the cameraman said: 'God, the camera loves you.' It was just pathetic. Is that what it takes? A wig and a bit of lipstick?

When I left home for college, men, and the whole ability to attract men, were fascinating. After being trapped for so long, all of a sudden I was free, although I didn't really sleep around as I was shy in that respect. I flirted and I enjoyed men's attention, because it was something new, it was a toy, but now it bores me. I think it's something about being older; it's boring to find an idiot who fancies you, there's nothing in it. But I'm truly, truly interested in men who ignite something in my mind. Sex is psychological. The best sex, the best partner, is someone who turns you on mentally, and that's what I'm interested in.

I didn't have sex, or a boyfriend for over a year. It's a conscious choice in the fact that I haven't found a man that I've wanted to get involved with on anything other than a platonic level. I've had offers, but what does that mean? If you don't find a person attractive even for a one-night stand . . . I was in the gym recently and there was a girl in there, and I just could not take my eyes off her. She was tall, muscular, short blonde hair, not masculine, but strong. And she was staring at me. I found her so attractive. I was shocked at myself. I saw her once more, but we never talked and I haven't seen her again. Since then, there's another woman that I also find attractive now, and it's like a new awakening which I'm actually scared of . . . because I didn't know that these things existed within me. I tend to pay attention to women more than men. But I never thought of myself as fancying women until recently. Quite a revelation. I don't know how far I'll take it. I think men are jealous at the closeness women can share.

I'm going through a phase right now where I'm very angry; not anti-men, I'm not scared of men – I love most people, well, not love, but I'm happy to let people be what they are. I'm going through a phase where I don't want male attention because I'm so busy trying to discover myself, and I know that if a man gets in the way I'm going to get distracted. The band is just too important. There's a song that we've just done, 'Father, Ruler, King, Computer', the title of which is taken from Germaine Greer's *The Female Eunuch*. There's a line in the song: 'The half-a-couple fantasy . . .' It's a celebration of female independence, it's not an anti-male thing. I'm just happy to leave them out of my life for the moment and sure, there'll come a time when I need . . . it almost scares men, the fact that I'm not interested; they're threatened by the fact that they're not important right now.

Feminism is still considered a dirty word among some women as well as men. There is still a great deal of discrepancy between what is openly accepted and people's secret views. I grew up in a family of four women to one man (Mum, three daughters and Dad). All the women in my family are pretty strong-willed and I suppose that I am too. My mother has probably never used the word 'feminist' in her life, but her sense of self and her no-nonsense nature have always been central to her personality. Despite the inevitable culture clashes between us, she has helped instil in me a sense of self-belief, which borders on the stubborn.

I do consider myself to be a feminist – I want equality through mutual tolerance and understanding. I am interested in the concept of yin–yang. A few years back I had a heated discussion with my karate master of the time, on the 'role' of the sexes. I argued that his views, which stemmed from traditional Japanese culture, objectified women and kept us down, ironically by putting us on a moral pedestal. I accepted his belief that male and female strengths are fundamentally different, in that men are immediately physically stronger whereas women's increased pain threshold and longevity are the root of our strength. I believe that the heavy value placed on immediate strength in our societies is an important factor in understanding the prevalence of sexism. Who knows, maybe human history is cyclical – the ancient female fertility cults and futurist philosophy may once again celebrate female strength and sexuality.

Some say that the reason why women are so openly portrayed as sexual objects is because we are more aesthetically pleasing in a physical sense. I feel that this is a cop-out and often an excuse for sexist exploitation. We have plenty of top-shelf porn magazines in this country depicting women in 'legs astride' poses and yet it is illegal to have a picture of an erect penis.

It's all very well talking about my upbringing, but although it has moulded my character, it's not that important. Everybody thinks the song 'I Don't Belong Here' off our first EP is a song about my personal alienation, but there are only a few lines about me. It's very limiting to write about personal experiences and it's also very difficult, because there's only so much you can ultimately say. You always have this feeling in the back of your mind that it's boring for other people if you impose your own personal angst on them. Most of my songs are written in a voyeuristic sense. I'm the ultimate voyeur! And a lot of them are quite heavy; not dirty, but in a sexually explicit way.

'Centipede' is about incest. I have always been fascinated by the fact that people who've been sexually abused must have a huge problem with the fact that they might actually be attached to that person. It's not simply about hating, that straightforward black and white: 'I hate you, I hate what you've done to me.' But how do you cope with the Lolita complex, with the fact that you might actually have loved them, when they're doing that to you? 'Bellyache' is about a friend who had an abortion. Her way of coming to terms with it was to deny the effect it had on her emotionally and to equate it with a trip to the dentist.

When it comes to lyrics, I get these feelings – it's the same sort of thing as the feeling when it's twilight and I start getting lonely. I could be on a bus, or driving to a gig, all rock 'n' roll and wonderful, and the guys are being complete idiots, and it's brilliant, but I look out of the window and the sky is blackening, and my heart sinks. It lasts a second and then it's gone, but it's always there. I don't want therapy, I don't need it, but it's always there, and it comes from my parents leaving me. It comes from my childhood. When we first came to London, we lived in one room: my sister, myself, my mother and father slept in one bed. I have this memory that will never leave me, of looking up – it must have been one of the first few nights that I arrived in England – I was lying on the bed, I looked up, and there was a suitcase on the wardrobe, and I still imagine it. I see the suitcase on the wardrobe, the suitcase that took whatever clothes we had from India to England.

It represented the act of being torn from the only home I knew to this horrible place that was cold and grey. England was totally grey after India – the rainbow colours, the noise, the smell. It's unbelievable, the sun . . . And then you come to England. It's grey, people are less friendly. Everything about it was colourless compared to a three-year-old's vision of home. I have this horrible memory, of the suitcase, of India, the airport. Just flashes, it's really . . . stupid, to even think that it can still affect me, because it's over now. I should be grown-up and totally mature about the whole thing, but it doesn't go away.

I watch programmes about Auschwitz or whatever, and I sit here with Glenn, who's blonde, Swedish, blue-eyed, and he's like: 'That's fucking terrible, what's on the other side? Let's watch that instead.' I'm left with a stone in my heart, and I think: 'My God, can you imagine being there?' I can't watch horror films, because every

SONYA AURORA MADAN & DEBBIE SMITH

time I see something horrific, I'm *there*. I put myself in the situation. At my age, I can't sit in a room alone and watch a horror film, because I'd dream about it for days. It's really pathetic, I get so engrossed in the whole thing that I can't detach myself from it. I always thought that as a child, if you can't sleep with the light off, or you're scared of going to the toilet, or getting a drink of water, it'll go away when you're an adult. But it hasn't gone away yet. I'm still scared. I don't even know what I'm scared of. I'm so envious of the fact that most of my friends seem to have had totally comfortable, warm, normal upbringings and although mine hasn't been too bad, I always feel that I could have been trapped, but I escaped. I don't know if it's knowing that I could have had an arranged marriage by this age, but it's there.

I have a recurring dream. There's a house I can make out, and when I dream of the house, I know what's going to happen. Sometimes it's a good dream, and sometimes it's about to turn nasty, and hopefully I wake up. Different things happen in this recurring dream. Once there was a huge staircase shedding golden light, and I was climbing to the top, and it was all very wonderful, and then it suddenly turned nasty and I woke up. Another time, I was trying to cross the road outside the house and was just about to get run over by 'ee-aw, ee-aw' – here it comes, and I wake up, heart palpitating, in a cold sweat. I don't know where the house is. I just recognise it when I'm there.

The only thing that hasn't gone away is that loneliness. And also now, for the first time I'm on my own. I don't have a boyfriend, a few of the girlfriends that I was close to seem to have drifted, and my parents went back to India in April 1993. I don't actually have many close people around me at this time. I find that I don't get close to people easily – although I'm very good at getting on with people, and I can bend my personality to get on with a person, very few people become close to me. But when they do, they become part of my extended family. Now my parents are back in India, I would do a lot for my close friends, and I expect the same from them. That's another Indian thing, or maybe it's just me, but I do feel I have this hunger. I don't give a shit about anyone else as long as my friends appreciate what I'm doing. The few people that mean a lot to me can move me really easily, I'm far too sensitive for my own good, and I feel like I need their support. I'm close to Glenn, but there's only so much you can talk to the band about. I think they'd be there for me if I needed them, it wouldn't be a problem. But still the loneliness, the isolation, doesn't seem to have gone away.

It's not the music, the lyrics, the poetry or the art that's important to me. It's not what makes me laugh, it's what makes me cry. Lots of things can make you laugh, but when it really hurts, when it touches you, you take it with you for the rest of your life. I was so chuffed when Morrissey was quoting my lyrics to me. The song 'I Don't Belong Here' – 'We are dreamers, dreamers a nightmare apart' – I was touched by the fact that he likes my lyrics. I don't have a problem with anyone saying we sound Smiths-like: we are not trying to be the Smiths, but if there are elements in there then that's because they are one of our influences. None of our songs is about one strict subject. You find that little sentences sneak in by themselves. I do take it seriously, I don't feel I always have to apologise for it, but I'm really – not impressed, but *surprised* by my lyrics. Almost as if I haven't written them. I sit back and I read them, and I think: 'Oh my God, that sentence is saying something about me', although it was written about something else.

I wrote this song called 'Talent', that's really vitriolic, where I slag off people I've known in the music industry. I really try and make an effort with people and I'm aware of the fact that I can talk to anybody. But I'm totally impatient with stupidity, I'm so shocked by the amount of people, men – not only men, though – in the music business who have not got a clue. A&R, marketing . . . just total chancers. They never see what's going on on the street, and then they pick up on it too late and sign the wrong bands. 'Talent' could piss a lot of people off. It's got lines like: 'Sell your soul, to papers that cater for cock 'n' roll.' I'm shouting out against sexist terms. The line in the chorus – 'Any offers, any pre-sales, we're the Umm & R' – is about all the A&R 'posse'. In 1993 we went in and out of A&R offices continually, we were the hot new band to sign, and the majority of these guys are egotists with portable phones. They didn't understand what the band was doing. I remember having this meeting with this guy in a pub, and he was asking: 'So what are you going to wear?' He hadn't even signed the band and he was insinuating that he'd like to see me in a dress, for me to be a little bit more titillating. It's like: 'Fuck you!'

SONYA AURORA MADAN & DEBBIE SMITH

I didn't say anything, I just looked at him and that upset him more. If I'd answered back, he would have been defensive. I just looked and thought: 'I'm not even going to bother.' But immediately I knew I didn't want to sign to that company.

I feel that people are so much stricter and more opinionated when it comes to women. If Polly Harvey was as conventionally pretty as Kylie Minogue, would she be allowed to do what she does? And if not, why? That's the ultimate sexism. It really upsets me that you are allowed to be . . . Tracy Chapman, for want of a better example, and write meaningful lyrics, or you can look like the woman in Saint Etienne and not be able to sing particularly well. You're allowed to be one or the other but why aren't you allowed to be everything? There's a great line in the film *Night on Earth*: 'Men – can't live with 'em, can't shoot 'em.'

But there are very few female artists that would make me think: 'Yes, I'm proud to be a woman.' Female musicians from Billie Holiday and Ella Fitzgerald to Patti Smith, Bonnie Raitt, Chrissie Hynde and Deborah Harry have all left their mark as artistes in their own right. I don't think that they ever considered themselves to be martyrs for future generations. Women have been wailing since the dawn of civilisation! The first time I spoke with our American press agent, she mentioned her involvement in an organisation called SWIM – Strong Women in Music. I have not heard of anything comparable here in Britain. If anything, it's going the other way. I've heard that the New Wave of New Wave scene was concocted by a handful of male journalists during a pub discussion. I have very little to say about it apart from the fact that I ignore the term. It has limited relevance to what I do. We were initially roped into this celebration of macho posturing because I wore a T-shirt with a Union Jack on it. (It's called irony, boys.) Now the same journalists seem to be sulking because we've been extracted from the clique. Fuck it, I'm used to not fitting in. I'm still looking in from the outside. Society is still coming to terms with strong, sexy women, Madonna being a prime example. How much criticism did she receive about her book *Sex* after people had a good look at the pictures? Regardless of whether we like Madonna, being in control of her own image seems to intimidate people who require female sexuality to be portrayed in a traditionally passive role.

Polly Harvey is really brilliant and I get off on some of her stuff, but at the same time it's too limited for me. There is nobody out there. I want to be as important to people as Morrissey is to me, because that is the only way to be. I see myself as a potentially great lyricist, not a pin-up. I'm really trying to take steps to avoid that sort of thing. I want people to read my lyrics and think: 'Fuck, yes. I know what she's saying.' That's the most important thing. 'Give Her a Gun' is about the fate of Asian and Arab women – 'Half the population/One per cent of the wealth.' At one of our gigs, three girls came up to me and sang the words of 'Give Her a Gun' back to me and it was brilliant. That's what it's all about.

Debbie Smith

I was born in 1968 in Victoria Maternity Hospital, Barnet, north London. At the time, my mum and dad were living in my aunt's house in Bounds Green. I grew up quite happily. There was always music on when I was little – my dad had a record player and a big reel-to-reel tape recorder in the living room. We had loads of reggae and soul records and we used to tape the Top 40 – I could memorise it by the age of three and I used to sing the Top 10 to my parents. It was my total obsession until I got bored with it at around 14 and started to think about playing music. My father bought me guitars every Christmas and birthday and me and my brother used to tie them to trees down the garden and shoot them with our bows and arrows. We'd play cowboys and Indians and pour fake blood all over them.

My brother Simon wasn't really into music. He really got into *Fame* when he was about 12. He's a dancer and he was always obsessed with dancing. He liked musical films; to this day I can't abide musicals 'cause he used to prance about every Sunday afternoon and sing *Carmen Jones*. Not the men's parts but the really high falsetto and soprano women's parts, but his voice was breaking. It was hell, absolute hell.

I remember when Elvis died in 1977. It was the same year my grandmother died and for some reason I wanted to know all about Elvis. I bought loads of records and joined the fan club – I wanted to

49

Debbie Smith and Sonya Aurora Madan

be Elvis, I suppose, till I was about 12. Only the young Elvis, not fat Elvis. It was the way he looked, he was so cool: the gold lamé suit and the pink and black clothes. Me and some friends at primary school wanted to put on a tribute to Elvis in the school hall, and we had loads of time off lessons to rehearse it. Somehow we never quite made it, but after that I started picking up the guitar and twanging on it a bit.

I used to be obsessed with *Top of the Pops*, and I remember seeing Suzi Quatro doing 'Can the Can'. She was dressed head to foot in black leather and she was the lead singer with this whacking great bass. That was it. I thought: 'Right. I want to play the bass guitar.' She was the first woman musician I really remember being fired by, and then it was Siouxsie. She was a really strong presence, she just was the ice queen, very haughty and arrogant. Patti Smith and Janis Joplin came a lot later – the first bands that I really listened to apart from all the chart bands were the Slits, the Raincoats, the Au Pairs and Blondie. I was immediately drawn to women's groups.

I had no idea how to play until I was 14 and I went down to Argos and bought a Spanish guitar for £14, a chord book for £1.99, sat in my bedroom with a copy of *The Scream* by Siouxsie and the Banshees and didn't stop till I learnt it. It was really exciting when I learnt my first chord. I put my fingers on the fretboard at random and it sounded nice. I used that one chord for about a year, sliding it up and down the neck, which is what the Banshees mostly did. It was really hard work, 'cause all the guitars I got my hands on were cheap and nasty or the neck was broken or I'd put steel strings on Spanish guitars and really fuck my hands up. But I learnt; I never had any lessons, it was just me and the chord book.

I used to go to loads of gigs, first in school halls in north London and then at proper venues. There was some really terrible eighties thrashcore band at the Clarendon in Hammersmith, and there was also this band Ut playing downstairs who were excellent. I'd never seen a band comprised of mostly women, with a man on drums. They were playing these really weird atonal songs, hitting their guitars and playing violins with bits of wood and stuff like that.

When I was about 17 and doing college A levels, I met this boy Josh in the guitar class. He was extremely quiet and everyone considered him the nerd but I really liked him. When the teacher asked us what kind of music we wanted to play, a voice at the back shouted: 'Siouxsie and the Banshees!' I looked round and it was the nerd from hell. I started hanging out with him and we used to go to little post-punk gigs in north London – Poison Girls and people like that – and go round to each other's houses and play Siouxsie and the Banshees and the Cure.

Our first ever gig was at a garden party in Bounds Green. I think it was a bar mitzvah. I was probably a total mess in those days, turning slowly and painfully into a Goth. I straightened my hair and sprayed on loads of extra-hold hairspray to stock it right up. I looked a right sight, terrible. But I thought I was the bollocks then.

Josh had this little Casio keyboard, I had my Vox guitar and my little amp, and we played Siouxsie and the Banshees covers in the middle of the afternoon. We were pissed by the second number. Then I played bass in a band called the Siren with these serious Goths from Salisbury who were into Sisters of Mercy, Siouxsie and Simple Minds. We did about six gigs and then the band split up very acrimoniously.

At about that time – I was 17 – I came out. I was going out to lots of gay places and I started going out with this woman Theresa, who was a drummer. In the fullness of time, with our mate Debbie Wright and Theresa's identical twin, Anne, we formed this group called Mouth Almighty – the drinking lesbian's band. There were only half a dozen dyke bands around, and we were a total legend in the lesbian music scene, mostly for our world-championship-level drinking. We played loads of benefits, for things like Clause 28, and didn't care about money; if there was beer, or preferably Scotch, we'd drink it. We farted about for about four or five years, did a couple of straight gigs, including one supporting Blur which was quite funny, and after that we totally split up.

I joined a band called the Darlings, which consisted of me, Lesley Woods from the Au Pairs, Ellyott who is now in Sister George and another woman, Elise, who played bass. We were all at a loose end and we thought it would be a good idea. Lesley had come back from the ghost of the Au Pairs and we thought we'd conquer the world, but we didn't. That was 1990. We made one or two demos and played six gigs. It was just too many different directions – me and Ellyott were: 'Louder, faster, harder . . .' Lesley was in her mellow blues period – after the Au Pairs, she decided to be a barrister and she's doing her pupillage now.

I got really depressed towards the end of the Darlings and I was looking in the *Melody Maker* and *NME* for auditions. I found the advert placed by Dean [Garcia] and Toni [Halliday] – 'melodic, rhythmic guitarist wanted. Into My Bloody Valentine, Ride, Dinosaur Jr' – rang up on Wednesday and that was it, I was in Curve by the Friday. It was the first band I've been in that was in any way successful. It had been hyped before I joined, with the release of the 'Ten Little Girls' EP. There was quite a lot of money being chucked at the band so I got all my equipment bought for me, £800 guitars and expensive effects. I didn't even have to pick up my guitar – a roadie would put it round my neck and hand me the plectrum. I kept thinking: 'Wow! I'm a rock star!'

I knew that Curve were going to split up at the end of the American tour. We'd already been told to feel free to look for other work when we got back, so I did, to no avail. Then I started getting friendly with Echobelly – oh yes, I fancied Sonya – and we went out a few times and got on really well. I went to see them in Coventry the night that her majesty [Morrissey] was there, and on the way back Alex the bass player asked me down to a rehearsal for a jam. Nothing happened, but a couple of weeks later I got a phone call from Sonya saying Glenn had broken his arm and did I want to join the band for the tour? I thought: 'Yes! Yes! Yes!' I was constantly listening to the 'Bellyache' EP and imagining what it would sound like if I was playing. And then it bloody happened. It was just the most amazing break, exactly what I wanted. We did some rehearsals and Glenn's arm was healing up – by the time the tour came he was OK to play, but in the end they added me on the other side of the stage and liked it so much they decided to keep me. That was really sweet.

Being in Curve was basically . . . boring. Like dictation. I always liked playing live but there was no real creativity there, apart from when I did my sonic blasts. With Echobelly, from day one if I made an interesting noise or improvised, it was taken on board.

53

SONYA AURORA MADAN & DEBBIE SMITH

It's difficult to pinpoint what the differences are between an all-women and mixed-gender bands, 'cause women have egos and problems as well. There's some basic understanding in an all-women band. When you've got boys in the band there is automatically a masculine, more aggressive side – but then I'm happy to be a lad, it's an acceptance thing. Boys generally tend to give it a bit of attitude, which I find quite good to play up to.

I've never, ever experienced homophobia in the press or from anybody who's actually come up to talk to me. I've always been out; if anyone asks, I'll tell them. It should be obvious to most people. Never mind the T-shirts that I constantly parade about in. A lot of people say: 'Yeah! It's really good that you're out. I thought you were a little guy, but you're not, are you?' That still happens with Echobelly. I walked past somebody in some pub the other day and they said: 'Hey! That's Mr Echobelly!'

When I started playing in bands I was generally the only girl in the group. I was also usually one of the best musicians in the group so they used to respect me for that. It was only when I played in strange pubs that roadies would say, 'Ello luv, shall I get your amp? That's the thing that you plug into the wall and the sound comes out of.'

I did worry a little about how I actually perceived myself as a black woman playing what is generically white, middle-class, male music. I still don't know how to reconcile it, but indie-pop – that's what I actually play best. People have found me intimidating. I've been called 'that fucking tank girl', mostly by blokes. Once when I was in Curve, a boy of about 16 came up to me and said: 'When I go home, I'm going to get out my Curve records, stand in front of the mirror, slick my hair back, put on my guitar really low and play like you.' That was so weird. This 16-year-old boy trying his best to be a black dyke guitarist!

I've had groupies once or twice . . . maybe. My first ever groupie was with Mouth Almighty. We did a European tour and stayed in Eindhoven in a massive squat. One of the girls there, who didn't speak a word of English, picked me out after our gig and said (obviously in Dutch), 'You're sleeping with me.' So I did. I had no choice in the matter, really. On the very first night of a Curve tour, in Nottingham, this girl came up to me and started chatting. I could tell she was a dyke. She was really nervous, and when we were going back to the bus she said: 'Can I come back to your hotel room?' I said: 'OK then.' We had a few drinks and she came back to my hotel room with me. I'm very passive in these situations!

I saw Huggy Bear on *The Word* and thought: 'Fucking hell, yes!' I went and saw a few bands and really got off on the energy. It was like when I was younger and used to go to all those anarcho-punk, crusty-type things. It was a vibe, everybody was really into what they were doing. It was spawning a lot of new bands and lots of women were getting up on stage: some of them were terrible, some were quite good and some were excellent. But it was encouraging women to play, which I had nothing against.

I'd read a lot about Huggy Bear, and the way they were being written about annoyed me. I could understand exactly why Huggy Bear refused to talk to the music press. The way Riot Grrrl was being treated: 'Oh yes! girls can pick up guitars too!' My flatmate Janis and I were arguing for hours because the press we'd read was so muddled – the idea was that Huggy Bear had invented feminism, a new, improved feminism and they were girls playing guitars; not very well, but they were still good. That's exactly what people used to say about the Raincoats and the Au Pairs. But their legacy was hardly mentioned at the beginning and that really fucked me off.

New Wave of New Wave was definitely a total female castration of Riot Grrrl. The music press couldn't handle the woman power. What is that bollocks anyway, how can you have a New Wave of New Wave? I learnt from being in Curve that there is a definite time span to being in a band; sooner or later the press are going to get really tired of it. The Happy Mondays, for example, were total press darlings and then that Steven Wells [*NME* journalist] piece came out and that was it – they were totally reviled. That's going to happen to people like Oasis; it's almost exactly the same thing. Working-class Manchester lads. And it *is* a reaction to Riot

SONYA AURORA MADAN & DEBBIE SMITH

Grrrl – lads and fights. Fighting, beer, football. There's so much of that these days, especially in music.

Kim Deal – what a woman! Best thing in the Pixies, several million light-years ahead. When I first saw the Pixies, she came on stage with a cigarette in her mouth and plonked her can of beer down, which is exactly what I do. I met her once, at a Lush gig in Brighton. She must be one of the coolest women *ever*. There's nothing as good as Kim Deal. Polly Harvey comes close musically, but she doesn't have the same personal charisma. Kate Bush is another woman I really admire – she was the first woman to top the British album charts with songs she wrote herself, at the age of 19. She got the piss ripped out of her at the time, but she's still here, doing the same thing – only now she's respected for it.

    I can't help but be cynical in thinking women-in-rock is just another fashion, something that has come into vogue over the last five years. It's always been happening but recently it's boomed and I'd like to think that women will definitely stay in the limelight now. That they'll have just as much rights and say from promotion to creation. Women artists are still marginalised or compartmentalised. Sonya is now being touted as the first Asian woman pop star, which is true, but it creates a defining set of rules which she's got to some-how 'obey'. She's got tremendous responsibility now she's in the limelight; she's got to behave in a certain way and no one should have to think: 'I can't do this because people might copy me.' I'm certainly not going to change because I might influence somebody. In fact, I quite like the idea!

Björk

björk

I travel all around the city
Go in and out of locomotives all alone
There's no one here
And people everywhere.

('Crying' from Debut)

Ten minutes before the agreed interview time, I arrive, ring the doorbell and hear a child's voice shout, 'Yes?' Sindri, Björk's eight-year-old son, pokes his head round the side of the house and squints up at me. 'Yes? What are you here for?' To talk to your mum, I say, and follow him into the small back garden. He sits down on a bench and spins his globe-cum-football, hiding his eyes under the peak of his blue baseball cap. 'She's gone to the shops,' he eventually says. 'This is where I'm from,' he continues, pointing at a tiny island north-east of the UK. 'Iceland. This is where I've been.' He points with dirty fingernails to Thailand, Germany, Italy and a dozen more countries. He tells me the highest mountain in Europe, that Italy and France are at present arguing over a piece of land which separates them, and discusses different oceans and seas. I feel half his age.

His mum comes down the alleyway and he shouts something in Icelandic to her. Björk is holding a carrier bag, wearing a big red coat, a long, purple-grey satin dress, a light blue jumper and blue (no name) sneakers. Her hair is tied back, her face brown and freckly. Björk and Sindri talk (fast and loud) in Icelandic, as she unpacks the food in the kitchen. She drops two pita breads in the toaster, pours some orange juice, slices the pita breads open, spreads cheese in them. Sindri eats his lunch outside, talking to a friend who's wandered in through the back gate. Björk takes big bites of bread, chews a little then laughs, open-mouthed, before she's swallowed. Cream cheese is smudged round her mouth. I feel twice her age.

She chats about living near Little Venice in west London (she bought the house in summer 1993); the local weirdos and snobs; feeling content that Sindri is safe to play outside because of the huge communal garden they back on to; Sindri's vast, encyclopaedic knowledge which he regularly recites, 'without showing off, thank God'; searching out a good school for him. Pretty normal, huh? Björk Gumundsdottir does a convincing impression of a single mum in her late twenties whose début solo album just happens to have sold two million plus copies – until she starts talking about music.

Björk, who was brought up in a hippie household in Reykjavik, can't remember a time in her life which didn't involve music. She attended music school between the ages of five and 15, made her first album at 11 (simply called *Björk*, it sold 7,000 copies and became a platinum record in Iceland – the country's population is little over quarter of a million). She was constantly in and out of bands, until the Sugarcubes formed in 1984. The group was never meant to be the indie success it turned out to be; Björk, Thor (Sindri's dad and Björk's former husband) and four other similar-minded musicians, painters and poets who were part of Reykjavik's alternative art scene formed the band, got drunk a lot, had two memorable singles (the gorgeous, sensual 'Birthday' and the hypnotic 'Hit') and a couple of dodgy, waywardly experimental albums before splitting up in December 1992.

What made the Sugarcubes special were the gasping, childish, untainted, almost naïve vocals and the heart-shaped, cheeky, grinning face with a wrinkled-up nose behind them. Björk was always going to be more valuable alone than as part of the Sugarcubes, and moving to London and teaming up with producer and technical whizz Nellee Hooper (who previously lent Soul II Soul, Massive Attack and Sinead O'Connor a touch of class) was the most astute move she could've made. When a few preview cassettes of *Debut* leaked out in early 1993, it was immediately clear that it was going to be one of the albums of the year. Björk and Nellee Hooper had created a work of fractured genius, a quirky set of pop, clubby and occasionally jazzy songs mixed up with soft, tender and simplistic love songs and a song spontaneously recorded in the Milk Bar's toilets while Björk was out clubbing one night.

Solo Björk is very different from Sugarcube Björk. As her own entity she has become a superstar, a 1990s package of songs, image and soundbites – the *Sunday Times Magazine* went as far as running a headline in February 1994 which claimed that her 'fans hail her as the new Madonna' and although they are musical chalk and cheese, there is something very knowing and even manipulative about Björk. If her success is in part man (as in not woman)-made – Judy Blame, stylist for *The FACE* and *i-D*, dressed her up; top photographer Jean Baptiste Mondino shot her; Nellee Hooper produced; Graham Massey remixed – she has ultimately stayed in control. Perhaps she is an alternative Madonna, the child-woman to La Ciconne's whore-woman, deconstructing her clothing rather than Catholicism.

Björk's image seduced her fans and the media alike with its kookiness. People with nothing better to do talked about how her name was in fact pronounced 'B-yerk', but then continued calling her 'B-york' because it sounds less pretentious. Ms Gudmunsdottir is the first to admit that she enjoys being thought of as kooky. 'I like the weirdo tag I've got. It's quite flattering because it makes me seem more interesting than I am,' she told the *Sunday Times Magazine*. If she wasn't from this weird country where the sun sometimes shines for 24 hours a day, Björk might not be quite such a mysterious curiosity – and her accent certainly wouldn't be peppered with its mad mix of Icelandic and London.

Sitting on a chair made of wood and rope, Björk fidgets constantly as she chats: squashing her face, sticking a finger up a nostril, wrinkling her nose and making loud phlegmy noises, pulling her dress up around her underwear, stretching the arms of her jumper, yanking on a bra strap. Her face is freckly, clear and make-up free. She is at her most intense when she talks about music, moving from hushed tones to loud and squeaky exclamations. She stutters and goes all coy when pushed to talk about her first boyfriend and uses a mystical, book-at-bedtime voice when telling the tooth-house anecdote. She pours strong coffee from a silver flask into two espresso cups painted gold then forgets to drink any. Looking around the living room – all whitewashed walls, stripped floors and big windows – she smiles and says it reminds her of a summerhouse.

Sindri appears in the living room, singing something in Icelandic. He scowls at mum and walks out again. Björk is taking him to Regent's Park Zoo – 'you can't get too PC with kids' – and is running late. She opens a walk-in wardrobe and pulls out a pink, cropped babydoll dress, which she tugs over her satin dress. She tosses off her sneakers and steps into outsized hiking boots then takes the band out of her hair and shakes it free. Sindri sticks to shorts and a baseball cap. When they step out of the black cab in front of the zoo's entrance, Sindri is wrenching his mum's arm, anxious to see the animals, oblivious to people elbowing each other and loudly whispering, 'Look! Look! It's Björk!'

62

There was always music around when I was a kid. It was on very loud, 24 hours and I was the only kid. There was ten . . . *bohèmes* . . . hippies, whatever. To avoid misunderstanding, they actually worked. It was more like a house downtown than a commune; it was really big with seven or eight rooms and all these people living there, sharing the rooms. There was always a queue by the record player and you had to argue to get to play your records. You had to make a statement with the record you put on. They played a lot of Johnny Winter, Cream, Eric Clapton, Frank Zappa. And then we had a revolution; when I was seven I was really getting into Sparks and driving them bana . . . nuts, 'cause they thought that was really bad quality pop. I loved it. I got into a lot of really good children's music like Thorbjörn Egner – this very brilliant person who writes plays for children and creates all these different characters. Egner's music is so brilliant, it's like Stravinsky for children, it's like Stravinsky pop – completely angular, full of life and anyone can sing along with it. It's really simple. And all the different sides to it –

the happy song, the sad song, the aggressive song, the sweet song for the sweet person. And then my grandparents listened to jazz and I used to stay at their house a lot. When I started music school – from five to 15 years old – I was obviously being brain-fed the classics.

I really loved the classes where you could play things, like xylophones, or write your own stuff with the other kids. That has always been what turns me on – to get really in tune with someone, to be the same person, feed off each other and drive each other mad with these little exciting messages. I really love all that. But of course the classical thing is obviously very snobby and: 'Just shut up and listen for an hour . . .' All that garbage. Being a single child who was really spoiled and running barefoot with butterflies in my hair, there was no way I would agree to sitting still. But I really liked the fact that in the classical music school I could either be the jazz freak, bring some jazz records and be really angular or bring Jimi Hendrix or right-out pop tunes. And I'd go to the hippie place and play them classical things to show them there was actually more than what *they* listened to. Then go to my grandparents and play them Sparks, Ravel, or something. I really liked being the outsider coming in with something: 'Did you know that there is one more thing?'

I had so many little families – my mum's from a small village and my father is very conservative and hard-working. I would always go to different families: I was the hippie at my grandparents' place and then the conservative person at the hippie place. That's probably why it suits me to be here from Iceland. I was very happy. I don't think I felt special. It was more a case of feeling like a kid who could really watch things and no one was bothered. Grown-ups talk about a lot of things that they think the kid won't understand. I saw so many different things going on that I realised none of it was necessarily right, correct. Musically, people tend to think that one thing is correct and the rest is rubbish. It's not that simple . . . My dad's lifestyle was probably as conservative as it gets and my mum was completely the opposite.

It wasn't just music . . . it wasn't till I reached 15 or 16 that it really started to bother me that there were so many things going on in my head that I couldn't see anything. You know that thing you get when you're around that age and you can't identify with anything?

63

BJÖRK

That's when you get really thirsty – to find a synonym for what's going on in your head. I was very lucky because I met a lover when I was 16. He was part of Medusa, which was the Icelandic surrealist movement. They were completely into literature and read everything – he had a house full of books; he had nothing, he was really young, but he had about 10,000 books. I was really lucky, I could stand up and say: 'Listen, I want to read something that's kind of like, hairy and dangerous with a nice female character.' And it'd be like: 'Here you go.' So you didn't have to buy twenty horrible books in a shop and feel insulted because you were reading something and taking something in that wasn't part of you. That was brilliant and I've read heavily ever since. The ones I liked most were those which made me realise that I wasn't mad. I guess everybody's got books which saved their lives in their teens. Books like *Story of the Eye* by Georges Bataille or *Demon Flower* by Jo Imog, this German writer. There were a lot of other books that maybe weren't as important, but I got the nutrition I wanted.

Thor was my first boyfriend. My girlfriends were always mad about boys, and they didn't get treated very nicely. They'd be heartbroken and I'd have to go and solve it all . . . It pissed me off and I couldn't be bothered wasting time with things like that. At that age they're just not very interesting. There were lots of really interesting girls you could talk to for nine hours but when it came to boys, it was really rare to find stimulating ones. So I always thought that boys were no good – except for bands, because they can play the drums, guitars and so on. From the age of 11, when my album came out, I was obsessed with the idea of starting bands and getting going. I was hyperactive and shouting: 'Yeah, yeah, I've got a rehearsal room!' Buying PAs, rehearsing, starting a band and another band, always searching for something. Boys were good to be in bands with, but the minute you started going out with them . . . I never did, I just knew if I did, something would just go wrong in the band. Also, most of them didn't really interest me. I had a lot of crushes, but crushes in the same way that you have for girls, more a mental thing. As a kid, I always had this thing, which I guess everybody does, when you meet someone who's thinking *exactly* the same as you are and it's electricity and madness and wow! And you usually call each other five times every day – always thinking all the same things. Which I like just as much. I like to admire someone both physically and mentally, but the mental thing's what triggers it off. Both boys and girls.

There was a lot of peer pressure in my school: everybody had to have exactly those shoes and exactly those jumpers and hairdos. I didn't take part in all that. I was the odd one out really, wearing my mum's orange sheets. I cut a hole in them, put a funny hat on, had green hair. I didn't care about things like that. I've since met teachers who taught me when I was five and six who say I was eccentric then. But I was never teased for anything, 'cause I always had several really, really good friends and I was always respected for having a happy-go-lucky kind of character. There were so many people who were considered eccentric who got really lousy, no mercy treatment, but not me. I remember people coming up and calling me 'Chinese', 'cause I look different, not really Icelandic, and I just went: 'Really? Great! I'm one of them? Cool!'

When it came to playing music, I always got together with this one person and there was just something going on here, in my head, between me and that person musically. You just have to do things together, it's like electricity. That gives you so much nutrition and feeling – casual sex up a wall somewhere is just nothing, nothing compared to that. But when I met Thor, it was love at first sight . . . It's kind of personal, a lot of it. I guess I can tell you, skipping all the really personal things. I met him and . . . apart from having quite similar brains, he was just very . . . magical. He was four years older than me, which is a lot when you're 16. And . . . I don't know what to say, it's so precious all of it. We were together for five years. Got married . . . Yeah, it's true about the contact lenses. In Iceland, 25 per cent of people's wages are put aside from the age of 16 to 25 or to whatever age you get married, so you can buy a house – or contact lenses. You don't get married if you've got no reason. It was like: 'OK, then.' If you're in love with someone and you've lived with them for many years, you don't suddenly walk in one day and say: 'Let's get married then.' There has to be something that triggers it off. Especially when obviously everyone's terrified of getting married.

We didn't want a big wedding; we just nipped off and signed in the registry, and then we didn't really tell anyone. Just one person, and that person told everyone. It was really good, 'cause we both had really big, complex families – my son's got nine grandfathers and eight grandmothers – so we had about ten wedding parties. One would take us to the most expensive restaurant in town, and the next night another would, so we just had two weeks of eating out every evening. We thought it was over after a week, but every night a distant uncle or something would call up: 'Listen, I hear you've gotten married and haven't invited me, so you're coming to this restaurant, whether you like it or not!' That was really great.

There were all sorts of mystical and magical things around it. I ended up going to this antique shop and buying this big, long, white, wedding dress which was ten times too big for me. At the time we were staying in a place that I rehearsed in. Thor's connection was all the literature people and mine were sort of punk. We slept in the corner of this office, with cigarettes and chewing-gum on the floor, and I was getting pregnant. Then this brilliant thing happened. Our house was at the end of a curvy street, and because it was a squat thing, we were told that any minute our house would be torn away. One morning I woke up with a pain in my tooth, so I went to the dentist and he pulled it out. It was a really strange feeling, because I don't like injections, I've never had one. It didn't really hurt; it was like having one bone taken out of your body without any pain. It's like a really empty feeling, it's really strange. I was all funny about it and high on the experience. Then I walked to the house and it was the same – it was the same curvy street but the end house which we lived in had been taken away and there was this big hole in the ground – just like in my mouth. I was standing there going: 'Hey! My wedding dress was in there!' That was the only thing I had in there. That was funny.

I had the baby. It was an accident, but I knew I wanted it, it was just an instinct thing. Everything practical was against it, but it was just such a strong instinct thing. We bought a house, and I was a housewife, listening to the Swans just to balance things up a bit. Got a vacuum cleaner and got completely obsessed with the Swans. I was happy, but it was like waiting for the baby to be one and a half. I wanted to be with him. I did a lot of jobs with him on my stomach: selling books, three little jobs at once and being in a band as well. I never thought having Sindri would stop me from making music; it was a good time to have a kid. It's got to be either 18, 19 or 35. That's what I've seen with my friends; that works best. I only had to make a choice once – that was the first tour I took him on with me. I was very aware of: is he or isn't he going to like this? If he can deal with it, it means I can do this, otherwise I just won't be able to travel abroad and I'll just have to make music in Iceland. Sindri was born for it – he was really excited, so basically he toured with me for five years. He was always really outspoken, really clear about how he felt. When he was five or six, he made an announcement: 'I don't want to travel any more.' That was it. Now he either stays with his dad in Iceland or he comes with me, but he doesn't like the travelling.

He learnt a lot from being around adults, especially with the Sugarcubes. Half of them were intellectual poets – it was brilliant, they were just kind of fantasising with him on 12-hour bus rides. It was like a family thing; all these other people who had kids too, came along as well. It was quite natural.

In Iceland, there was a group of people who'd been working together since they were 14. We were on a mission for teenage rights; we were going to change these towns. I guess Britain had the punk thing – but it was different in Iceland, it was basically people putting out poetry, records, radio shows. On a mission. Doing normal jobs in the daytime and then doing that in the evening – a lot of it was crap, but a lot of it was good. It was probably the healthiest way to spend your teenage years, 'cause it was about pushing each other: 'Put out a record. Now! You can do it, I'll support you.' It couldn't have been better, really. The Sugarcubes were just a joke. If we were on some kind of mission to become world famous, it worked. What we wanted to do was plan a bad-taste company in Iceland and change Iceland. Tell me if I'm boring . . . You don't really talk about your past like this unless it's your best friend or you're drunk.

Leaving the Sugarcubes was always a courage thing. It was also about being protective towards my relationship with myself. What kept me sane after a nasty day was coming home, when everybody was asleep, and writing these little tunes and lyrics, and not telling anybody about it. It kept me sane, honest. It was like, if I

BJÖRK

showed them to people, the magic wouldn't be there any more – it was almost too private. I knew that with the Sugarcubes I would write a song in the afternoon, or at a rehearsal, and it'd be really precious to me. Then I'd have to spend a year going through the whole process of putting it out and repeating that one afternoon 900 times. Getting it recorded, doing the legal things, the music business – that whole bollocks. I completely lost all interest.

There were several other things. First of all, I was getting completely pissed off going to local record shops and not finding anything that I liked, and walking out with one more Miles Davis record. And during the five years I went out with the Sugarcubes, I met other bands and realised that 90 per cent of them were lazy and taking advantage of the easy life. Not pushing anything, not taking any risks. It just pissed me off, 'cause the ingredients, the possibilities, were there. At the end of the day it doesn't matter how insecure you feel about what you do, you just get pissed off 'cause there are no records you can buy and it's: 'All right, I'll do it myself then. I'll do the dirty job.' It was very much that housewife angle: 'No one's going to do the cleaning – guess I'd better!' Also, when I started feeling a bit older – I'm not saying 26 or 27 is very old, but you get one brain cell in your head saying: 'You've been a teenager now for fifteen years . . .'

So all these things were going through my head which had never been documented and if I didn't do it then, they'd have gone away. And living a great life in Iceland, having a house, the most gorgeous set of friends – my lifestyle there was just so brilliant. We'd go swimming in the morning, play music, meet this person, that person, if I needed a job I'd work in an antique shop. It was a very, very happy life. Travel with the Sugarcubes, go abroad for a free holiday. I felt I had to do one thing before I die. It was a bit of a mission thing.

One more factor which was very big, and which made me go ahead and leave was this. How many times in the evening have you sat back and read a good book that saves your life; put a record on and everything just clicks, makes you feel: 'Yes, this is what it's about.' That's what music and books and films do to you. And sometimes you can't live life really easily – you have to make sacrifices. Almost in a religious sense. Be unselfish, not think: 'Hey, I'll go and get drunk with all those friends.' Leave the country with my child, live where I don't know anyone – just go on a mission. I had that urge. To not take anything for granted, not play it safe, not do an easy record. Get down what it takes and do it with integrity. It probably started when I was 25 or 26 and then it took a year or two; I started organising and collecting together all the ideas, writing everything down, every sentence, every chord, everything. Then, in a way, *Debut* was really, really easy to make; it couldn't have been easier. I just sat down with a lot of diaries and books and I was almost like an editor. I had so much material to choose from it was a joke. And the songs were all really formed, with an intro, a bass line, chords, music, melody, lyrics – it was mapped out.

I accidentally got to know Nellee through the London club scene – I didn't really know about his past, although Soul II Soul was on the radio all the time; there was just that electricity. We would go to the corner of clubs and talk like lunatics and then I'd go on tour with the Sugarcubes and we'd just go on sending each other faxes in the middle of the night with ideas. It was like a musical love affair. The process of the album took two days, on average, per song, both to record it and to mix it. Which, nowadays, is unheard of. It was partly because I had so much material to choose from and partly because we're both very, very different, but we both work in the same spontaneous way. If it doesn't work first time it was like, forget it. Nellee also seemed to know exactly what was going on in my head.

I don't know what *Debut* would have sounded like without him. He gave it an extra flexibility and smoothness. What I tend to do is quite angular and almost clumsy, and he made it all flow. For me, the album was completely 50–50. I felt really secure about songwriting and making up melodies – I could express more than half a song with those. I felt more insecure with the music. It was like me going out hunting and coming back to the kitchen in Nellee's house and saying vaguely what I wanted it to be cooked like. He cooks it and I watch him, saying: 'No, not that direction, that direction,' and he does it. I'd love to work with him again. We call each other a lot, just with advice on what I'm doing and what he's doing. At the moment I don't know; I shouldn't say anything because I've got so many people in mind that we are all going to write nine albums together! Which is good to have that longing, to do that with people, but it's good not to say anything until it's there for sure.

BJÖRK

There's a certain naïveness about *Debut* that is not going to exist on future records, partly because some of the songs, like 'Human Behaviour', are ten years old. I've changed a lot since then and also it was about me being completely shy about the equipment. Now I can be more flexible and more relaxed with the equipment, but at the end of the day I couldn't even sit down and say I want the next album to be brilliant. It will become what it becomes.

I'm not nervous about making the follow-up to *Debut*. No, I'm having the time of my life. I feel very, very lucky. I not only have the money now to do the album I want to do, but also there are a lot of people I respect who I can work with. *Debut* was such a virgin thing; it was about not taking any risks because there were so many things I didn't know how to do and playing it really safe.

I started music in a very good way. I wrote songs in my head for ten years and they became an inside thing, something which had been locked inside a cupboard for too long and which can't really look at the light. The main difference between music that is played on machines and music that is played by human beings is that it's an outside and an inside thing. Most music with computers is all about the imagination; you can get away with making the sound perfect and flawless if it's something you imagined clearly in your head. If you imagine the perfect man, or the perfect ice-cream or something like that, it *is* perfect; it's a picture that's in your head and machines are really good at reproducing it. When it comes to 'not imagined' things, but things that are real, talking to people and daily life, for instance, then I think that you need musicians and wooden instruments, organic things.

So with *Debut*, being introduced to machines by Nellee and a programmer called Marius [De Vries], was the perfect thing. The album had been in my head for ten years, it almost had a life of its own inside the cave, and it would be too much to push it out like 'der ner ner ner': it just wouldn't work like that. So the album was still quite inside that cave but then I found Marius – the person who's perfect with synthesisers – and I could say: 'Listen, I want a sound like that fluffy bit on top of a coconut.' And he'd respond: 'You mean this?' Marius was so good at understanding things like that.

Looking back on it, *Debut* was the most perfect thing that could have happened in the end. Now I want to move more into organic things; the next album won't be something that I've had in my head for ten years but that I write in daily life and it'll be like outro, not intro. I'm now much more into getting lots of musicians – I've spoken to Evelyn Glennie the classical percussionist, and all these people that have organic instruments. I don't know if I'll use technology as well; I'll have to take it as it comes. But I like extremes, I really like saxophones, really hard, really loud Public Enemy-stylee things. And then the opposite, like sophisticated harp and synths. So I like things that are very instrument-like and also very techno – I don't like the things in the middle. I think I'll just mix it in the way it sounds.

I have always had a certain song in my head, a certain chemistry of sounds. I've always liked to sing noises since I was little, but then again everybody's like that. But with writing songs – I have actually learned to talk and express myself in lyrics and it took twenty years. I started off experimenting with lyrics with a band called Kukl, half of whom became the Sugarcubes. We always sang in Icelandic and we didn't even write the lyrics down, we improvised them. We were existentialists, it was a joke – we just had a vague idea what the song was about and then we changed it every time we sang it. It became plain to the four of us that we weren't getting anywhere by playing in Icelandic, because the rest of the world doesn't speak Icelandic, so we started just to put one sentence here and there in English. Then later, with the Sugarcubes, we'd do the Icelandic version first and then translate the whole lyric into English. It was a very slow process.

Now I always write the two languages side by side. They're almost equal; it's gone that far. I still think in Icelandic 80 per cent of the time, unless I have a whole day of doing interviews in English. I was so pissed off with the world for not speaking Icelandic for a long time, and then I would try and translate the lyrics to mean exactly the same thing in English and it wouldn't get there. They're two different things, they're never going to be the same. You just have to focus on the emotion, and emotion is exactly the same in any language. So now I use it as a tool; I write in Icelandic and when I

BJÖRK

translate it, it adds to the words. First of all, it becomes ten times simpler; the Icelandic lyric is five pages and it becomes ten words in English. I like it like that, it says everything I want in three words – almost.

There are piles and piles of words in Icelandic that don't translate, but it's eleven years since I started in Kukl and I've always set aside a lot of time for writing. I could always write music fast, but, as I said, lyrics used to take me days. Writing has become much more natural for me now; I've come a long way. I write about whatever is turning me on at the moment really, I don't decide that my lyrics should always be about any sort of thing. I was more into words in films and books when I was young; the only music and lyrics that I admired are in jazz songs like 'My Funny Valentine'. They're just so so simple, like pure pop, but in a completely cool way, with all the passion and all the heat. Songs like Chet Baker's 'Let's Get Lost' and 'Cry Me a River'. They are my favourite. But it was poetry that I used to admire. At the moment I'm obsessed with a poet called Jeremy Reid, I really recommend him, he's English and our age. He's got one book called *Black Sugar: Love Poems for Heterosexuals, Gays and Lesbians*. I can't get enough of him. I'm really bad; when I find a book I like, I always give it away. Then I buy another one and I give that away too. So I haven't got any books that I like, only those I don't.

I guess I've taken being a woman for granted and decided early on that the only thing for me to do was just ignore it. People used to say: 'Wow, she can do all this *and* she's a woman.' That upset me – fuck you! Also, when I was growing up and making music I never wanted to work with people because they were boys or girls. It was: 'Does that woman turn me on with her ideas or not?' All that female thing bored me to death. Being brought up by feminists who refused to even go in the kitchen. They were making things difficult for themselves – although I understand that they had to go through that to change things. I'm lucky to be this generation, that I didn't have to go through all that 'no, no, no' business. I instinctively knew a lot of things like 'Don't make love to your fellow guitarist' because that will mean that you will lose some power, and he won't work with you on an equal level afterwards. It's very easy to deal with guys on an equal work level, and I never even thought about physical gender differences. I'd be really proud of carrying the equipment, and always say, 'I carry my own equipment.' It's very important to have ten years of pride.

Every time I met a record company person or a lawyer, it'd be a few days of: 'OK, so she's the cute one.' Until they realised. But a lot of that is just a patience thing, and knowing that you can't win it in one, 'pouffe'. You have to hang around and wait till people actually realise exactly what you're doing. But it's never been a struggle for me, it's never been like: 'I can't deal with this . . .' And I've never hated guys. Ever. A lot of times I prefer them. When it comes to Madonna she's obviously not a musician, and that's why most people slag her off, because she can't sing. But that's not the point of Madonna, it never was; it's just taking her too literally to look at her in that way. She's changed so many things and sacrificed her life. She must have sacrificed a lot of things to do what she's doing and go all the way in that area.

For me, Madonna is up there with Bette Davis – with the really strong women. The most important thing for me about Madonna is that once she moved into the power thing, she had the guts to say: 'I'm the one in charge.' Which for men is probably the most unsexy thing about women. But she actually allowed herself to be a character: 'I'm not gonna be your fucking kitten – I'm gonna be a character. I'm gonna be Madonna, who likes to do this, not this.' For me she's got ten times more character than – I could name fifty women singers – and she's allowed herself to become this persona which is not necessarily sexy. People say that she's used sex to get her where she is, but it's almost the other way: she's had the guts to throw away the whole sex kitten thing and be strong, and I think that's brilliant. She does things I don't necessarily agree with, but that goes with being a character. It's like with friends: you don't like those red trousers they wear all the time, but you're never, ever going to say anything 'cause they wear what they want to wear.

I've said this 900,000 times but, because I got so heavily involved in music when I was 11, I feel as though I've been in a seventeen-year rock school. In Iceland it's obviously on a much, much smaller scale; it's my home, all the people are important to me and I don't get crude judgements all the time. 'She's great! She's horrible! She's a genius! She's an idiot!' I've almost grown immune to the media attention and distortion now, so it no longer bothers me. I've learned a lot from those years in the business.

I never planned to start so young. Things always kind of happen. Suddenly they're big and I'm like: 'What?' I realise five years later what really happened because it's all too much at the time. Looking back on it, I feel really grateful because what I'm doing now is really, really complex: I'm arranging and writing music with people. And also all the other aspects: the photographs, the travelling, the business and stupid things like T-shirts and albums covers. If it had only started this year, I would not be sane. With seventeen years of training I just managed to get by, but I was on the edge of not being able to deal with it. It makes you begin to understand a person like Kurt Cobain, who was obviously like, ten times bigger than I am and it all happened to him in six months. What I'm trying to say is that I've got nothing to complain about.

I really feel like I've got the hang of running the whole thing now – doing twenty faxes a day, making all the decisions. That was what got to me first: spending a week thinking about making a decision. I had to learn to decide 'now!' If it wasn't the right decision – me to blame. I got the hang of that pretty quickly and pressure doesn't really scare me, but what pisses me off is how people think of me. Not friends, or people I'm working with, but people who I don't know so well. Just the hypocrisy – because I'm in a good position socially, I get a lot of people that want to be my friend. It really gets to me, it frustrates me. I can tune into that really, really quickly. I've had it since I was 11 with people in Iceland, people who just want to hang out with me because they'll get to the right parties. I know the minute I meet them what they're after. When I go to a bar, a seventh [sic] sense tells me when someone's trying it on. Then there are people who honestly are interested in talking. It's all that garbage; I don't have to go into it, you know exactly what I mean.

I was asked to perform at the Brits Awards in February 1994 and I insisted on doing a duet. They suggested Meat Loaf. So I said I don't want to do it . . . there was so much politics involved. The only person I could imagine doing a duet with, 'cause it was an English thing, was Polly Harvey. She was so cool about it; there was so much garbage around it, all the sorts of things you hate most in the world are present in that single event. She was in my team against the rest. It was really, really cool. We did one song, and she came and sat next to me through the whole thing and it was just a sort of support thing. With Polly, you just look at her and you know. She's really really cool. She reminds me a bit of Clint Eastwood; her spirit – everything's understated. She's the kind of person you don't have to talk a lot to. I like her.

I never had any icons when I was growing up. Maybe it's partly my character, but it's also my hippie upbringing – you always should believe in yourself. You shouldn't imitate anyone, just be happy with what you are – all that stupidity. It was never told to me straight in the face, but that was obviously in the air. They were all having therapy courses. Which is brilliant, but I think a generation of people had to do that to make the revolution. It's a joke that before the hippies, all the attitudes and lifestyles were only 5 per cent a boho, arty vibe, and for it to go so quickly into the mainstream, a major revolution had to happen. I guess therapy comes in there. I mean well, but being brought up by hippies there are a lot of little things to giggle about. All this: 'I'm sorry I can't come, but my moon's in Virgo.'

75

Louise Post and Nina Gordon

nina gordon &
louise post

Veruca Salt

Keep her down – boiling water
Keep her down – what a lovely daughter
She is not born like other girls, but I know how
     to conceive her
She may not look like other girls – she's a snarl-
     toothed seether.
               ('Seether' from *American Thighs*; lyrics by
                                   Nina Gordon)

Tiny trunk stop
You lay me in a towel
And savour me like a lamb
You smell of corduroy and lemondrops
And reds pulled from a can
I dream in black and white
I've long forgot
Exactly who I am.
               ('Spiderman '79' from *American Thighs*; lyrics by
                                   Louise Post)

At a small venue in north London Veruca Salt takes the stage. It
is July 1994 and the Chicago-based foursome are doing their
first gig in the UK. Bass player Steve Lack stands in the middle of the
stage, head down, hair flopping over his face; drummer Jim

Shapiro's curly mop is just visible. It is the other two members of the band who rock out. Nina Gordon and Louise Post – both vocalists, guitarists, songwriters – steal the show. Their guitars are menacing, confident and exhilarating, their lyrics spunky and sinister, their vocals simultaneously tough and soft. 'Seether', their début single which sold out the gig, is a furious pop tune with Joan Jett riffs and snarling lyrics that attack a bullying boyfriend; 'Spiderman '79' a sweetly sung love song with chugging guitars; 'Fly' slow and fragile; 'Sleeping Where I Want' gentle, lazy pop.

Nina and Louise were introduced to each other after Nina's close friend the actress Lili Taylor met Louise at a New Year's Eve party at the end of 1991. They hit it off musically and personally – so much so that they often get mistaken for twins – and spent 1992 writing songs together. At the start of 1993 Nina and Louise placed an advert in a local Chicago paper for a female rhythm section, describing themselves as a dreamy grunge band with distorted guitars and ethereal vocals. Committed feminists, they initially wanted an all-girl band, but finally had to put talent above gender and, after bringing Steve in, Nina's brother Jim made up the quartet. The band's musical references range from My Bloody Valentine to the Pixies and the Breeders. 'Seether' was to 1994 what the Breeders' 'Cannonball' was to the previous year: a heady indie rock record which reached out beyond an indie rock audience.

The band's name is stolen from Roald Dahl's *Charlie and the Chocolate Factory* and the spoilt brat who screams 'I want the world and I want it now.' When they discovered what a 'verruca' is this side of the Atlantic, they decided to label their music 'wart-core', although others have had less imagination: one American journalist described the band as 'waif rockers', which in turn pushed Nina and Louise to reject 'babe appeal' in favour of a tomboy jeans and T-shirt look.

Despite both being in their late twenties, Nina and Louise are refreshingly free of cynicism. While stopping over in London for a few days either side of their gig, they hunt out limited-edition Hole, Nirvana and Dinosaur Jr vinyl in Camden market, feel guilty about not going to art exhibitions and stay up till 5 a.m. two mornings running to discuss their monologues with each other. They worry about being judged harshly for their feminism, want to talk to other female musicians about being on the road, feel unsure of male journalists.

A month later, after Courtney Love has just invited the band to tour with Hole and fellow Chicago musician Liz Phair has asked them to support her on tour, Nina and Louise sound breathless at the other end of the phone. Their first album, *American Thighs* (a skit on AC/DC's song 'You Shook Me All Night Long', which included the line: 'Knocking me out with her American thighs') is about to be released and, with the help of a new manager who used to look after AC/DC and Metallica, they are preparing to dodge the media spotlight. That little brat Veruca Salt may have wanted it all at once, but the band are willing to wait a little.

Nina Gordon

My father played guitar so there were always guitars around. In the early seventies, when I was little, this guy – we call him Johnny 'Free-love' now because he was living in our basement in some kind of 'hippie freelove' arrangement that my parents had worked out – also played guitar. It's funny because I think that in my mind I have confused my father with Johnny. I have these distinct memories of someone singing me to sleep and playing guitar for me, and I always assumed that it was my father. I later learned that it was usually Johnny.

79

Both my parents were really into music. We used to move around a lot, and one of my earliest memories is of being in Boston, dancing around the dining room and singing along to Donovan's 'Barabajagal' record – my favourite song was 'I Love My Shirt'. Then, when I was about two, *Abbey Road* came out and my parents played it incessantly. I think it was a really accessible record for little kids because there are lots of sunny, childlike songs on it. I obviously didn't understand the genius of that record then, but I responded to it and loved it on a very basic level. I had a little record player from the time I was three. I'd listen to whatever my parents were listening to – the Stones, Jimi Hendrix, the Band. My dad was a serious hippie and quite radical and my mom had a more conservative streak in her, and although she loved music, she liked poppier, less scary stuff. I was always really into the Beach Boys. They were the cheery side of music.

It was strange being a little kid in the early seventies because there was a lot of really dark and creepy music which I associated with scary images that I saw on TV, like Vietnam and drugs. Also at that time things were very unstable within my parents' relationship and I know that I picked up on that. A lot of the music from that time I associate with all the fear I had, and how out of control things were within my family. But my parents took me to see the Beach Boys when I was about six, which was the most amazing thing – it was my first concert. My most vivid memory is of seeing people twirling those neon sticks around, and being really mesmerised by them. I don't really remember what was going on on stage.

My parents gave me an acoustic guitar when I was seven. I learned to play about three chords so I could play 'Nowhere Man', and maybe a Creedence Clearwater song. I really wish that at that point somebody had tapped me on the shoulder and whispered in my ear, 'You know what, you should stick with this because when you're in your twenties you're going to want to be in a band, and you'll want to be a good guitar player.' But I totally dropped it. I'd basically pick up the guitar once every six months and play the same three chords, get frustrated, and that's as far as it would go. It seemed too hard for me and for some reason, I didn't want to spend the time.

My brother, who is two years older than me, played guitar and piano and I was always begging him to play songs that I wanted to sing along to. Sometimes he would play and sing with me, and those were that happiest times for me – it's when my brother and I were closest – singing in harmony together. But he and I had kind of a complicated relationship, so if I begged him to play for me too much he would refuse. But I wanted desperately to have an accompaniment and to be able to sing along with him.

I read an interview with Courtney Love where she said that every New Year's Eve she'd make one resolution: to just *shut up*. I love that. I was a really loud little girl. My parents were always telling me to calm down, and my brother was constantly telling me to shut up, but I always wanted to sing, and scream really loudly. It's funny because now we're playing really loud music, it's a great release for me and I'm definitely not the loudest person I know any more.

It wasn't until high school that I realised that rock could be an outlet for me. When I was younger I wasn't really aware of women who rocked. I never heard Debbie Harry until Blondie's disco phase, but when I was 12, the GoGos' *Beauty and the Beat* came out and I paid attention. I spent hour after hour with headphones on listening to it, singing along and fantasising about being one of them. Then someone played me the Pretenders – I don't think I was aware of them in the late seventies when they first appeared, but when the second album came out I was blown away.

I was with this guy who, in my high school, was known as 'the little girl corrupter'. He deflowered all the young girls. It was a status thing: 'Have you gone out with him, and have you . . .?' It was really gross. I didn't have a lot of experience with guys, but he suddenly took an interest in me when I got my braces off. I remember hanging out with him and feeling pressured into an uncomfortable situation. We were in his bedroom and he was obsessed with Van Halen, so he played me these David Lee Roth interviews taped from the radio. David Lee Roth was obviously saying all these really cocky, sexist things – about scoring chicks after shows or being on stage and pointing out women in the audience to the stage manager: 'I want her, her, her and her.' I remember feeling really uncomfortable. Like, I'm here in this guy's room, and I don't really want to be here and he's playing all these creepy interviews. Then he said, 'Oh wait, have you heard this? This woman has the sexiest voice.' And I thought: 'I don't know if I want to hear this. What is this? Why is he playing me some woman he thinks is *sexy*?'

He put on *Pretenders II* and I remember being completely floored. I heard that voice, saw the picture of Chrissie Hynde with her guitar, and I learned that she had written all the songs. It was melodic, but really powerful, and there was nothing cute about it. I had this moment of feeling really daunted and alienated – how did she know how to do that? But from then on there was an increased awareness that maybe this was something that I could do one day. Again, I was too lazy to learn to play guitar – it just seemed like too much of a struggle.

Anyway, this guy was trying to score me, and I was a virgin at the time. I remember feeling – and maybe this will sound corny and like I'm reading too far into it – empowered by Chrissie Hynde and

NINA GORDON & LOUISE POST

the sound of her voice, and I was thinking: 'Fuck this asshole – forget it!' His ego was so bruised because he prided himself on being this huge Casanova. A little girl corrupter, like David Lee Roth. In a way he blew it by playing the Pretenders for me. But I fucked up the next day by lying about the whole thing, and I can't believe how severely I buckled under teenage girl peer pressure. I had always been the cute little kid of my class, way smaller than everybody else, completely flat-chested, freckles and braces. But the summer I got my braces off, suddenly guys were noticing me for the first time. I was totally inexperienced and young – just a baby. This guy was two years older than me and was paying all this attention to me and I was really excited about that. When we were in his room, I was really into making out with him – that seemed really cool, but I didn't want to have sex with him. So it didn't happen. He was furious, told me I was a tease, and drove me home in silence.

The next day I went to school and told everybody that we *had* slept together. It was so stupid. I lied to my so-called friends because they didn't take me seriously – they thought I was uncool because I was so inexperienced. They were these really mean and tough backstabbing teenagers. They had really long nails and purple nail polish. I wanted to be accepted by them, so I lied and said that I had slept with this guy. Rumours spread fast because my school was so small. It got back to him and he denied it. He told everybody that I was lying. I don't know which one of us people really believed, but I was totally humiliated and deeply ashamed of myself for getting sucked into that kind of bullshit behaviour. I couldn't wait to get out of high school. I felt trapped.

I still love Chrissie Hynde. She's gone through a lot of changes with her band, but I totally admire her and respect what she does. She has paved the way for all of us. She may deny being a feminist, but she obviously did a great thing for women and has made her contribution. Maybe she doesn't want to call attention to her gender because she doesn't believe in singling out women in rock as if it's something out of the ordinary. Why focus on it? It's not the same for me, but I can understand that mentality.

I definitely don't have a problem with saying I'm a feminist. I grew up like many people my age thinking: 'Yuck, feminism.' For some reason, all the associations we had when we were growing up were wrong and feminism was something we all pushed away. I associated it with hairy armpits and unshaved legs, and because where I went to high school the aesthetic was that girls were demure and pretty and wore make-up, feminism seemed like a bad word. Now I have no qualms. But it's hard, because it's not something I want to focus on; I certainly don't sit down to write a song thinking I'm going to write a feminist anthem or a song from a woman's perspective. Obviously, that's my perspective anyway. For most of the women I love and respect, I know that songwriting couldn't be that self-conscious otherwise it would end up feeling and sounding forced. Maybe some day I'll decide I want to write a song about a specific subject, but usually it's just about what happens when I play chords and what comes out of my mouth at that moment.

When critics label our music 'post-feminist', it's like some crutch, a way of writing it off. Our lyrics are a lot more complicated than that because, as I said, there is no plan. They're not part of an agenda. Few women have written about us, and I feel that the term 'post-feminist' has become easy jargon, it's become a tag and it doesn't mean anything. I don't know if I really understand what post-feminism is anyway.

I think the press, especially the male press, can be really lazy and it's frustrating. Veruca Salt is already getting lumped together with other bands fronted by women because there are so few getting recognised. We get compared to the Breeders, Juliana Hatfield, Belly and Liz Phair all the time.

When I was nine, I had a friend who played the piano and we used to write songs together. I actually still have a cassette of one of them and it's pretty hysterical. Obviously we'd never been in love, but all the songs we heard on the radio were about being in love or being heartbroken so we just mimicked those words. We would just write clichéd songs about being lost and sad and our hearts being broken. I didn't really have any way to write songs on my own because I didn't play an instrument. Finally, when I was living in Paris during

NINA GORDON & LOUISE POST

college, I bought an acoustic guitar for $40 and learned how to play over the phone. I'd call my brother in New York and write down his instructions on how to play chords. The first songs I ever really wrote on my own were when I was in Paris. Now they just seem silly and naïve.

When I went back to college for my senior year, I left my guitar in Paris. Then, for my 21st birthday, my brother bought me an electric guitar – a cheap copy of the Gibson SG I play now. It sat there and gathered dust while I focused on school. After college I moved back to Chicago and my mom still had one of Johnny 'Free-love's' old guitars – a really beautiful tiny-scale Martin acoustic made for a child. As I didn't have an amp, I couldn't play my electric, so I played this little ukulele thing. I was lonely and for the first time I started feeling like I had to write songs. My brother got me a four-track, and I started recording some of my songs, but it became clear that I needed to play with somebody. I needed that support. I became pretty depressed, feeling alone, sitting in my apartment playing these songs over and over for myself.

On New Year's Eve 1991, my friend Lili went to a party over at Louise's house. Lili had given me this pep-talk days earlier telling me that I had to play music, focus on guitar, maybe take lessons. I felt really weak at that time. Guitar was like math to me, something I was never good at, never had the patience for. It seemed too technical and forced, not organic the way singing was. When Lili heard Louise's songs, she basically sent us out on a blind date together. From that time on, my life totally changed. From the moment we met there was a feeling that we were going to bolster each other as women and as musicians.

Originally we wanted to be an all-female band because we thought that would be a more empowering and exciting situation to be in. That it would be comfortable and feel better for us. Louise and I connected so immediately as friends and as musicians that we assumed we'd be able to find two other women who felt the same way and who we could connect with in the same way. All the people we met, we really liked, but it just didn't happen musically. Steve answered the ad for a female bass player. He liked the bands we'd listed – Pixies, My Bloody Valentine, Big Star – and he turned out to be right for us. We were desperate for a drummer and we'd played with a bunch of women and it just didn't happen. So my brother said he'd buy a drum kit and play with us. Which he did. Now I feel fine about it, I don't feel like I miss the two other women that I was hoping to be playing with, although I think it could have been great too.

When we played our first couple of shows, Louise and I definitely dressed up a little bit more. We felt: 'We're performing on stage, this needs to be special.' But as soon as the spotlight was on us, as soon as people started paying attention partly because we were women, we began to shy away more and more. We became more low key in the way that we presented ourselves. Here's a perfect example: we played this concert in Austin, Texas where there were a lot of industry people who noticed us for the first time. Immediately afterwards someone called us 'waif-rockers' in this industry magazine called *Hits*. Now, in many articles, they've called our music 'waif-rock'. At first I thought, 'That's funny, that's stupid, whatever . . .' but then suddenly it dawned on us. 'Wait a minute, why are they jumping immediately to our body type?' It seemed really creepy. I don't see that with a lot of bands fronted by men – with the exception of maybe Tad [fronted by a huge Seattle grunger], who I've heard someone call that 'fatcore'.

It struck me that the press deemed it more important to focus on our bodies than our music. I remember reading about kd lang and how she masks her body on stage. I guess she has a full figure, she has large breasts and she wears clothing that would never expose that. She doesn't want her body to be part of her image. At times I can relate to that. Because we're on an independent label, we don't have people talking about our image or pressuring us to do certain things or wear certain clothes.

I read an interview with Kim Deal and Tanya Donelly where Kim was talking about the pressure from the industry to wear lipstick and dress up and she wasn't into it, while Tanya Donelly would more naturally go in that direction. That pressure is definitely there, but we don't feel it right now. I'm so impressed by women who are strong enough to reject and resist it and not care.

I remember when Bananarama were around, male friends of

NINA GORDON & LOUISE POST

mine would refer to them as 'the pretty one', 'the horsy one' and . . . whatever the other one was. I suppose I could be the one with the big nose. I'm sure it will happen: people will tag us, talk about our personalities and what we look like, compare us to each other. It's something that we haven't given much thought to yet. I hope that by that time I will have enough confidence in the music and faith in the songs for it not to bother me.

I wanted to work with Louise because she was a woman, she was my friend and I loved her music. Women are pitted against each other constantly, but I'm hoping our friendship is strong enough to combat that no matter what anybody says. It's part of the beauty myth, and we all work against it every day – I'd hate for any of that to seep into my relationship with Louise, because it would be really dangerous. I've felt it in my lifetime, obviously, with other women; you can't escape it and you're made to feel that you are in competition. Up until this point Louise and I have just been so connected, and have had this very singular vision together . . . I'd be so scared and disappointed if the press created something competitive: it would be a disaster.

It's funny, because when I first met Louise I saw her nose and I thought, 'I don't know if I can be in a band with her, she's so pretty and I'm going to be known as the one with the big nose.' We constantly have this struggle when photographs are taken of us 'cause I see her perfect little nose and face, and I'm sure she'd say she has complexes about me. I'm very up-front about it, but honestly, when she walked through the door I thought, 'I don't think I can handle this.' But of course I can, and will.

We are lucky to get a lot of positive response after our shows, but I've noticed that there's a certain type of cocky, proprietorial male fan that keeps surfacing. Guys who think that because they see women up on a stage, they have some sort of claim to them. Maybe these guys are confused by the power that we wield on stage, by how loud we are, and they don't know what to make of us. They come up to us after shows and stand there in all their glory as though they think they mean something to us. Like what we really want is *their* attention. I love it when young women come up to me after shows; in a way it means more to me. We've played some all-ages shows, which are the best because when a 16-year-old woman – girl? – female person? – comes up and says, 'Ooh, that was so great, I play guitar and I want to do this too', it's a really cool feeling. It's inspiring to feel like you may be inspiring somebody else.

I sometimes feel that I'm going to get tripped up by saying something that a certain kind of person is going to jump on and say, 'OK, she's calling herself a feminist but she's not really because why would she talk about *that* if she were?' Just like it's some sort of club with strict rules where people have to say the right things. It's so silly, because for me the whole idea of feminism boils down to just believing in the power of women, just supporting women, period. Sometimes it seems to be more about criticising other people's visions of feminism than supporting each other.

Louise and I have been talking about this incessantly for the past 24 hours while thinking about this book – about the fear of being a spokesperson. I can understand how someone might feel uncomfortable, even if they feel comfortable writing lyrics. That's your craft, your art, so you can feel safe about it, and having those words spill out of you feels really natural. But suddenly, when you're asked in an interview to state these things in a non-poetic way, in a political way, I can understand how that would be scary. Being forced to comment on your culture, your society and your gender may not be what comes naturally. Shrugging it off is a different thing – that's not something I can imagine doing – but I can definitely imagine feeling uncomfortable talking about it. Ultimately, though, I feel a responsibility and a desire to do it. Again, it's about supporting each other, bolstering each other, and sharing our thoughts and experiences with each other. Sustaining this dialogue is definitely in everybody's best interest.

Louise Post

When I was really young and growing up in St Louis in the seventies, the older kids in my neighbourhood were doing a lot of drugs and listening to the bands of the time – Led Zeppelin, Pink Floyd, David Bowie, the Doors, the Beatles – these were my rock 'n' roll roots. I was in love with Davy Jones and *The Monkees* was my favourite show. I called up the radio station and won a two-album set, which I imagine is worth a lot of money now . . . or maybe not. I played it to death, and even though all their songs were written by Neil Diamond, I just loved their pop songs. Recently my brother said, 'Louise, I realise why you liked Davy Jones so much – he looks like he's ten. When you were little it made perfect sense that you would love him.'

The first rock record I had was the Beatles' *Abbey Road*, which my older brother Ken gave to me when I was about eight. We'd just been given a stereo, which we positioned in the sun next to the window, and I listened to *Abbey Road* constantly. At one point the record was warped, I was hysterically upset and was convinced my brother had switched his record with mine. I didn't understand that the sun could warp vinyl and I felt really foolish when I realised that and I had been blaming him for the demise of my favourite record.

I used to save up to buy my own records. And at Christmas in my family, there's always been a lot of record exchanging. We're a big, musically oriented family and we take our rock very seriously. That pretty much goes for the rest of St Louis – classic rock is taken very seriously. It's the axis on which the city spins. We played in St Louis recently in this bar called Mississippi Nights – where I used to go a lot and see my boyfriend's band – and it was really a thrill to play there. I knew that we had something when these kids gave us their seal of approval – it was a serious triumph. I grew up going to a lot of concerts and everything up to this point in my life seems to have led to being in a band.

I started going to shows when I was 11. My first was Jackson Browne, which I went to with my mom and her boyfriend – my parents got divorced when I was eight – at a huge outdoor pavilion. I was so excited. Actually, I think my sister took me with her friends to an outdoor festival when I was eight. I remember her shoving me into these straight-legged blue jeans and I was really upset because I wanted to wear bell-bottoms, but as far as she was concerned, bell-bottoms were out – she wanted to show up with her little sister in straight legs. I was upset, but she was really concerned about my fashion so I had to comply. The next day I went out and bought two Jackson Browne records. 'Here Comes Those Tears Again' became my anthem. I'm sure it helped that he looked a little like Davy Jones, but older. I also listened to the Mamas and the Papas and Fleetwood Mac's *Rumours* like crazy and worshipped the photos of Michelle Phillips and Stevie Nicks.

The summer before sixth grade, I went to see the Cars. It was when feathered hair was in, Farrah Fawcett-style. I had a huge crush on this guy, who was actually a younger brother of my sister's boyfriend at the time, and he didn't notice me or my feathered hair the whole night, but the Cars were awesome. Later, I went to see REO Speedwagon, Charlie Daniels Band and Styx, all these classic rock bands. My best friend, Emilie Lucas, and I got tennis shoes just like Tommy Shaw, who was the other singer in Styx. He had these light brown Nikes and we wanted to dress just like him. We were into arena rock, and we would bring our lighters religiously.

That was a dark time in my family. We had moved and I had switched schools. When I met Emilie and her family, I basically moved in. We were hanging out with her older brothers and their friends, collecting 45s and playing foosball [sic] in her basement. Emilie and I would act out duets like 'Paradise by the Dashboard Lights', 'Don't Go Breaking My Heart' and songs from *Grease* in her bedroom. I remember her brother T.O. was in a band that played covers like 'Born To Be Wild'. They were only in the eighth grade – about 14 – but they seemed so old and we idolised them. The summer after sixth grade, one of Emilie's older brothers killed himself after a Marshall Tucker concert. It changed everything and everyone. I think that was when I started associating people's sadness with rock 'n' roll.

I think I always fantasised about being on stage, but I don't think I ever thought about picking up a guitar and writing and playing out. I started singing in choirs and musicals when I was in grade school. I played a little guitar when I was really young; my mother had a guitar and we used to sing at family parties before my parents got divorced. We did a few duets and sang harmonies together – it was a really nice thing that we shared. My parents met in a choir so it follows that music figures heavily in our upbringing. My dad and I have always sung together. We used to sing and dance around our living room. I would walk on his feet.

89

NINA GORDON & LOUISE POST

Then I started playing the piano when I was seven and I loved it. I used to sleepwalk a lot around the time when my parents were getting divorced and I took to sleepwalking down the street in my underwear. Nightwatchmen would find me and send me home; it was horrifying. I also used to sleepwalk down to the piano and bang on it. My parents would come down and wake me up, although they never knew whether they should wake me up and scare me, or just guide me back to bed.

At high school I was in a bunch of musicals. I loved singing and dancing and the spirit of musicals, as sappy and silly as they are. Then I got into an R&B band with my brother Eric when I was 16, 17, and I was singing Vanity 6 and Go-Gos covers. A guy from an R&B cover band came to one of our practices, liked my voice and asked if I would audition for his band, who had been together for six years. So I ended up spending a year in this excellent, funk cover band who were doing really well in St Louis. We played at proms, at college dances and at bars, when they would let me in.

Here's a nice little anecdote. When we were younger and my parents were still together, we belonged to this exclusive country club in the suburbs of St Louis. I remember roast beef dinners and having a lovely, very privileged, comfortable life. Anyway, there was a real intolerance of anything other than white Anglo-Saxons at this country club, and when a cousin of ours, who was three, took along a three-year-old black friend of his, they made the kid leave. My family withdrew membership. About ten years later, when I was in this R&B band, we were asked to play at the country club. I was the only white person in the band. It felt really good to return there with that band and be paid to play.

As I was in a band, I didn't want to go to college; my mom was begging me to at least consider some courses, but I was really involved in the band and we were going to get a major deal. At the time it seemed huge and unfathomable and exciting – I was caught up in it all. But the band somehow sensed that I would end up going to college so they took me less seriously and it also happened that I wasn't being very well received at black clubs. They got a singer for those nights, and I ended up feeling really gross, like I was just used for the white shows. I got the lead in *Hello, Dolly* at my high school and, eventually, the band thing petered out. Since then, they've signed to Capitol and one of them is touring now with Bootsy Collins. Around that time, my brother Eric had been listening to early Cure, Tears For Fears and Velvet Underground records and my tastes took a dramatic turn. I still love Velvet Underground; each record is a collection of gems.

I went to college in New York City at Barnard where I joined this a cappella singing group, which was excellent. I guess it was my version of a sorority without all the formalities and bullshit. I met a lot of cool women. We toured around a little and sang all the time. I majored in English, but because my boyfriend of the time was living in St Louis, I wasn't fully embracing New York or college. He was in a band that was doing really well in St Louis, and I think we both envied each other, 'cause he was throwing over college for his career in music and I felt I was missing out on something crucial by going to college. As time went on, the relationship fell apart. Meanwhile my musical tastes were evolving.

Right at the end of college, I got into this poetry class that I loved; that's when I began to learn how to exorcise pain through writing. I won these two prizes at the end of the year, which for me was a huge compliment and my biggest honour in college. I wasn't a great student and I spent more time on poetry than geology, for example, so it was like I had accomplished something significant. I was dubbed by one of my teachers a 'love poet'. In a grade report, he wrote: 'Maybe when Louise works out some of her issues concerning her relationships, she may have to change into a different kind of poet or she may have to draw from some other source, because right now, her poetry focusses mainly on love.'

The poem that won the prize was called '110th Street Station.' It was written from the perspective of a man on the street who is committing a violent verbal assault on a woman in New York City. That is partly why I left. Being constantly harassed walking down the street hearing guys saying: 'I wanna suck your pussy', is a really distressing part of living in New York. That city can be intensely inhospitable to women. In spite of all of that, I love it there. In a way, it's the place where I feel most independent, confident and powerful and, I guess, autonomous, whereas in Chicago it's a different way of life altogether – I'm much more linked with people.

I left New York when I finished Barnard and went back to St Louis, partly because I needed to remember that there was a world outside New York where foliage prevailed and you could actually smell clean air. My relationship dragged on interminably over the course of the next year and then I moved to Chicago with a bunch of bags and found a place. I had one friend there who was in a theatre company, and I thought that I was either going to join a band or act. I felt inclined to do both. I auditioned for the theatre company and ended up being involved in really aggressive, challenging, improvisational commedia dell'arte theatre. I felt like I could do it, but I was terrified. I performed in Dario Fo's *Accidental Death of an Anarchist* but I had some political differences with the people who were running the company. The company chose plays which had very few roles for women and I wanted to do my own thing, to express myself in my own words and be in control as much as possible.

It made more sense to me to write songs. A good friend of mine was talking me through my decisions. I guess I was having a personal crisis, not knowing what I was going to do. I'd been playing acoustic guitar for about three years and I'd started to record on a four-track around the time that I was in the theatre company, but I wasn't taking it really seriously. I guess in the back of my mind I knew maybe this was what I wanted to do some day, because I would dream songs, wake up and record them sort of half awake. I'd be so excited about them that I'd play them over and over again just to absorb the sound of my voice, the sound of my guitar, and, in a way, to make sure it was really me.

I had started playing guitar when I was at college in New York. My sophomore year, a friend of mine down the hall lent me her acoustic. We were living in this old welfare hotel really far off-campus, a strange place to live: really dark and depressing. It was an odd dynamic to have young, financially comfortable women living next to these elderly people who had been living for ever in tiny fixed-rent rooms; it was unsettling and pretty eye-opening. At that time, I spent a lot of time sleeping 'cause I was really down – a friend later told me I was sleeping the whole year – but when I wasn't in bed or at class, I was playing guitar. Strangely, I was also obsessed with aerobics, so I was going to aerobics three hours a day and then I would come home and play guitar. Playing made perfect sense to me, and the following summer I got an acoustic. From there, I played acoustic for the next three years.

When a friend gave me their discarded Les Paul copy – an Electra – I got a small Fender amp and I was so happy. Right when I started playing electric guitar, the Smashing Pumpkins' album *Gish* came out. I didn't know them; I didn't really know anything about the Chicago music scene – I just went to plays all the time because all my friends were in theatre. I was so freaked out by *Gish* that I had to turn it off after the fourth song. It was too close to home. It was something that I imagined myself doing, but I didn't know how I was going to get there. I didn't necessarily want to play their music but I was so daunted by them. I've had other, similar experiences. Like after hearing the first side of PJ Harvey's first album *Dry*, I was so overwhelmed I had to turn it off. Now I love the record, but it's in its place. I understand what it is and I'm no longer threatened by it. I now know what kind of music I want to make and it's different from both of those bands, but at the time I was just starting to play electric guitar and it was too overwhelming.

Pretty soon after I got my Electra, I met Nina. I had a few songs ready and she had some too, and we hooked up. I guess we really spoke to each other, our music made sense to each other; I felt I could have written her songs, and vice versa. It was such a relief to meet her, renewing to say the least. I like to think that there was some magic involved – a dear friend of Nina's introduced us so it was just really lucky. We started playing together, our voices matched each other and the whole thing made sense.

Things have happened so fast to the band, and in some ways I expected this. I was so proud of our music, and my friendship with Nina feels so magical to me that I could only imagine something really special coming out of it. But there's also a certain amount of disillusionment that goes along with it, as it becomes one's work. Now I understand that being in the studio is gruelling, and going on the

NINA GORDON & LOUISE POST

road is not that great. You start to give big chunks of yourself away every night and then you find yourself at three in the morning lying in some weird hotel room, half empty. It's really fun and I love to travel, but it is fucking hard. I miss my cats and I get a little teary when I leave them. I also realise that we're in a great position because we're playing clubs where people don't really know about us – so we just get to surprise them and hopefully blow them away.

I imagine that with an album coming out, the loss of anonymity must be hard. I don't know if that will happen to us, we could remain comfortably anonymous – or maybe uncomfortably anonymous! It's just a real adjustment, and in some ways I feel prepared to make whatever adjustments are necessary because this is the most meaningful way I can imagine living my life and I feel so lucky to be able to do it and potentially support myself doing it. In other ways, I feel incredibly naïve.

I felt paralysed for a while. When we were in the studio recording the album, I couldn't write anything new until we were done with those songs. We have so many ideas and we want to go in different directions. I want to keep experiences flowing, and not be tripped up by the business end of things. There's just so much to think about and so much to learn. The whole thing about record labels, the technicalities and the transition to treating your music as a business. It's really distracting to me; I just want to write songs and play shows and travel. If I can do that, I imagine I'd have reached the point where I'd love to be.

We've been dubbed 'post-feminists' in a number of articles written about our band. My theory about this is as follows: if we are 'post-feminists', we are perceived to be less threatening, as feminism can then be considered a thing of the past, which is absurd. The tendency for people to place women in a box and store them where they are safely out of the spotlight is all too tempting – it's universal. I hope the term 'post-feminism' will become obsolete when people start recognising that there is nothing 'post' about feminism. It is an ongoing struggle for acknowledgement of our equality with men, which is not conveniently going to come to a screeching halt when a certain catchphrase comes into fashion.

GRRRLS

As far as my songs go, I don't try to be political. I usually write about whatever's on my mind – whatever comes out when I hit a chord and I realise what I'm thinking about, what's bothering me or what's making me happy. The craft part comes in when I try to make it into a cohesive, coherent song. But it starts with whatever I'm thinking and feeling. Nina said something recently which really struck me – that being alone writing songs was when she felt the most at one with herself, the most connected to herself. That's how I feel too in writing music; that it's the most intimate time I have with myself. Things just spill out, whether it's a cool guitar part or groove or just a beautiful chord. Often I shock myself with what I say because I'm not realising that something's really bugging me and it just pops out and I go: 'Shit, I have to deal with that . . .'

A lot of my wanting to do this book is the fact that it includes Kim Gordon, Courtney Love . . . Those are some of my role models. They have forged new terrain; really paved the way for us in a lot of ways. I respect them immeasurably and I'm honoured to be in their company in a book. I certainly don't want to publicly dismiss or reject or criticise other female artists, unless I am personally offended by them.

I have a definitive answer to the 'do the press try to pit women against each other' question. That would be 'Yes'. We really hadn't discussed it or reflected upon it absolutely until talking for this book. I had an experience last night where I realised that I felt manipulated, and that already people have been asking me far too much what I think of all the other female bands around. Like who the fuck cares what I think of them? Everyone wants a cat-fight and I'm just not going to play that game. I'm determined.

Women need to be more tolerant of each another. Recently, upon returning to Chicago after being out on the road for three weeks, I discovered some mean graffiti about my band in a bathroom stall in the club where we were playing that night. It really hurt that in the place designated for and sacred to women, a woman was moved to take a pen out of her purse and slam my band in print. I have to learn not to care, but it still sucks.

People have really rigid, strict and inflexible ideas of what feminism should be. I'm learning, I'm having to figure out how I want to express myself and I guess the bottom line is that I want to express myself as naturally as possible and I want to be allowed to find my way. I'm not necessarily coming to the rock world with a feminist agenda that I want to dole out to people, and yet I do have a lot of really strong opinions and ideas which I want to let grow and develop as I do. I want that to be both inherent in my music and separate from my music. They are inextricably linked, but I don't want to feel as if I have to be a feminist spokesperson before I'm an artist.

That's something that I think a lot of women in rock bands now are running into – feeling like they are being put on a pedestal or that they are being put into a situation where they are being looked to as role models. I know that because I've been personally disappointed by some women whose music I've really liked but who, politically, won't take a stance. There's a certain way of categorising people, specifically women, in order to understand who they are. This whole issue is so frustrating to me, and we're in such a vulnerable place right now; I think we've been approaching everything with fear of how we're going to be perceived. I've found myself talking a lot about feminism in interviews. We haven't been interviewed a lot, but just in the few we've had, I've felt: 'I was so conveniently pegged just now.' And, as a feminist, I can be as ridiculed by people who are feminists as people who are not. It's just frightening to come out politically, to know that one is going to be bashed and then set aside.

I do think I'd be equally attacked for being passive as for being opinionated. Society really looks to rock idols; at this point, people don't really read much any more, certainly in America, and rock has taken much more of a poetic place in people's lives. It's important to see women playing music, and rock music specifically . . . I don't really know a lot about the bands that are in the Riot Grrrl movement, I'm not really familiar with the basis of it, I don't live in Olympia or Seattle and it kind of bypassed me. Yet I do understand that the feeling of just picking up a guitar and making noise is a really powerful one and why should it be relegated to men – why should men have a monopoly on loud music? Women playing guitars should be just another . . . bold step for womankind.

Gina Birch and Ana da Silva

gina birch

Raincoats

I'm not glamorous or polished
In fact I'm no ornament
It could be my bodyshape
I wonder if I'll ever look right

('Odyshape' from *Odyshape*)

The story of the Raincoats is a story of tributes. They formed in London in 1977 at the height of the punk era. Gina Birch had moved down from Nottingham to London to study but was more excited by seeing the Slits play their frenzied live shows than by her art course. Ana da Silva had just moved from Portugal to London and was going to the same college and gigs as Gina. Spurred on by the Slits, Patti Smith, X-Ray Spex's Poly Styrene and the DIY nature of punk as well as a love of Velvet Underground, Gina bought a bass, Ana a guitar and they formed the Raincoats. After several unsuccessful mixed-gender line-ups, they settled with Vicky Aspinall, a classically trained violinist, and Palmolive, the Slits' ex-drummer.

Gina and Ana didn't really know how to play. Their style was experimental by necessity, their understanding of music grounded more in instinctive, gut feelings than considered responses from trained ears. The Raincoats were avant-garde punksters, out there with the likes of Captain Beefheart on a weird, eccentric edge. Their first single, 'Fairytale in the Supermarket', was released in 1979 on the new indie label, Rough Trade. Its primitive, jerky sound immediately attracted an audience and captured music critics' imaginations. Writing in the *NME* in April 1979, Paul Morley exclaimed: 'I'm so happy. This scrawny, noisy Rough Trade maxi-single . . . has some of the tenderest and harshest music since Nico sang with electric guitars . . . play this next to the new Patti Smith single and feel a whole lot better.'

Their self-titled début album was lo-fi and shambolic, held together by nagging melodies and Palmolive's tough drumming. The songs had a textured, layered sound which constantly pushed back musical boundaries. The Raincoats were not badge-wearing feminists but their lyrics reflected their concerns. 'Off Duty Trip' on the first album describes a soldier raping a young girl:

> It's not just a kiss you owed me with all this ammunition
> loaded
> I bought you a drink and, well . . .
> Woman you're pinned up on the wall in front of you
> A soldier's life is very tough
> Need tender loving when fighting's through.

They did a deadpan cover of the Kinks' 'Lola', further confusing its already confused gender and sexuality.

On the third album, *Moving*, released in 1984, 'Animal Rhapsody' addressed image with a beguiling simplicity:

> I get to know my body
> Like I know my mind
> It makes me feel so good, feel so fine
> Bless my soul, I'm in control!

Palmolive had left the band after the first album, and was replaced by a series of drummers, including Robert Wyatt. *Odyshape* was as fluid as the title suggests, its gentle, jazzy, off-kilter instrumental combinations more knowing and developed than on the first album. Vivien Goldman, one of the few female music journalists around at the time, was inspired to write in *NME*: 'I love the way the Raincoats are taking liberties'.

By the time their third album, *Moving*, was completed in 1984, the Raincoats had announced that they were splitting up. Although they held on to something of the DIY punk ethic, they had lost the momentum of the early post-punk years. Some thought *Moving* too accomplished, but the accolades kept on coming. Graham Lock's *NME* review paid tribute: 'The Raincoats made pop an adventure close to home. They sang in forbidden voices and drummed out *"taboo beats"*. They opened the door for a new kind of women's music and . . . others will surely follow. Epitaph for the Raincoats – they chose their own fate.' The lyrics on 'Animal Rhapsody' – 'Bless my soul, I'm in control' – said it all.

The Raincoats were relocated to the annals of punk his-story (they were mentioned in punkumentaries, but not at length). Gina went wilfully commercial and slick for a while in a very dodgy early 1980s band, Dorothy, before going back to college to study film. Ana worked in an antique shop in west London. Vicky Aspinall started a dance label while Palmolive moved to Texas and became an evangelical Christian.

One afternoon almost a decade later, grunge's royal family stepped into Ana's antique shop. She didn't know who Kurt Cobain or Courtney Love were. She remembers Kurt saying: 'The Raincoats make me want to fall over', and asking how he could get a copy of their first album. Although Ana would have liked to talk more, there was another customer in the shop and she was feeling slightly harassed. She duly sent Kurt and Courtney a copy of the album, complete with photos, cuttings and autographs. Kurt invited the Raincoats on tour with Nirvana. He gave them an immediate injection of hipness and suddenly they were being revived big time.

Rough Trade re-released their albums on CD and Kurt's involvement secured a deal with Nirvana's major label, Geffen, in the US. Although they were hardly the initiators of dirty rock sound-scapes, the Raincoats were (proudly) tagged 'the godmothers of grunge' because so many bands associated with grunge name-checked them. Sonic Youth's Kim Gordon (the true godmother of grunge) wrote the sleevenotes for the reissue of *Odyshape*:

I loved the Slits because of their boldness and that they actually had commercial songs but it was the Raincoats I related to most. They seemed like ordinary people playing extraordinary music . . .

GINA BIRCH

They had enough confidence to be vulnerable and to be themselves without having to take on the mantle of male rock/punk rock aggression . . . or the typical female as sex symbol avec irony or sensationalism.

But even before Kurt's royal seal of approval, Riot Grrrls, inspired by the DIY music and gender-conscious concept, had been citing the Raincoats as a major influence, alongside the Slits. Writing in the sleevenotes of the reissue of *Moving*, Voodoo Queens' Anjali gushed how 'No One's Little Girl' made her feel 'extremely contented'. Hole covered 'The Void' (from the first album) in a John Peel session. The Raincoats went on the road again at the start of 1994 with Sonic Youth's Steve Shelley on drums and Anne Wood on violin. When they were supposed to be supporting Nirvana, they were supporting Liz Phair in America and dedicating a song 'to Kurt, forever'. He gave them new life before taking his own.

I never idolised people when I was young. I never really had a particular favourite Beatle. My brother Nicky, who's two years older than me, introduced me to lots of music; I used to hear Bob Dylan and Melanie through his bedroom wall. When he tired of a record, I'd take it into my bedroom and play it even more to death. I rarely went to concerts and never strongly identified with the characters – except maybe with Melanie! I had this live concert album where she chatted between songs and I knew everything off by heart. Then I got heavily into the Velvet Underground and Prince Buster – I listened to a lot of ska in my teenage years. I always lived in and around Nottingham. We moved out to the country at one point, and when I was between 12 and 16 I used to cycle three miles to go and see these 16-year-old male twins who had the use of the ground floor of an old building, where they ran a club. I used to go there to dance and drink. There was this really groovy Methodist minister in another nearby village who used to let some of the local kids all go and play records in his garage.

Getting up on stage and playing now, I wonder however did we start, how did we ever have the nerve to get up and play all those years ago? When I was a kid, I never in a million years thought I'd be a musician. I used to like singing a lot when I was young – my first appearance on stage was in the Brownies, when I was about seven; there was a little fairy doll on the piano and I had to crouch down behind the piano until it was the fairy's turn to sing. That was my first taste . . . in fact, I probably haven't got as much pleasure out of anything since then – joke! Anyway, I followed the art school path and thought I'd be a painter or a sculptor. I remember on the first day at art school in Nottingham in '76, I said I wanted to design bathrooms. How punk can you get? I was completely and utterly bowled over by discovering conceptual art and stuff that had some kind of meaning. Ridiculing the world and looking at it in strange ways.

Later on that year, I applied to Middlesex Polytechnic. The previous summer I'd seen the Sex Pistols playing in London – these guys playing five songs, completely self-destructive, and then disappearing. It had such a profound effect on me. But when I came down to London in September '76, Middlesex Poly felt dead as a doornail – lots of rich girls doing painting, very little conceptual art going on and only video of any interest. So my life and soul was discovering the Roxy Club. We'd go down to Neal Street three or four nights a week, to this little club where loads of punk bands played and there was a reggae sound system. All these art students wore strange things like bin liners and some had tampons on their ears – just generally being outrageous. Not in a totally camp way; they were just very committed to breaking taboos.

Ana and I used to go to these gigs and we became friends; by that point I'd been to see the Slits and hundreds of other bands. People you'd see in the audience one week were up on the stage the next. Bands were being formed at a really fast rate. Sometimes the atmosphere was more exciting than the music. Ana and I started joking that we were going to form a band; we formed a band in our imagination way before we ever got to play. I suppose 'The Raincoats' came about as a name because Ana's from Madeira and she was fascinated by London and the rain and dreary old days. It was never my ideal name but she was so keen on the name that I went along with it.

GINA BIRCH

At the time I had no idea how to play any instrument whatsoever. One day we were at an exhibition at the Acme Gallery and at lunchtime I went out and bought a bass guitar – it cost about £40, quite expensive then – and I got a tin of car spray-paint and sprayed this nasty dark brown bass sparkly bright blue. I suppose I'd bought it 'cause I wasn't getting what I wanted from art school. I was really heavily involved in the music scene and I thought, 'I'm going to try and learn how to play – I want to be in a band.' But that's one idea and the next step is actually *writing* a song.

I had this really crappy old Dansette record player, and the only music that I could actually hear the bass on was reggae. I had this Toots and the Maytals record, so I taught myself the bass line to 'Funky Kingston' and thought I was a living genius! Little by little we started to get a band together. It was horribly intimidating when we got up to do our first gig, and although it was a time when so many people were getting up and doing it, if it hadn't been for the Slits I don't think I would have had the courage. Their shows were anarchic and boisterous and good fun; they were just such an inspiration to me. One night, the second time I saw them, I was with Palmolive's sister, Esperanza, and we ended up doing backing vocals to this song, standing in the audience with a microphone singing: 'Sellin' it, sellin' it nine to five.' About us all being prostitutes . . . about selling your soul to the City of Woolworth's or whatever.

Being in the Raincoats was difficult at first, 'cause Ana's a much more serious and dramatic person than me. I'm more of a maverick, good-time girl – well, this is how it polarised. So a lot of stuff we did at the beginning was very serious and I wasn't sure if I was in the right place, and I was slightly confused. I don't know how much of me was in the very early stuff, but Ana always cajoled and encouraged me. I stayed at art college for two years and then left to be in the band full time. It was a slow process really; at our first gig one of the tutors from college came and said: 'Well, ho, ho. Come back to college; you're wasting your time.' But three gigs later, we did a show at the Chippenham – a room in a pub in west London – and we used to play this thing called 'Instrumental in E' where we'd just play anything that went with 'E' – a drony noise. Various people, invited or not, came up and ranted over it, and it ended up with a version of 'We're Gonna Have a Real Good Time Together'.

That particular night we got these two performance artists called Reindeer Werk to come up on stage and they kind of rolled around on the floor. They were behaviourists – look it up! I always felt that the Raincoats were more on the serious side of punk; not in the sense that we were ever highly confrontational, only in that there was no compromise in the sound. We tried to be ourselves; we didn't take on the punk Sid Vicious stance, we tried to fight our way through it and make sense of it. Anyway, this guy from Poland was at the show and I think we were the first punk band he'd ever seen. He invited us to go and play in Warsaw where he was organising an international performance art festival. Before we knew it, we'd packed our bags and our fifth to ninth gigs were at this festival in Warsaw. It was really fascinating – these performance artists from all over Eastern Europe and hardly any from the West. Poland was terribly starved of music; they were used to rock and folk/jazz but nothing more outrageous, so when they saw us they just went potty. That was totally exciting. That was the moment that I recognised that I really wanted to do it, to be in a band.

I think, being women, we got a lot of shit from people, particularly because we didn't always come across as rowdy and boisterous, good-time girls. We gave the audience a harder time in terms of coping with our music. We took ourselves seriously. People were annoyed we didn't give a little more. In that respect, that was them responding to us as girls. 'If they're girls, they've got to be this or that.' But that's only a percentage of the audience. We had a huge number of fans and I would probably say that the larger percentage of them was men.

But in a way, gender helped. Had I been a guy, I probably would have tried to play a guitar as a teenager, or a child. I don't know, I suppose plenty of girls have guitars. I feel quite proud of the way I got up and learned how to play in *public*. I was totally inspired by the moment. I used to say: 'We're so lucky to be alive and living in London at this moment!' I was really carried away on it. It's not nostalgia. It was a brilliant feeling: all these comparisons were made with Dada and stuff, which was a bit idiotic, but at the same time the feeling was so intense that I really thought something profound was

GINA BIRCH

going to happen. Not only in music but in the world – there was a huge sense of optimism for making a world that we could live in. A better world, our own kind of world. In a way, we created a little enclave that kind of was like that. Then when it all died out, I was so depressed and disillusioned. I felt I had conned myself, how could I have been so naïve? But then I think, if you don't have these dreams and beliefs and those pure, intense feelings . . .

I never felt like a girl, or a woman. I was always tall so I never wore high heels and I always dressed in an odd way. I remember my brother brought home a girlfriend and she said, 'Now I know what Nick meant when he said you wore strange clothes.' I had these boots from Olaf Daughters – a Swedish (I think) shoe company that had these soft leather boots that looked nothing like anything you could buy in Nottingham! – which probably wouldn't look so weird now. I'd spent some time in London, after I first left school in 1975, and I'd met this girl who gave me this really weird and beautiful dress from Afghanistan, with kind of embroidered fabric. I used to wear strange things because I was attracted to them. I never wore what other girls wore; my mum was always trying to take me out shopping and buy me things but I never liked them.

When I went to art school at Trent Polytechnic, I really went to town and dressed as weirdly as I wanted to. It was full of Jackson Pollock types and fashion students – there were weirdos from all over the place. We united and felt like normal. When I came to London, I carried on in the same way; I had stuff from thrift shops, stuff with holes in it, things that didn't fit, I mismatched things, wore huge dresses with belts . . . It didn't matter if it was a size 18 if you liked the fabric. Or I'd chop something up the side and sew it up roughly. But mostly I wore trousers, even if I'm making it sound like I wore dresses all the time. As far as image goes, I think the Raincoats probably would fit in more now than we did then, although I think the Slits were much more conscientious about what they wore. Ari would wear knickers over her trousers and Viv would always wear pretty, but kind of outrageous dresses. We wore idiotic things. Like when we came back from Poland, I had two pairs of these white waitresses' boots that were very strange, they kind of expanded to fit your feet – sort of orthopaedic . . . I was always attracted to things orthopaedic! I did knitting – I'd knitted this jumper which was all kinds of different shades, very subtle, but a really weird shape, and I wore this thing for God knows how long. I'd get attached to something and wear it until it rotted on my body. I was never really working out what I was going to look like as such. I'd just be attracted to something and put it on. I don't think I ever had a full-length mirror.

Punk was a very asexual time. I'd always had a boyfriend up until that time and when I came down to London I didn't want or need one. Instead, I wanted all these brief encounters. It was very much a time to stand on your own two feet and I wasn't very aware of being a girl. I'm sure there were all sorts of things that were annoying about being a girl, but my stronger recollection is of feeling strong, tough and empowered by the situation. I suppose since I discovered alcohol I'd always been fairly boisterous, and I felt I could be my own person. Punk gave me a space to do that. To not be afraid of saying what was on my mind.

There were a few young boys who followed the band around. We became friends, really. I probably did sleep with a lot of people, but not with anybody who came up to me and said: 'I love your music. Let's go off to bed.' It doesn't work that way. I've slept with quite a few people in my time, but in terms of groupies I don't know how it works for women. I don't know how it works for men. Maybe if you're in the Rolling Stones or something. These groups that have these dead sexy girls who go backstage and want to go off and screw the band. Have a blow job in a doorway. I've never had a blow job in a doorway, either way. Not through the Raincoats anyway. It was never like that, I've never got sex for being in the Raincoats.

We did a shortish, 28-day tour just before we recorded the first album with Palmolive playing drums. She'd discovered her religious side at that point and I think by the end of the tour she'd decided to leave the band – I think that during the tour she'd been deciding that she no longer wanted to be in a rock 'n' roll band, a punk band. There was Kleenex and Spizz Energy in the van, and it

GINA BIRCH

really was quite a weird nightmare. Three bands stuck in this tiny little Transit van chugging from down south, to up north to down south again because we weren't booked properly. We came back and recorded the album, which was great. Then Palmolive left.

There were the three of us left, me, Ana and Vicky, and we had to recruit a new drummer. Vicky had joined shortly after Palmolive. She'd seen an advert in Compendium bookshop in Camden which was for a violin, keyboard and guitar player. The key words were 'strength not style', which everyone but me thought were really important words. Maybe it was someone to carry my bass amp! Do we really need another stroppy person in the band?! Anyway, along came Vicky who played violin and keyboards, and soon learned to play guitar. She had been classically trained but had been interested in Brechtian theatre and had also played in Jam Today, a feminist band. We wrote a lot of new material – I think there was a sense of relief at first, 'cause she was a lot younger. After Palmolive left we recruited a young drummer called Ingrid Weiss, who was very good, but there seemed to be a lot of tension between her and Ana, so after working with her for about nine months that ended too.

Being in a band is a really painful thing, especially when you're young – at first it's really exciting, it seems to encompass everything you want. Then you realise there are other directions you want to go in, the band starts pulling apart, people want to start doing their own thing – the Raincoats were no exception. Over the three albums you can hear that we were pulling in all sorts of directions. It was very painful, because you want your own way, yet you don't want to break up the band. So it becomes a compromise. It must have been in 1982 when the Raincoats went to play America for the second time. We decided that we didn't want to continue things as they were. Shirley, our manager, persuaded us to record the final album, but it was a horrible time for me. My relationship had broken up – the first time I'd ever been left. That kind of situation can completely overshadow everything and it took me ages to get over it. The punk thing had become far from tribal – I suppose it was only really like that for the first year or so. I think I had taken all my records to the Record & Tape Exchange by then.

My sadness, I suppose, led me to spiritual stuff, but the nearest I got was reading a lot of Zen Buddhism. I did two weekends of this thing called Mongolian overtone chanting, which was quite strange and not terribly helpful for me. I didn't go off and join the Moonies or become an evangelical Christian but I did write songs at that time that were trying to get in touch with my spiritual side. I got it off my chest in an artistic way. I hope I won't have to do that again. But I can strongly recommend a good therapist in those circumstances!

We were writing songs which were getting weirder and weirder. Songs like 'Rainstorm' on the *Moving* album were spiritual and getting into Zen Buddhism. *Odyshape* really has very little connection with punk apart from the fact that it was a vehicle for us to become musicians and to write material. I was still going to gigs but our relationship in the band was increasingly rough and tumble; somehow it lost its complete thrust and energy. Not completely, but it had certainly lost its edge. By the time of *Moving*, I was getting more interested in studio techniques. Scritti Politti had gone pop; way back, all these bands which had been committed to punk ideals were beginning to 'embrace the enemy'. They were saying that infiltrating the system was the only way to break it. Around *Odyshape*, I was listening to loads of weird stuff as well as punk. Strange instruments, South American music, Eskimo music . . . But by the time of *Moving* I'd got more into the idea of a pop sensibility, of what was going on with a lot of my peer group.

When *Moving* was finished, I thought I'd like to write smoother music that somehow 'fitted in'. I turned the screw in my own destruction, really. In 1985–6, Vicky and I formed Dorothy, and did the total pop bit. It was quite a trauma though, 'cause I thought we could handle pop culture, that we could have some kind of control over it and be whatever *we* wanted to be. One day you could dress up like this and be this person, the next you could dress like that and be that person. In fact, you get very consumed by it, by selling records. It was a nightmare. Dorothy was the person that either of us could be if we felt like it, a kind of *alter ego*. The music was poppy ironic. Songs like 'Frog Prince', which was based on the romantic fiction of Barbara Cartland. The chorus went: 'You've got to kiss so many frogs before you find your prince', and the verses had whispered lines like: 'His warm lips pressed down upon hers . . .' Another was about falling in lust with your psychiatrist, another was a cover version of the mildly masochistic 'Hurts So Good'.

GINA BIRCH

Geoff Travis at Rough Trade had a label through Chrysalis records to whom we signed, and for the first time ever I made a living wage through making music. The problems began though when I started listening to Radio 1 to see if our record was being played. It became a torturous obsession and one which drove me crazy. I hate the world of pop music, it's a nightmare. During Dorothy, I started to be involved in directing pop videos. I had made super-8 films during my three years' fine art course at Middlesex Poly and suddenly I felt like I had come home: the film thing was a language I understood. When we got dropped by Chrysalis – EMI bought them out – I wanted a complete change and so I worked more in film. I directed a few pop videos then started an MA in film direction at the Royal College of Art [RCA], where I graduated in 1983. While I was there, I directed videos, including a couple for Daisy Chainsaw – for 'Love Your Money' and 'Hope All Your Dreams Come True'.

While I was at the RCA I didn't really have anything to do with music: didn't talk about it, never went to see any bands play. We were all so wrapped up in making films, it was such an all-encompassing thing. I met up with an American guy, Tim, who was on my course, who came to see the Raincoats play in New York recently, and he said how weird it was seeing me play. That this person he'd spent two years with had this whole other history that no one had explored or knew anything about. He had been to see a lot of bands in London, perhaps because he was in a foreign land and made more effort. But it did make me much more aware of my history and that it is important to confront it and to integrate it into what you do now.

When I left the RCA I got taken on by M-Ocean Pictures to direct promos and commercials and I have been working on and off since then. I am still working on drama scripts and want to make a long film some time in the next three years, but during this period of the Raincoats' revival there is only so much time in a day.

There had been talk over the years about re-releasing the CDs, but times have been really hard financially for small labels like Rough Trade. Things really didn't spring into action until August 1993. We were going to play a couple of songs at a party to coincide with the release of the first album on CD, and then suddenly we were invited on to the Nirvana tour. Although we didn't know that much about them, 'cause neither Ana nor I had really been listening to music, we thought it'd be stupid not to do it. Then things started to hot up a bit, to get more serious. Geffen put our records out in America because of Kurt's interest. They said that if we did the Nirvana tour it would be good if we also did a little American tour, maybe one on the East Coast and then come back and do one on the West Coast. Then we got invited to do Lollapalooza and we just went: 'No way!' We couldn't imagine being on the road for two and a half months.

It was really a slow process of recognition, because we kept saying to each other: 'Well, we don't know if it's going to be fun.' We'd broken up for a reason – because it wasn't fun any more. Ana and I weren't getting on brilliantly, musically, and we didn't know how we'd get on now. I had stayed friends with Ana over the years. We live very close to each other, although we didn't see a huge amount of each other . . . It was amazing when we got together after eleven years. I'd been doing a little practising with a keyboard and a sample/sequencer which I'd been playing bass lines on. So I hadn't actually picked up the bass for so long, it was just brilliant . . . it wasn't quite like riding a bicycle again, I had a lot of relearning to do. The first time Ana and I got back together, we could only play part of a couple of songs. We were just so hopeless – just falling about laughing. How can we possibly do this in public again? We were thinking that the first gig we do is just going to be like our first ever gig. But actually, we got it together and auditioned for a couple of violin players, and by that time we'd become quite respectable.

Going out and playing has been so fantastic, partly because I feel much more focused about what I want out of it and what I can put into it. I've got my other things – doing filmmaking and promos and stuff – so it's not the be-all and end-all, but it's a really important part of what I do. We've got on famously; such a revelation, really. And there's all these other women's bands playing, a few of whom really like what we did. Because by the time the Raincoats split up, we thought that we'd run our course and couldn't see the value, really. I think Ana always felt that the music never got as much attention as it deserved, and I always felt that that was it – we'd done it and some people liked it, some didn't. I hardly met anybody who'd ever heard of us and for a time, if anybody asked me what I

111

GINA BIRCH

did, I wouldn't mention the Raincoats because it didn't seem relevant.

We both resent bands reforming, because it's a hideous thing to do. Most undignified. But little by little, as it became such good fun, it also became irresistible. It's been so great that I don't think we were wrong to do it. We wouldn't have done it if it hadn't been for Nirvana and if it hadn't been for Ana and Shirley [O'Loughlin, the Raincoats' manager] dragging me out to see all the Riot Grrrl bands. Seeing Skinned Teen, Voodoo Queens, Mambo Taxi and Huggy Bear made me think: 'This is amazing, it's really good again.' It was such a brilliant feeling seeing all these girls getting up and doing it with their own sound. It's weird, 'cause having an all-girl band is a statement. One thinks that it's probably a phase that one goes through, but there still aren't that many. In the eighties there were bands like the Belle Stars, and there were a hell of a lot of women fronting bands. But not many with guitars or other instruments.

When you compare the Riot Grrrl movement to seventies punk bands, I don't remember us being very supportive of each other. I adored the Slits but didn't take much interest in some of the other groups that were going around, like the Modettes, the Delta Five, the Au Pairs . . . I liked them, but I didn't go crazy about them. We were constantly being thrown together in articles and being compared to the point where it divides you. We never went out with a sense of sisterhood, we never toured together. The idea never entered our heads. We were as supportive of male groups that we liked as female groups. Gender wasn't an issue for us, which perhaps it should have been. That's what I first liked when I heard about the Riot Grrrl thing. I always felt there was an intention to be mutually supportive and an awareness that that was important.

Whether Riot Grrrl actually worked in practice or not, I don't know. It seems to have broken down and a lot of people have fallen out with each other. But in any intense organisation, whether it be a Marxist-Leninist group or a housing co-op, where you have a common cause, one can fall out over the most ridiculous things. The tiniest details sometimes become major issues. But for us, that was never even a consideration. We never even thought of it in those terms and now it seems weird. We talked a lot about women in the Raincoats, and I would have said yes, we were feminists, but the actuality was that Ana and I were doing what we wanted to do: finding our own identity as individuals in this movement that allowed people to be people. When Vicky joined the band, she'd been in a feminist band and she was much more politically aware. She came in and said: 'You are feminists and it's very important that you recognise that.' As soon as the word was mentioned once in an interview, it was thrown back at us every time. Then we'd say: 'What do you mean exactly by "feminism"?' It still annoys me that people are terrified of the word. One would like it to become, well, like the word 'socialist' – I don't think they're redundant words. They're as dangerous as they ever were.

I would still call myself a feminist even though I think that all women's organisations have terrible problems, and that feminism has got an awful lot of things wrong. But we're working it out, we're trying to work towards some kind of better future and, slowly but surely, the world is taking some of those things on board. As a term, 'feminism' still confuses me. I wish that it could become such an integrated term as anti-racist. Practically no one would want to admit to being racist yet so many people feel the word 'feminism' is an affront to their femininity/masculinity. I see it as giving women the opportunity to voice their grievances about language and deep-rooted prejudices and to raise awareness of what women can bring to the world if men would only stop and listen. For God's sake, we might still not have the vote or be able to show our ankles if it wasn't for feminists.

Kim Gordon

kim gordon

Sonic Youth

I was out in the backyard
With the harvest spoon, now
Cosloy and Keanu coming down the street
And I got me a quick one
On the outskirts of town, yeah
Right outside of guyville
Well it's gonna be a 7"
And I gotta hard-on for it

('Harvest Spoon', Free Kitten)

Kim Gordon is perched on a stool at the back of a small room. A Riot Grrrl band is shouting and smiling and banging instruments on stage. The gig is full of expectant young women with pigtails, clear skin, short skirts and long, stripy socks and young guys with T-shirts and sloppy cords. Maxwell's, in Hoboken, New Jersey is a mini-mecca of alternative rock where every band plays at some point on their way up. At the end of the gig, Kim talks to Kathi Wilcox, bass player with Bikini Kill, America's premier Riot Grrrl band. Kathi is drunk and emotional, Kim sober and serene. The godmother of alternative rock carefully climbs down off her stool, arches her back and puts a hand on her swollen tummy. Seven months pregnant and checking out new bands, Kim Gordon is the original Riot Mom.

Kim moved from the West Coast to New York in 1980. She had an art school background and her first jobs were in galleries. She first found herself on stage when conceptual artist Dan Graham asked her to put a band together for a performance piece in Boston. Thurston Moore had moved from Florida to New York in 1977; Kim went to see his band, the Coachmen, and they hooked up. Sonic Youth made their début in 1981 at Noise Fest, a mini-festival Thurston put on in the gallery where Kim was working. The band (with Thurston as vocalist and guitarist, Kim as bassist and sometime vocalist, Lee Ranaldo on guitar, Richard Edson and then Steve Shelley on drums) emerged musically from the No Wave scene in downtown Manhattan. No Wave was otherwise known as 'art punk' – it was loud, aggressive, provocative and occasionally pretentious. Their first, self-titled album came out in 1982 on noise jazz composer Glenn Branca's avant-garde Neutral label.

In the past dozen years, Sonic Youth have made ten albums. Their music has developed and evolved then gone back to its 'art core' roots. In 1986 they released *EVOL*, a confident album with the odd unashamed pop song ('Starpower'); two years later they had their first indie number one in the UK with *Daydream Nation*, an ambitious and inspired double album packed with great rock songs. At the turn of the decade, Sonic Youth went overground, signing to Geffen (home of Guns n' Roses) and releasing *Goo*. The album's cover borrowed from pop art, showing Raymond Pettibon's black and white illustration of a cool, young couple wearing shades, next to the melodramatic words: 'I stole my sister's boyfriend. It was all whirlwind, heat and flash. Within a week we killed my parents and hit the road.' Talking about the transition from indie to major label, Thurston once said: 'There's money in the mix, but we still don't sound like Foreigner.' For a band who once used power drills on stage to increase the noise factor, *Goo* was subtle, but there was nothing about it which suggested a stab at commercialism. As on previous records, the music mixed controlled chaos with layers and textures of experimental sound.

Sonic Youth's lyrics are sometimes as difficult as their music, and neither Kim nor Thurston is prepared to explain them. On 'Flower', a 12-inch single released in 1986, Kim sang with angry and emotional vocals against a background of feedback:

> Support the power of women
> Use the power of man

Support the flower of woman
Use the word: *fuck*
The word is love.

In the video for 'Kool Thing' (a track on *Goo*), Kim dressed up as a rock chick stereotype and sang about the relationships between black men and white women. Public Enemy's Chuck D, guesting on the song and in the video, rapped about his 'fear of a female planet'. 'Tunic (Song for Karen)', also on *Goo*, paid tribute to the late anorexic 1970s star Karen Carpenter. Although Thurston is often called Sonic Youth's frontman, Kim's contribution is fundamental. On 1992's *Dirty* (another double, produced by Butch Vig, who gave Nirvana's *Nevermind* its razor-sharp edge), Thurston gets political on 'Youth against Fascism' while Kim gets into gender politics on 'Swimsuit Issue'. The song tells of a secretary defying her boss's sexual advances ('I'm not gonna give you head . . .'), followed by a list of supermodels' names slowly spat out, set to juddering rhythm. On 'Bull in the Heather', one of the poppiest songs on their last album, 1994's *Experimental Jet Set, Trash and No Star*, Kim rails against playing a part in a male-dominated culture, deciding instead to be passive.

For such an influential band – they are constantly name-checked, by Grrrls and boy rock bands, once by Nirvana, now by Pavement and Sebadoh – mainstream success has eluded Sonic Youth. They have watched those they've helped along the way succeed – Nirvana, Hole (also tipped off to Geffen, and Kim co-produced their début album, *Pretty on the Inside*), the Breeders (Kim co-directed their 'Cannonball' and 'Divine Hammer' videos). And, despite the re-emergence of punk chic in the 1990s and the band's major label status, they have remained an experimental art core band on the periphery of punk, rock, pop and art. Like Patti Smith and Yoko Ono, Sonic Youth are successful in their embrace of rock and art. Andy Warhol would probably be a groupie, were he still alive. But, as Kim once said, they don't write singles, and each time they make a vaguely polished album (*Dirty*) they return to fragmented albums made fast to sound cheap (*Experimental Jet Set*, etc.) They may make concept albums, but each time they verge on the pretentious they haul themselves back with humour – in 1989,

KIM GORDON

Sonic Youth's alter ego Ciccone Youth released the sassy 'Into the Groove(y)', with Kim taking on Madonna's seductive pop vocals.

Kim had been in Sonic Youth for two years before Madonna released her first single, but even with a young baby daughter [Coco Hayley Gordon Moore, was born on July 1 1994 and within days was wearing a 'Question Authority' T-shirt] she isn't about to give anything up. She is happy with the young audiences Sonic Youth draw, flattered when young women write to her saying she inspired them to start their own band, amused on the occasion when two girls approached her after a show and asked, straight-faced: 'Will you be our mother?'

Having started music late like Patti Smith and Deborah Harry before her, Kim is now 40. She's married to long-term lover Thurston, is in a second band and has recently taken up fashion as a serious sideline. Free Kitten is Kim's girl bonding band. With Julie Cafritz, one-time member of punk slacker band Pussy Galore, Kim completely escapes the confines of a regular band set-up. The two friends make what Kim calls 'anti-commercial music'; it centres on her and Julie's vocals and guitars, with sporadic help from Yoshimi (drummer with Japanese punk band the Boredoms) and Pavement's Mark Ibold on bass. *Unboxed*, 1994's collection of EP imports and live tracks, is experimental noise which sounds like Riot Grrrls warming up for a gig they know no one will turn up to.

With Julie's sister Daisy von Furth, Kim runs the clothing line X-Girl. An offshoot of Beastie Boy Mike D's skate/hip hop label X-Large, X-Girl produce (affordable) shrunk T-shirts in bright colours alongside jeans and little skirts. Kim and Daisy put on a street show during New York fashion week in April 1994, with model/singer Donovan Leitch (son of 'Mellow Yellow' Donovan) compering, Sophia Coppola (daughter of Francis Ford) producing, Zoe Cassavetes (daughter of director and actor John) and Donovan Leitch's sister Ione Skye modelling. Donovan decided 'we're kind of like Warhol's Factory' and, amongst others, Linda Evangelista turned up with her man, Kyle MacLachlan. From Riot Mom to fashion bum.

Kim Gordon is seriously cool, an ice queen by her own admission. During lunch (skewered sandwiches and mineral water) a few days after the X-Girl show, she is clearly a little bored with selling her songs, and although she is pleasant enough, she is also slightly aloof. In the SoHo loft she shares with Thurston, she talks enthusiastically about their kid-to-be, dismisses the fat, stripy cat as Thurston's and introduces her tall, gangly, boyish husband (he's five years her junior) when he wanders in with armfuls of rare records. Later that evening, outside Maxwell's, Thurston, all jeans, T-shirt and sneakers, leans against a car and chats with some friends. Kim, in a tight jumper, short skirt, white tights and low-top trainers, is a (bleached) blonde and blue-eyed beauty who is hard not to stare at. She raises an eyebrow as Kathi Wilcox lurches past. The original Riot Mom is so cool it hurts.

I always wanted to rebel. I was always rebellious as a teenager, but I had nowhere to put it. I would just do things like stay out all night for the hell of it, just 'cause my mom said I couldn't. I hated school and I would read Nietzsche in my classes 'cause I thought that was really rebellious. Not that I really understood what I was reading. I had an older brother who read all that stuff. He was into music, though he didn't play an instrument; he just played records all the time.

My brother is three and a half years older and I used to really look up to him even though he was mostly an asshole. He became a paranoid schizophrenic in his twenties. As well as turning me on to Dylan and sixties stuff, he played a lot of jazz records – everything from be-pop to Coltrane to Ornette Coleman. Much of my rebellion had to do with the double standards for him as a boy and me as a girl. You know, staying out late, etc. In the late sixties he used to wear all white, carry a bible and live in Malibu. He studied classical literature and wrote sonnets about maidens. It was very Renaissance Fair-like. His friends were like followers – almost Manson-like. All that stuff was in the air at the time. He had a girlfriend in high school who was killed by the Manson family.

My parents had jazz records; Billie Holiday, things like that. I think I was around 12 when I first started really taking notice. We

KIM GORDON

lived in Hong Kong for a year and I had this English boyfriend who was a drummer, although I actually never saw him play in a band. My brother had this friend whose band opened for Herman's Hermits in Hong Kong. Going to see them was really exciting. I also remember going to these clubs in hotel bars and they'd have these Chinese girls playing Beatles songs and wearing weird party dresses. I always seemed to have musician boyfriends, and it took me a long time to figure out that I wanted to be able to play the music. I was really intrigued by it, even though I had no musical training.

Steve was my first boyfriend. I was 12. He was English and I was heavily into the Stones at that time. We would make out in his room for hours, then get up and have a formal lunch served by their Chinese maid. It was very colonial. I was very developed for my age and sailors would proposition me walking down the street. I read every Ian Fleming novel that year. I was heavily into daydreaming and escapism – nothing felt better. I guess that's a totally normal teenager. My mother explained to me that boys will like a girl longer for her brains than her body, and instilled a key neurosis.

I didn't completely become a juvenile delinquent 'cause I came from a nice academic middle-class family. My father was a Dean of Sociology and Education at UCLA [University of California, Los Angeles]. My mother made custom clothes and did tailoring for people, but was basically a housewife. I went to the University Elementary School at UCLA till I was 11. It was an experimental laboratory school, so there weren't any grades, it was all based on creativity. When I went to a public school, I really didn't know how to fit in; there were all these girls in their little white socks, and I was used to wearing whatever I wanted. I didn't know how to dress myself. Somehow I ended up hanging out with the white trash, listening to Motown records and stuff. I was blonde, developed for my age . . . I guess I was sort of nerdy. I was either nerdy or I was setting my hair and wearing make-up. By ninth grade you wore bright lipstick and had roller cards in your hair. When I went to high school, there was no make-up and it was more hippyish.

I didn't go to any gigs – no, that's not true, I used to go to the Fillmore in San Francisco when I was 14. It only used to cost $10 to fly there on Fridays and we'd go with some friends we'd met in Hong Kong. I took acid and saw Jefferson Airplane and the Grateful

Dead, Moby Grape, all those bands. But I never went to the Sunset Strip; Los Angeles was so different, it was really heavy. My mom would never let me go up to the Strip. Had I known what I was missing . . . In high school I started listening to more jazz and going to jazz concerts – Archie Shepp, the Art Ensemble of Chicago, Don Cherry, Miles Davis.

It wasn't until I moved to New York that I really realised I was more into music than art. I came here because of art, then I saw people like Glenn Branca play with his group the Static; Lydia Lunch; DNA. But I really missed the heart of it. I missed the early days of No Wave; by the time I was here, the Contortions had turned into James White. Thurston used to come here when he was 17, so he saw everyone – Patti Smith, Television, New York Dolls, Sid Vicious. I arrived right before Sid Vicious died. It was weird, it was kind of like: 'Everything's over.' It was like the end of an era. New York music was in limbo then, so Thurston and I were more into all the English singles – the Jelleys, Girls At Our Best, Au Pairs, Young Marble Giants, the Raincoats, the Slits (of course), A Certain Ratio, Delta 5 and the Pop Group.

When I was in art school in Toronto, I was in this band that we made up from members of our class. It was really fun, but we'd get so drunk that I couldn't continue playing on a regular basis. Then when I came to New York I was friends with an artist called Dan Graham who had this performance piece he wanted to do with an all-girl band. I asked Miranda – a bass player – and another friend called Christine who played drums, and though I'd never played guitar, I had a go and we wrote these songs. We took the lyrics from ad copy. There was this one song called 'Cosmopolitan Girl' which used text straight out of a magazine. Something about why I love being a *Cosmopolitan* girl . . . then there was another song about lipstick. So we did this one gig with Dan, but Miranda and I used to play and rehearse endlessly with other people. That's how I met Thurston.

Thurston was playing in a band called the Coachman. I went to see their last show. There was something special about him, like he exuded this air of boyish wildness but incredible goodness. We became involved fairly quickly and started playing music together, with this other girl, Ann – also a friend of Miranda's. I guess it was love at first sight. He has such faith in things. It's not that I'm a pessimist, I like to question from all angles. We're opposite in that respect, but his faith gives me confidence to question and have something to come back to.

Doing music was so much fun that I started wondering: 'What am I gonna do now? Am I gonna pursue art?' I was kind of turned off by the whole thing, the whole commercial aspect of art. I was working at a gallery and I think I was really afraid. I was afraid to put my own ego out there. It's very cut-throat, the art world, and I guess being in a band is different, it's not just your ego out there. You feel more protected. I like collaborating. I didn't feel like a rock star on stage; it was the morning after, when you just felt like you'd spent all this energy. Being on stage is very visceral, just feeling the power of your body. Maybe it's sexual, but not as in: 'I feel like a woman' or 'I feel like a man.' I think the closest explanation is being at one with everyone. You lose your self-consciousness, you're not really thinking about what you're doing, you're just doing it, and something is carrying you along.

But at the same time, it felt really unnatural. The only thing I could relate it to was when I used to dance. I used to do ballet and modern dance and physical, tomboy stuff before that, so because I had no musical training, I related physically to playing music. I felt unnatural about my lyrics for quite a long time – until quite recently, with a few exceptions. Part of it was because of the way the music was always written. Like: 'Here's a weird piece of music. OK, you can sing on this one.' As I don't have a real singing voice, I think of other ways, usually rhythmically. I always liked the Shangri-Las, I liked the presence of their voices when they weren't singing, but speaking about some melodrama; the way a word would have space around it.

We remastered all the old Sonic Youth records recently and it was the first time I could listen to them and not cringe. Even though they're flawed, they hold up, in a way. It's funny listening to them in the context of the music people are doing now. I'm surprised at all that our records have been consistently well reviewed. Our music is a far cry from mainstream. The whole Nirvana thing – I can't believe that people actually thought anything similar would happen to us. That's preposterous. Also the whole way of thinking that happens so suddenly when you sign to a major label – everything is about competition. Your whole reason for being is to have a Top 10 record. If you don't have a gold record, people perceive you as somehow having failed, as if your music is no longer valid. In a way, it's too bad 'cause it takes the whole meaning away from the fact that we're 'alternative'. Alternative now just means a radio format. We always operated independently. We always had our own little goals: we go on tour, make a record, get more distribution, whatever. But it wasn't ever, like, world domination . . . I don't really recommend anybody signing to a major label, unless they're going for Top 10 success. The bands that just put out one record and sign to a major label, that's such a waste, 'cause they miss such a good part of their career and their life as a band and they can never go back. I look back on those times with fondness.

Maybe the weirdest thing about signing to Geffen in 1990 was going to a corporate place and seeing the secretaries. They're all women, they all dress the same, they all get flowers on Secretary Day. But they don't seem in line to move up to higher positions. That whole notion made me really feel patronised as a woman, like they didn't know how to treat me. We talk to everyone in the record label now, but there was a period when we didn't have a manager and I was ringing up and dealing with everything, but no one would have a serious conversation with me. The only women are in publicity, art . . . There are women in A&R, but they don't have any power.

I guess that's why I relate to Japan – people are so repressed there! It's probably one of the most fun places we've toured, because it's culturally the most different. Americans have a fascination with freedom. All the commercials are about freedom, youthfulness, lack of history, guilt, etc. Americans are deeply repressed, they just hide it. Japan has made an art form of repression. They admit to shyness or show embarrassment over small things. I find it refreshing and liberating to know there's a culture more repressed than ours and that they're so honest about it. They won't let people get up on stage or anything; they bring out the police if people get up on stage. But it's

KIM GORDON

fun to go there 'cause of all the fans, they're so into detail. That's a little scary. But unless you're Michael Jackson or Madonna, you'll never be as big as Japanese pop stars. Unless you're super-big they just ignore you 'cause they've got so many of their own pop stars.

Anyway there *are* more women, it seems, getting attention playing music. I don't have any real role models for the kind of music I do. The closest one is someone like Patti Smith, who retired and had kids. Which is always an option, I guess. It gets me down when people are malicious about age, and when they have double standards for men. I could name a number of men in their mid-thirties who people rarely discuss in terms of age. Even, for example, with Neil Young, the response is: 'Oh, he's just getting better as he gets older.' With women, it's more like: 'As you're getting older, you're losing it.' I think also that if you do a certain kind of music, more dissonant music, people think it's inappropriate to be beyond a certain age. You get away with more if you make more melodious-type music. At least in England, that seems to be my lasting impression. In America, the mainstream doesn't consider you if you're a woman making what they see as annoying music. That's why people like Chrissie Hynde were never a role model for me. She fitted right in.

I don't think that anything's going to change radically overnight as far as controlling the media or the way things are perceived. I think that the mainstream is conservative and that women who get recognised in the mainstream are even more conservative. I don't really care about that. But we can see the difference with bands like Bikini Kill and Huggy Bear. I don't want to make generalisations because so much is based on people's personalities; the fact that Kathleen [Hanna, singer-songwriter with Bikini Kill] has the kind of personality that she has means she's kind of a leader in a way; she's really outgoing. Her more militant side is balanced with her kind of musical comedy side, her entertainer side. I think that people are far more influenced by personalities than by movements. I was really interested in Riot Grrrl, but at the same time I really felt totally irrelevant to it, 'cause I didn't feel musically involved. I mean Huggy Bear were aware of something, but I didn't feel that Bikini Kill were necessarily that aware or influenced musically.

Huggy Bear seemed to be more experimental in their approach,

124

whereas Bikini Kill seemed more in the trad punk rock mode. Both bands were, I think, influenced by National of Ulysses, a [Washington] DC band. Since neither band seemed influenced by Sonic Youth, I always feel weird when journalists ask how it feels to be a role model to those groups. It seemed to be more about late seventies punk rock and early nineties third-generation DC hardcore. I've gotten to know them – I felt like I really wanted to make contact and I was also glad that they're bratty and strong, independent. I'm not sure if I would have been a riot grrrl if I was just starting off; it sounds clichéd, but I've really never been one to join groups. Because of my background as an artist, I've always been wary of groups, Although, really what Riot Grrrl came out of was the friendship between two or three people. I totally relate to that, and it seemed like that was really fun. Yeah, actually I think I probably would have been involved.

I hope my daughter grows up to feel that she can do anything she wants to do. Of course, I have fantasies about her sitting playing guitar . . . If she feels no need to be creative that's OK. When we were in Melbourne, Australia, we went to this place called Rock 'n' Roll High School. It's a place where girls can go and learn to play rock, meet other girls and form bands. It seemed like most of them were high school age, and it was founded by a young woman named Stephanie to help girls with the self-esteem that they lack going through puberty. They seemed to be into indie rock music – it was very logical, but very surreal.

It maybe is easier now for me, as a woman, to do something like a clothes line without being seen as vacuous. Daisy von Furth and I have been friends for a few years. We've always hung out and gone shopping. Daisy is Julie's sister – they are very close, so we all hang out together. The [Beastie] boys who run the hip hop clothing label X-Large wanted to design a line of girls' clothes because they saw the competition doing it. They thought that we would have good taste so they asked if we wanted to do it. Daisy is one of those people who, since the age of six or seven, has been reading fashion magazines; she knows all the editors' names and all the models' names. She's been preparing her soundbites literally for years. It's fun

KIM GORDON

to do it with her because I don't feel all the pressure's on me. Because I do have other things I do, the clothing label's not my passion. I love clothes and I love anything that's visual – I'm very visually oriented – but music's really my passion. Still, I don't like to do anything badly, and I do have the drive to be involved in X-Girl.

When we did the fashion show during New York Fashion Week, we were so happy because we just thought if our name gets mentioned once in a paper, it'd be good. But then people actually took us seriously and reviewed it . . . It was odd because we don't really think of ourselves as designers: we just take clothes we like and rearrange them. Basically we make clothes that we want to wear. It comes from years of shopping and having to deal with visible panty-lines, or simply thinking: 'Oh, this doesn't work because of this.' I wanted to make clothes that didn't use Spandex and Lycra, that weren't body hugging but were flattering at the same time and could maybe be worn on a wider range of figures.

I am one of those people whose self-esteem is based on doing things. If I'm not continually creating challenges for myself or playing music, I feel like shit and I'm grumpy. Even though I'm naturally lazy I can't maintain it. I do admire people who are happy doing nothing but who have great charm. The song 'My Friend Goo' [on *Goo*] was about a girl who just felt good about her girlness but didn't feel she had anything to prove. I always feel strong in the midst of action. After it's over, the accomplishment is too – that's why I have to keep doing things, get involved in different projects.

Working with Tamra Davis is fun. We met when she did our first video, 'Kool Thing'. She let me look through the camera to give me a sense of confidence about how things looked and to understand what I wanted to get across. She has since done three other videos with us. It turned out we had a lot of friends in common. Actually, we met a couple of years before she shot 'Kool Thing' – I knew her sister – we just became friends over the past few years. We like the same kind of books. She is probably the most high-powered, driven, female friend that I have. I admire the way she deals with male authority – with studio or movie heads – something I have little patience for. We've been working on a story for a movie, but these things take so long. I don't think I'll make any more music videos unless something really moves me. I don't have the discipline just to do it as a job and I can't deal with MTV politics. MTV in America is much more conservative than in Europe.

I don't know how long Sonic Youth will go on. I find Free Kitten very exciting 'cause I get to play guitar; it's just me and Julie and it's really easy. It's easy working with another woman who's my best friend, and maybe it's easy because it's not my main band, and I don't need to depend on it to make money. But it's definitely a lot of fun going on tour and recording. Yoshimi flew over from Japan to play drums and we spent a week recording for a new record in a rehearsal space with an eight-track. We basically just wrote the songs there and then recorded them. Working with Free Kitten is also much freer than with Sonic Youth because we don't have any history. Free Kitten works because of our shared sensibility and the fact that we're friends. Julie and I are very similar in our laziness. We don't have a fan-mail address. We're really bad, we don't reply to fan mail. We've only done a few interviews, 'cause we're not really so into doing all that extraneous stuff around the music that, with Sonic Youth, has become kind of a drag.

127

I don't think I've had to be stronger than Thurston in dealing with fame, but I think Thurston was born to rock 'n' roll. I read his high school yearbook and almost all the inscriptions were about becoming famous or becoming a criminal. I'm more the overly sensitive type. I'm either much more emotional or I make myself into an ice queen when I feel most picked on, like in England.

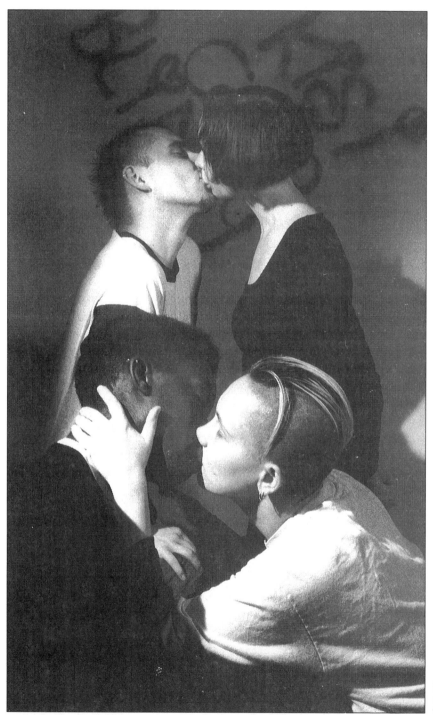

Sister George (clockwise from top left): Lyndon, Lisa, Ellyott Dragon, Daryl

ellyott dragon

Sister George

'This is earthquake country,' I laugh and point at
   my head
If I could only write again, I'd will this hunger
   dead.
People want me to be funny so I drink
Besides, you can't have two writers in one
   family, I think.

('Janey's Bloc' from Drag King)

It's Hip to be Queer, It's Hot to be Queer, It's the Gay 90s
(gay and lesbian slogan)

Ellyott Dragon, ex-Israeli army corporal, wants Sister George to
be as big as the Carpenters. She talks fast, in an accent which
mixes Hebrew, East Coast American and east London and somehow
ends up sounding Glaswegian. Born and brought up in Israel, Ellyott
hated the native music – 'total crap' – and instead fostered her love
of indie rock. At 18 she joined the army to complete two years' com-
pulsory service, and met her first girlfriend.

Bored with the limitations of being a musician in Israel, she
moved to London around six years ago and played with various
bands, including the Darlings with former Au Pairs singer Lesley
Woods and Debbie Smith (now guitarist with Echobelly). In Spring
1993, after seeing an advert in *Melody Maker* requesting a singer for
a 'Queer/dyke band' into 'Riot Grrrl, L7, Bikini Kill and Hole', Ellyott
met up with and joined Sister George.

Sister George felt alienated by the gay scene, enamoured with guitar rock and spurred on by Riot Grrrl. Lisa (bass), Daryl (drums), Lyndon (guitar) and Ellyott felt more affinity with working-class heterosexuals than middle-class gays and lesbians. They are not railing against straight, white boys rocking out so much as sneering at the 'pink pound' which buys cappuccinos, immaculate haircuts and designer clothes in Soho's guppie (upwardly mobile and gay) bars. For them ABBA, the Pet Shop Boys and gay discos like Heaven mean nothing. Big guitars, manic vocals, celebratory queer lyrics and gigs in England's scuzziest venues are all that matters. Queercore, Sister George say, is best characterised as 'an attitude problem'.

Queercore emerged in America in the late 1980s amongst gay and lesbian punks who felt isolated from both the disco and the 'alternative' scenes. *Homocore*, an American Queercore fanzine, wrote: 'You don't have to be gay; being different at all, like straight guys who aren't macho, women who don't want to be a punk rock fashion accessory, or any other personal decision that makes you a social outcast, is enough.' It wasn't until 1993, however, when news of Riot Grrrl began to filter from the US to the UK, that British gay and lesbian bands into punk rock rather than camp pop felt there was space for them.

In 1993 Liz Naylor read an article about Riot Grrrl in an American magazine, formed her own label, Catcall, and put out a Huggy Bear/Bikini Kill joint album. She recalls watching the two bands at a London gig when some people from Walthamstow came up and hustled her. 'They said they were going to form an all-queer band. I thought they'd never do it. I bumped into them a few days later at a Voodoo Queens gig and they invited me to their first show. I went along, thinking it would be awful. They were fantastic. They could really play – they sound like Pearl Jam.'

Liz was so impressed with Sister George that she began to manage them and put their first mini-album out on Catcall. *Drag King*, which came out at the end of 1993, is cheaply produced, but it captures something of the anger and passion Sister George generate during their gigs. Complemented by thundering drums and bass, grunged-out guitar and Ellyott's screeching voice, the band's lyrics ridicule misogynist gay men 'clone' culture – 'Hey there big girl's blouse/Wanna ride my handle bar moustache?' on 'Handle bar' –

while 'Janey's Bloc' was inspired by reading the writer Jane Bowles's biography.

Sister George have no time for mainstream lesbian icons – their pin-up is Sara Gilbert, who plays Darlene, the sulky-mouthed teenager with acid one-liners, in *Roseanne*. *Drag King* opens with a sample from *Poison Ivy*, a tacky American film starring Sara Gilbert, as does 'Let's Breed', a cynical look at heterosexual mating rituals: '. . . those lips. You know, lips are supposed to be a perfect reflection of another part of a woman's anatomy. Not that I'm a lesbian . . . Well, maybe I am. No, definitely not. I told my mother I was just for shock value. She said fine, just so long as you don't smoke.'

The 'lipstick lesbian' media fixation of 1994 had some women stumbling out of closets stinking of moth balls, but high-profile dykes remain a scarcity – kd lang came out with the release of *Ingénue* in 1992 and her sexuality is still a talking point. As rock has (too) long been the domain of the white boy, it has, from Mick Jagger to Morrissey, traditionally been easier for men to flirt with sexual ambiguity. Female musicians aren't 'supposed' to toy with lesbianism: Janis Joplin wore men's suits and occasionally fucked women, but lived in fear of her bisexuality being discovered and, three decades on, Elastica's three female members wore suits as a fashion rather than sexuality statement.

131

Ellyott knows that Sister George – and other UK Queercore bands such as Mouthful, Men Should Wear Mascara, Sapphic Sluts and Children's Hour – will draw attention to themselves by wearing T-shirts with slogans like JUST BECAUSE YOU'RE GAY DOESN'T MAKE YOU OKAY. She also knows that, as long as Queercore lasts as a trend, her band can easily maintain a media profile. But what happens when queer is no longer hip? 'I don't want the whole world to buy my records 'cause I'm a dyke, but because I'm brilliant.' There's a hint of a smirk as she smoothes her floppy bleached Mohican back over her stubbly head – but only a hint.

The band's name is taken from the movie *The Killing of Sister George* (1968), in which Beryl Reid is a maturing bull dyke actress.

ELLYOTT DRAGON

She is behaving badly, gradually being kicked out of her role as Sister George in a soap, losing her girlfriend to her female boss and moaning loudly. A dyke heroine.

There is all sorts of music in Israel – it's like a western country. Indie records are harder to find than chart music. Obviously everybody knows Nirvana and Pearl Jam, but Hole probably only sold a hundred copies, if that, of their first album. Indie and underground music makes its way quietly; you've got to know the right people and the right shops. Israeli music is crap, total crap. Quite eighties with a foreign language. Hebrew is a very hard language to sing in. When I wrote lyrics for the Israeli bands I was in, most of them were in English. Which is partly why I eventually thought: 'If you're singing in English anyway, what are you doing here?'

I listened to some Israeli records, but I grew up with classical music because my parents are into it. I'm lucky 'cause my parents have been together for thirty years and, so far as I know, they're totally monogamous and faithful. They're the perfect couple – a house in the suburbs, kids, a dog. They really love each other and they're best friends, so in a way it's released me from having to prove to myself that true love is possible. Anyway, for a long time I hated classical music and couldn't listen to it. Now I've come back to it and I really love it.

My older brother brought music like David Bowie home. I remember when I was 14, somebody bought me a big Bowie poster and I had it up in my room. Everyone was asking: 'Who the hell is this?' That was in 1980 and he *still* wasn't well known in Israel. My brother lives in the States now, where he's a total American producer – an over-producer – and he listens to ZZ Top, the Spin Doctors and shit. Ugh! But he's great, he bought all the first albums I got into. Then he stayed on the progressive rock thing and I went a bit more to folk, kind of singer-songwriter music. I discovered Velvet Underground, John Cale, Lou Reed and on from there to Patti Smith. I spent half a year in the States when I was 16, and I saw J. Geils Band and Aerosmith. Oh yeah! Aerosmith were great. They were both great, actually. I was living in a hick town in New England. It was scary – I knew I was a dyke and I couldn't come out.

I was out to my friends in Israel but not to my friends in America. You'd think it would be totally the other way round. I think I have to re-experience the States.

I joined my first band when I was about 15, at school. I was the drummer and there were two girls on guitar and a boy singing. We were the pits. The *pits!* We were absolutely horrible. But it was great, 'cause we used to get up on stage and do cover versions. We couldn't play or anything, but everybody seemed to enjoy it. They had no choice, really. When I was still in high school, I wanted to be a painter. But music took over more and more. When I was in the army, I was playing drums in my brother's band and we played a few festivals. Then somebody introduced me to three guys in a punk band – the only punk band in the country – who thought it would be cool to have a girl drummer. They were a really weird band, somewhere between being total misogynists and total feminists. They were all tattooed – nobody in Israel was tattooed at that point – and they used to take their shirts off when we rehearsed. The music was like Dead Kennedys, Butthole Surfers, which for '84, '85 in Tel Aviv was pretty cool. I practised with them for a year. We played almost every day, had one gig and split up.

After that, I did two or three gigs with an ex-girlfriend who played bass. We called ourselves Polianna Frank and everybody started to say that we were the 'great new promise of Israeli rock'. My immediate response was: 'It's time to leave. Fuck this, it's too easy.' I left Israel in 1988 and went to live in Europe. I returned briefly the following summer to record an album with Polianna Frank – which, by then, had my brother and a few friends in it. At that point, I was definitely the token dyke. I came out in Israel's biggest paper with the release of the album. My mum's response was: 'Argh!' But making that move took me a few years – I didn't feel able to come out in the media until I'd left the country for a while and sorted myself out. I think everybody's got to be 3,000 miles away from their mum before they can really start a revolution.

On the second album, which came out on CD and had a TV campaign and all that shit, people talked more about my voice than my sexuality. When you get a bit famous in Israel, people think they own you. You become public property, so if you're walking down the street on a Saturday afternoon with your mum or your

133

granny, everybody feels free to come over and tell you exactly what they think. I don't know if I handled it great, but I handled it. People would come over and say: 'I was in the closet – I was in the army, in the desert, camped somewhere and nobody would talk to me, nobody knew. I was listening to your record all the time, it gave me hope.' It is touching, and, in a way, it's hard to hear. Other people would come over and say: 'That's *the* lesbian, isn't it.' OK, fine, you know. England is a much bigger country, it's not like everyone's going to come over to me and stare. They probably whisper it behind my back. But I never thought of an alternative, I've never considered not coming out. No imagination whatsoever; I couldn't imagine what might happen to me, that maybe everybody would've hated me.

In February 1988, when I was 21, I came here [London] for a month. It scared the shit out of me. I'd been speaking English since I was eight or nine, but it made little difference. It was this massive city, it was so big, I didn't know where I was and it was so cold and dark. I thought: 'Shit, what the fuck am I doing here?' So I went to Amsterdam, which was cool at first. I was a roadie over there and I used to play gigs with various bands. I lived in a squat and had no money. A year later, I went back to Israel for a holiday and recorded some songs on a four-track with my brother. Some guy from Israel's one indie label heard it and they released it as a cassette. It did pretty well, so we did another album.

As I had already moved away, it was easier. I did my tour and then escaped back to Amsterdam, where nobody knew me. There is only a limited amount of success you can have in Israel; you get the few thousand people who make up the 'target' audience, and, unless you're willing to totally compromise, you'll never get more than about 4,000 fans. It's terrible, everybody there sells out immediately because there's no other way to make a living. They all have to do the Eurovision and shit like that. I knew I was going to leave from very early on.

I was having a great time in Amsterdam, but I realised I was never going to get enough music done. So I moved on. I returned to London; I knew some people by then, I had somewhere to stay. I

134

started to play drums in a band called the Darlings. Lesley from the Au Pairs was on vocals and Smithy [Debbie Smith] who now plays with Echobelly, was the guitarist, and Elise Gurley was the bass player. We worked together for about a year, we had some good times, but it didn't really work out. Then I was in another band called the Brendas for two years before I decided that I was wasting my time. I was the drummer and after a while I played so loud the singing was being muffled – I was drumming for Nirvana and the vocalist was singing for the Smiths. It could not be done! Eventually I left because they were just being boring and I didn't like their attitude. I was very depressed for about half a year until I found Sister George.

I saw an ad in *Melody Maker* which Lisa and Lyndon had put in. They'd been playing together a long time and decided it was time to start a band. The ad said something like: 'Queer/Dyke band looking for singer and drummer. Riot Grrrl, L7, Bikini Kill, Hole.' I wasn't going to ring up, but my lover hassled me and finally I did it. We met up in Lisa's bedroom and started writing songs. That was spring '93. Only one or two other people responded to the ad. Later, we put in another ad for a drummer. I went to Israel for a week or two and the day I came back, Lyndon told me they'd found a drummer. We all met up the next day for four hours, taught him all the songs, and the next day we had our first gig, in the Monarch in Camden. It was really good, the venue was totally full because it was this girlie Riot Grrrl night that Linus had organised. It was also Skinned Teen's first ever gig.

I remember seeing Huggy Bear shouting out on *The Word*. It seemed like they were having a really good time; they were going round the country making everybody mad and crazy, which was great. I'd been in an all-girl band before – the stuff I did in Israel in '86 was Riot Grrrl. Two girls wearing Doc Martens, standing with a guitar and bass on stage, who couldn't really play, doing three songs and taking the piss out of everything. I thought: 'Yeah! It's happening now!' When I met Sister George, we wanted to do Riot Grrrl but make it Queer.

Queercore probably couldn't have happened without Riot Grrrl. Credit where credit's due. But Hole influenced me and changed my life a lot more than Huggy Bear did. Huggy Bear

ELLYOTT DRAGON

opened the door, but musically Hole touched me a lot more. I saw Hole's first gig in Britain and that totally changed my attitude, it blew my head off. There was this woman, Courtney Love, on stage . . . I was totally smitten. Courtney is a total star; she's interesting, a bad girl subversive. She can out-scream anybody and she's never out of tune, even over all that racket. She's got my vote. If I ever have to make a compromise in the music business, I think I could face having an affair with Courtney Love to get signed to Geffen. I could sacrifice myself. I was in the Brendas when I saw Hole and I was very unhappy. That gig made me think: 'Fuck, I gotta do something.' The energy made me realise I could do it too. Riot Grrrl opened the door for it.

Even after Riot Grrrl, though, you're not going to see lots of girls by the front of the stage – no way. And you get weary of going to soundcheck when there are boys around – always, always boys around. With better equipment and always thinking they're so great. They're the ones who get the deals, who have a crew and who have roadies re-stringing their guitars in the back. You try to not see it, or if you do, you get angry and it makes you better on stage. When I was a drummer, other bands were always surprised that I could play – which was so patronising.

But while you are involved in changing the world, you can't really see the effect you're having. For example, I don't think that the Raincoats knew they were going to make a comeback and so many people were going to come out of their holes and say: 'Yeah, that was one of my favourite bands.' They didn't think Kurt Cobain was going to kick-start their comeback; you just never know who you influence . . . it's going to take years, there are going to be girls who were 13 when Riot Grrrl came out and when they're 20 and forming bands, they're going to say: 'Yeah, that's what sparked me off.' A lot more bands have got girls in them – isn't that what everybody has been fighting for? If you decide from the beginning that you're not going to change the world, you might as well just shut up, have a spliff, stay home and watch telly.

Every movement works on the principle of 'us and them', so with Riot Grrrl there had to be a 'them'. Polly Harvey fitted into the 'them' very well, and everybody fell for it. You need to hate people who talk against you in order to form an identity for a group. The identity of Riot Grrrl was so hard to establish anyway – and of course the middle-class girls took over. In every single music press interview in 1993, the Manic Street Preachers, Sonic Youth, any-body and everybody was asked about Riot Grrrl. It became: 'Sonic Youth love us, Manic Street Preachers love us, and Polly Harvey said we're crap.' That might have happened to Queercore as well, but not many people would let themselves be quoted saying that queers are crap just 'cause they're queer. It's not really 'in', it's not cool at all, is it? In a way, Axl Rose is quite unique in that he came out and said 'Kill homos'. A lot of people probably think it, but they won't say it.

Huggy Bear were great when they played in front of an audi-ence that hated them. That's when they were best, because of all the conflict. When I saw Huggy Bear playing before Hole at that women-only gig at Subterania in April 1993, I was bored. There was no conflict there. We've yet to face this. It's weird, it's easier for guys to take the piss out of Huggy Bear; with Sister George they sort of freeze and just stand there staring, not believing. We don't get shit, we just get frozen faces. It's worse if an audience ignores you. We want some reaction – say something, for fuck's sake. It goes back to Axl Rose.

I would call myself a feminist. Though probably by some people's definitions I wouldn't be. Feminism meant loads of different things to me as I grew up. If we're talking about the liberation of women – yeah, most definitely. But I've kind of moved on to other things. It gets a lot more complicated and a lot more personal. I don't have sexual relationships with men, I don't want to start a family. So a lot of the problems of the 'real world' which feminism tries to fight, I support, but those issues are not part of my life. We can fight our own little fights, that basically are feminist fights, like Riot Grrrl. Fighting for girls to be able to stagedive or simply to be listened to. It's just a different branch of feminism that the suffragettes never dreamt of. If you'd given them some records and explained what rock 'n' roll is, I'm sure they'd have said that of course girls have to be there. I used to hate it in the eighties when the first thing women singers would say in interviews was: 'Look, I'm not a feminist,

ELLYOTT DRAGON

but . . .' I think it's crap. I don't think there are many women in this world today who are not feminists.

I was a militant feminist about ten years ago; when I came out, I rolled straight into anarcho-feminism. It was great, that was my rebellion. I was 20, and I rediscovered and reinvented the world, I hated everything and everybody, 'cause everything was patriarchal. Everything was militant, at the time, like sitting in front of the telly saying: 'This sucks.' Talking about pornography. In a way, I've gone all the way round. People do their own personal little search and come to their conclusions.

I'd been smelling the whole 'lipstick lesbian' thing coming for a while, I just didn't know how hideous it was going to be. It started with Sandra Bernhardt being an out lesbian in *Roseanne*. I knew lesbians were becoming media icons in the States, so it was only a matter of time before it came over here. It'll go away again, and because we know it'll go away, we try and make the best out of it. If I thought it was here to stay – that from now on any attention Sister George gets in the press would be because of lesbian chic – I'd shoot myself! But it's not going to continue, so if it gives us an opportunity . . . Till now, nobody would pay attention to us because we're queer, so if because we're queer we get a bit of attention now, we're gonna put the boot in. Then people will listen to the music and at least judge it as music.

The dyke community is a closed community and there are specific rules as to what you do and don't do; basically, you don't wash your dirty laundry in public. You don't do a 'Camille Paglia', who said 'lesbians are not capable of being chic'. I think every subculture gets to the point where the separatism breaks and people start criticising the group in front of the outside world. You have to learn from it, face it and do something with it. The lesbian community has reached that point now. There are bound to be loads of fireworks before we see what has actually been achieved.

There is this consensus inside the lesbian community: 'Everybody who's a dyke is cool and we support her.' It got to the point where people said to me: 'Oh, Linda Perry from Four Non-Blondes is dyke and black – you *have* to support her.' And I'm:

'Fucking hell! Her music gives me a headache! Heartburn! It's terrible!' Why should I like her 'cause she's a dyke? I don't want people to come and see me just because I'm a dyke. No way! That is what Camille Paglia means when she says dykes become so non-judgmental about art and life. Israeli Jews are like that – any foreign band that comes to Israel, first question is always: 'So what do you think about Israel? What do you think about the Arabs?' They judge you on that. You could be the best band in the world and you say one wrong thing about Israel and that's it. Tunnel vision.

Because of where I'm from, I'm really paranoid about this 'us'. It's the easiest thing to fall into. Like people fall into starting families, getting married and having a mortgage. Then they feel safe. I can only say this because I've been there. Coming into this country as an immigrant and not knowing anybody, the obvious thing was to be part of the lesbian community or at least part of a sub-group. At the time it was a rebellious group, but now it's made its way to the mainstream lesbian and gay scene. Now I can look from some distance after a few years and judge the lesbian community critically. I don't think people can talk about being individuals if they've never attempted to be part of a group. They can never understand what it is to be disillusioned with the group.

I'm not so much of a going-out type. I've become so hateful of the lesbian scene. I hate the clubs. The music drives me up the wall. I find that techno touches me in a place I didn't know existed; I didn't know I could be so violent and nervous. It brings out the serial killer in me. We've only ever done one gay gig, which was in Heaven and it was very odd – great for a few songs then it was too rock 'n' roll for the audience, who like kd lang, Erasure and think: 'Oh, we liked punk in '76 and now it's dead.' The lesbian and gay community is totally, totally uncool about music – they don't know shit about music. Not what I'd call music. I don't want to only play in gay venues. We're out but we're not a gay band – we're not there for the gay community.

I'm not afraid of Sister George being accessible. A song like 'Let's Breed' is a pop song. When we first started working on it, we knew that it almost sounds like a piss-take of the Breeders. It's got a pop riff. Great. But we don't want any more than the odd pop song. It's what Liz [Naylor] always says – that we were born alternative, therefore we can't sell out. We live our lives for real, in the margin. If we work hard to achieve a tension and write great songs, we want people to hear them. Selling out would be too bloody Eurovision! Selling out would be doing a tour with Guns n' Roses. The target changes all the time. You get greedy and once you get to publicity and success, it's not a dream any more – it's reality. It's never quite as good. What is it Virginia Woolf said? 'The nerve of pleasure becomes numb very quickly.' That is so true.

Every time we get asked about middle-class values I go: 'Oops, I'm middle class. Excuse me!' I would never, ever say I'm working class. I've emigrated from my country, therefore my status has totally changed. Here, I am in fact immigrant class – I'm really poor, I don't know anybody and I have no connections. It's hard to say if my parents are middle class, 'cause in Israel the class system is not as clear as it is here. My dad's family has been in Israel for many generations, which in an immigrant country gives you status. My mum's family has been there since '39 – they escaped the Nazis at the last moment. Most of my mum's family stayed behind in Prague and they were all killed except for one cousin.

My parents have a house in the suburbs, they're both doing well. We never had loads and loads of money, but I grew up in a really rich town – in the suburbs of Tel Aviv. They had the money to make sure I learnt English, which gave me the opportunity to be here now. It's bullshit to try and escape that. But because I'm a dyke and I'm Jewish, because I'm a woman and a musician and I don't want to get married and do the whole mortgage stunt, I don't have the same status here that I would have had over there. In a way, I chose to move myself to immigrant status. Not working class. I'm not bothered about proving to people how hard my life has been, because it hasn't. The rest of the band are working class and they're genuinely angry about loads of shit – when they talk about class and stuff, I shut up for a change. What I see of the English class system, I hate. It's getting bad here, but it's also an interesting place to be in. Not like Amsterdam, which was like Legoland, all perfect and clean and lovely. Nah. It was too much for an Israeli: after twenty-one years of war and hot weather, it was too lovely.

I write the best songs after reading a really strong book. It's like your head is getting blown up from inside – a total tornado of feelings. If something really moves me to feel, then I'll stay up all night. The best songs only appear once every five years. I read biographies, history, fiction, fantasy crime, not real crime but stuff like VI Warshawski by Sara Paretsky. I also read Christa Wolf and Sherri S. Tepper. There's a song on *Drag King* called 'Janey's Bloc' about Jane Bowles which I wrote after reading her biography. With a good biography, the subject takes over you and you live their life for a week, two weeks – as long as it takes to read the book. I was totally thinking about her all the time. I was angry and fascinated about the way her life turned out and so I wrote the song. There are long periods in my life when I can't write at all and feel that I never will. Then it's really tempting for me not to get up at all.

I find it hard to write regularly – I'm a real lazy bastard! I could sit at home and moan all the time and not do anything, but the band pushes each other to write. I don't really go in for political lyrics; I could never have written [Tom Robinson's] 'Glad To Be Gay'. For me it's got to be the Bertolt Brecht kind of approach to politics – you find the little details, the way the political affects the personal, and you write about that. That gives people a way to identify with what you're writing without the lyrics being right-on. I could go on writing 'Please stop fighting', but it's useless, totally useless. I use humour and irony and cynicism. Or I try, anyway. I think that's the real genius – if you know how to do that. It's very rare that a band can sing 'I am an Antichrist' and make it work.

Israeli feminists push for the right of girls to fight in the army. It's rubbish, y'know? Being a member of the army is not a privilege, it's a punishment. No one should have to do it. It's changed now for women – if you say you're a pacifist and don't want to be in the Israeli army, they'll let you off. But still the stigma in Israeli society is massive; if you didn't go to the army, it's harder to get jobs or

ELLYOTT DRAGON

grants later on. Israel is a little ghetto country and they all think that they're fighting for their lives. It's full of scared Jews thinking: 'Never again the Holocaust, we're going to defend ourselves.' It's a country where being an outsider is so depressing, so hard. At 18 you've got to totally decide if you're giving up your future in the country altogether by not joining and emigrating – it's a big decision to make when you're so young. Some people decide it without really realising what they're doing. If you leave without doing your military service, you have to do a runner and you can't come back.

The only way to get out of the army used to be to prove that you were mad. And then who's going to give you a job? You spend the rest of your life hiding. When I was 18 dropping out was a massive no-no, so most people my age did it [army service]. But now, ten years later, it's possible to avoid it. Because Israel went through the Intifada and the Lebanon war – which was a sort of Vietnam – protest against the army was, all of a sudden, a bit more acceptable. So people who are now 18 have a bit more of a choice whether to go or not. I know my parents would have slung me out of the house if I didn't go. It was made totally clear that that is the last thing I could do. I could almost bring a Palestinian girlfriend home – so long as I go to the army. It's like – it's all right to be a dyke, so long as you don't smoke.

Here I am, talking as an ex-corporal in the Israeli army – it's true! How more un-PC can I get, right? I was part of an oppressive machine. My male friends finished high school at 18 and that very summer most of them went into the army to fight, 'cause the Lebanon war was going on. Many of them spent two or three years in Lebanon, watching behind their backs for snipers all the time. A lot of them have never truly recovered. Some people died, others were wounded or maimed for life. To see people killed, and to know that you killed too. To do that for three years. A lot of guys would blow their heads off because they didn't want to go back to Lebanon . . . but it's changing a lot now. Some kids don't go in the army but play in bands instead. There are only a very few people who are doing it, but it's a start. There are youth bands now in Israel, which you never had before. Most people start bands when they're 17, and when they're 18 would go into the army and you'd never hear of them again.

I was out from the start. Most people didn't dare give me a hard time. Most of the talking was done behind my back. I came out to my family during my army service, left home and got this terrible tiny room in Tel Aviv. I met my first girlfriend my first day in the army. In basic training. I was wearing a Lou Reed T-shirt, she was wearing a Bauhaus T-shirt. Love at first sight! 'Yes!' I thought. 'Mmm'. Her hair was red and orange and no one looks like that in Israel. Because they were never ready for punks, there were no written rules about that. If your hair was more than a certain length, it had to be ponytailed. With guys they were – still are – really strict about long hair. But the rules for girls are more about what colour of nail varnish you can wear. I think there's a rule that says your hair can't be more than one colour – I think they put that in later – but at the time, in '84, they didn't. I had patterns shaved in my head and it was dyed red. I always used to get stopped by the military police but I always argued and they couldn't actually prove I was doing anything against the rules.

Anyway, the girl in the Bauhaus T-shirt came to visit me with a bottle of vodka on my first night in my first flat, and ended up staying for a year. We weren't discreet at all, but we didn't serve in the same base. She was made to go into therapy by the navy – she was a gatekeeper at the Navy Headquarters. We kept each other alive through those two years. But I was really lucky in the army. There were too many girls and most were made into secretaries. I went for loads of interviews to get into the army radio station. They'd take twelve people every year and I was one of them. After six months, my brilliant career as a radio reporter . . . well, I was a real disaster. I was not running after the scoops or being a bitch, so they kicked me out. Big disgrace. I was called a 'demoraliser' and 'unmotivated' – two of the nicest things anyone has ever said to me. So I wrote propaganda for the army and drove a van. I found myself in all kinds of weird places – in a van in the middle of an army manoeuvre with things exploding everywhere. A lot of smoke and tear gas. Shit. I can laugh about it now, but at the time it was terrible. Stupid people telling you what to do.

We grew up knowing that we had to go through that experience at 18. Most people, till this very day, don't think it's anything but their duty, they're not even bitter about the time that's been taken

143

ELLYOTT DRAGON

away from them. Most of the people I knew back then are still in Israel. A lot of them talked about leaving but none of them made it. Only one or two out of all my friends. One of them, Dana Fainaro, lives here and is a brilliant theatre director; and the other, my first girlfriend, the one with the Bauhaus T-shirt, is a tattooist in Seattle. She got me into Nirvana – she used to send me all these compilations of Seattle bands. 'Nirvana are the biggest band in Seattle! They're really cool! You've got to hear them!' When she came to visit me, she left Seattle on the day that *Nevermind* was released. She bought it in the morning at the airport, brought it over, put it on and I was like: 'Yes! What is this? Fucking great!' Everybody in my house was going: 'Turn this shit off! What is this shit?' And half a year later it was the biggest thing and everyone had a copy.

144

Huggy Bear (left to right): Jo, Niki, Chris, John, Karen

huggy bear

Your burnt-out fucked-up attitude
Post-tension realisation that this is happening
Without your permission
The arrival of a new renegade girl-boy hyper
      nation . . .
Boy-girl revolution tease.

('Her Jazz' 7")

February 14 1993. Huggy Bear are invited to perform their thrash punk anthem 'Her Jazz' live on *The Word*. After they've played, the band stay in the studio and watch a filmed report on two American models who call themselves The Barbi Twins. Huggy Bear are incensed. They heckle presenter Terry Christian and can be heard by viewers at home. Christian, squirming at the build-up of tension, responds: 'I've just been called a woman-hater, which I'm sure will come as a surprise to my mother, my sister and my girlfriend. If these garbagey bands don't want to come on the show, that's fine by me.' The band are thrown out of the studio and a spokesperson for *The Word* claims that a member of Huggy Bear's entourage 'bit the face of a member of our production team'. The band, passionate to the last, insist their protests were only vocal and an instinctive response to the programme's 'trite, casual sexism'. The following week a still of Niki's face appeared on the cover of *Melody Maker* with the slogan: 'This is happening without your permission.'

That particular Valentine's night viewing turned Huggy Bear into Britain's most (in)famous Riot Grrrls. The paradox is that the four piece London-based mixed gender neo-punk band so rarely speaks out to the British public. They shun the media, going as far as trying to ban journalists from attending their gigs and turning down most interviews. This is not for a lack of things to say; it is borne of a lack of trust. Interviews mean misrepresentation and losing control and they are all about maintaining and regaining control, via dedicated, bookish 'zines (or 'bullet-teens'), gigs, (vinyl) records, 'girl positive' info nets, word of mouth.

Huggy Bear are DIY revolutionaries, full-on feminists, art terrorists. They put up posters at gigs inviting women to stand at the front. Slogans help put the message across; they write 'prophet' and 'slut' on their arms. Although into their 20s, they can seem like snotty, prissy kids throwing tantrums at the press, behaving like a conspiracy theory is out to get them and them alone. Niki (bass guitar/vocals), Jo (bass/vocals), Chris (vocals) and Karen (drummer) have often remained silent rather than defend or explain themselves. In some ways they haven't done themselves any favours, incurring the wrath of the music press with their snooty pouts. Huggy Bear would deny being awkward; they'd say they wanted to stay silent and underground so they wouldn't have the power sucked out of them.

Riot Grrrl has excited some, left others cold. Much of the criticism has fallen upon the 'clumsy' music they make, the apparent irrelevance to musicianship. Courtney Love has been quoted as saying she'd 'like to have a Riot Grrrl in the band, but I can't find one that can play'. Quizzed on Riot Grrrl in *NME*, Lydia Lunch said: 'It reminds me of '77 revisited . . . (but) the music is irrelevant – as a matter of fact, it's pretty sucky so why are they even using music? Get rid of the fucking raunchy bad rock 'n' roll! That's where girls should wake up instead of trying to cop second, third generation rock 'n' roll licks that were terrible in the first place.' Sonic Youth's Kim Gordon, widely regarded as a main Riot Grrrl influence, is more impressed: 'They're showing girls they can make their own culture and their own identity during those tender teenage years'. And original Riot Grrrl rocker Joan Jett has worked with both L7 and Bikini Kill.

Winter 1993. Huggy Bear want to talk about being in this book. They are encouraged by the words 'collaboration' and 'monologue'. Over the phone they say they can't actually pick one voice out of four to do interviews for a monologue. They want all of the band to be given the opportunity to contribute written or spoken words. They would like to meet up for a chat. One late Saturday afternoon in a Camden pub, Niki, Jo and Jon (former guitarist, now gone his own way) turn up with no money for drinks and talk feminism, music, Riot Grrrl, clubs, being poor, feminism and music for an hour. Jon smiles a lot and says perhaps three words; Jo is friendly but wary; Niki is amiable but spikey. The set-up feels like a three-on-one interrogation.

A few days later there's a message. Huggy Bear would like to be part of the book. They will interview themselves and write bits. Theirs will be the only chapter with a male voice, but what the hell, Chris is a feminist. A few months later they send a package – pages and pages of typed words which defy conventional use of grammar and syntax. When asked to answer specific questions, they are hurt and disappointed; for a minute the book is as much a part of the conspiracy theory as newspapers and magazines. They are reluctant to acknowledge or accept the importance of clarity and context. Niki says: 'We enjoy playing with words and language; it's not about being pretentious.' After considerable cajoling, they agree to answer the questions.

Huggy Bear's chapter is a challenging and jerky discourse. It is, exactly as you'd expect, part clumsy, part lucid and often wilfully obscure. There is, perhaps, a charm in their clumsiness; it confirms that they are human. Their personal revolution has reached out to those who have now formed bands because of Riot Grrrl, and their existence has sparked off debate, even if much has centred upon not-so-oblique condemnation. Riot Grrrl may have been a term as convenient a tag as Generation X, but at least they labelled themselves. In a climate of political disaffection, Riot Grrrl was – and the groups remain – vital. Huggy Bear's appearance on *The Word* was exciting and as empowering as L7's Donita dropping her pants and revealing all on the same slot some months earlier. Riot On.

19 July 1994. What follows is an explanation. Up to a point. What follows is just us kids talking. A conversation. It answers the

questions asked. What follows moves on, moves left and right, vertical and horizontal. What follows has no pretence to a *whole* truth. It is a surface. A surface so fucking obvious it is often overlooked.

The 3 Rs of rock 'n' roll: Repetition. Repetition. Repetition.

We do not want to remain in the past.

These questions have been asked.

Firstly the claiming of space is always expressive of powerful impulses and we see Riot Grrrl as connecting theory with action, connecting feminism with nothing less than the urge to live, which is something towards which we are impelled. The music, the literature, the hanging out – all reveal this relentless urge, the speed and seriousness of this impulsion. A call to any girl open to it. It would go too far, it could slip into the mainstream, but mostly, we feel, we're not concerned with that as we would, at this time, feel *real* punk rock feminism's reverberations, whilst the simultaneous thing of it becoming powerful in the underground. We know a lot of important stuff is happening in private, that there is a kind of gestation period going on and that a lot of stuff will come through in the future. Intimidation as inspiration.

150

Lineage of female musicians:
STP. BABES IN TOYLAND. KIM GORDON. DEBBIE GOOGE.
SYLVIA POTTINGER (STUDIO ONE).

Chris: Why Riot Grrrl started. This question pertains mostly or largely to the USA and how, in the UK, punk rock as naïve, terrible children is still stimulating to a large body of young people. Punk as fractured systems of communication was discouraged, or was always, as far as I was concerned, aesthetically poorly judged in the UK. There were no ideas 'cause no ideas were encouraged. We began to look to the US as if it were a one-sided mirror . . . as spectators. Girls wanted in, so they began to work towards inclusion. Unconnected, this seems to point to a general interpretative need for there to be large components rooted in punk, and an avalanche of bands/zines/shows and so forth ensued.

Jo: Our situation was different to the one the American Riot Grrrls were responding to. The underground in London had deteriorated totally, there wasn't really much of an alternative . . . 'indie' just became an abstract term for a style of music, not ideas or values, 'cause they were all signing to major labels. The notion of selling out wasn't important. Punk rock wasn't important. Fanzines were seen as a sad joke, so we had to explain stuff that might have been obvious to American kids but was alien to young British kids. The reasons for being independent were snorted at.

Chris: We as Huggy Bear had our feelings on a similar pulse. Felt the need and began to mobilise ourselves accordingly. At that time I was writing ideas, ideas which were to become songs or 'zines, trying to find out why these kinds of unholy music art terrorism were still remaining hugely important and stimulating to me. It truly felt – naïvely maybe – like a new time was about to happen and I strongly, obsessively wanted to be a part of that.

Niki: Riot Grrrl's roots are in American punk circles. It goes beyond that now. The important thing is that, like any feminist school of thought, it is open to *any* woman for interpretation and expansion.

Jo: Riot Grrrl was about inventing new titles. You think up some name for a fantasy revolutionary group of girls, spread the idea of it about and hope, for someone, it'll come true. With Riot Grrrl it did . . . I don't know why it should have caught on like it did, except that it was so much more of an exciting and alive idea of feminism than we were all coming across in books. It was imaginative and active, and it not only worked in theory, it also related to everyday life. Well, everyday life for punk rock girls anyway.

Chris: When Riot Grrrl needed a name, then that's how it should be. Of course the naming is important but it should never remain the same. But it attempts, via the explosivity of its name, to link up riot = upturn, girl = gender. It was the coolest thing and now the name's a stigma. But however it names itself next, and whichever activities it encompasses, it is still about upheaval, replenishment, action.

HUGGY BEAR

Niki: All women who create stuff should do it *their way* absolutely . . . the way they think/feel is right for them. Everyone is going to come at all this stuff from different angles and with wildly conflicting agendas.

Chris: Riot Grrrl to me in Huggy Bear meant mostly that I could be where I most like being in this time sense, amidst the people with the most radical ideas and attitudes – in this case, girls with a refreshing outlook. Action. I don't like and never did get major kicks from hanging out with boys anyway; always felt too compromised, wound up, let down, disappointed. I love that which needs to move, examine, attack, celebrate and continue to move and keep moving.

Jo: We're people with things to say, and we do write these things in pamphlets, but we've never written a manifesto in the sense that most people use that word.

Karen: People are convinced we must have one. It's been created for us.

Jo: We couldn't write a manifesto like the situationists or Nation of Ulysses could, because they could dump it the next day, move on to something new, and people would let them. We never had a formal manifesto, but the fact that people assumed we did, and referred to it, implies that there was a desire for our ideas to be simply identifiable. As recognisable and comfortable as a brand logo. We're allergic to being fixed, so we never complied with that desire.

Niki: MANIFESTO can be used more positively to create excitement and certainly discussion. An ideal medium, cheap to produce and run off in vast editions distributed by post or on the streets, so the REVERBERATIONS can be felt. Could potentially change everything. Though the implication is that they are fixed steadfast and not open to change, they are fun and energising too, and can give the impression (often the first necessary step to the real movement) that it actually exists. We can't really go into all this, can we?

Simplification/clarification are a pressure symptomatic of our culture's need to understand everything in a most basic way.

Niki: The most dramatic, exciting works for me so far, in feminist terms, are the writings of Hélène Cixous, Monique Wittig and Christine Brook, and they're all influenced by decades of European theory. It is important for me also to note and take courage from the fact that their work remains resolutely uncommercial.

Jo: Like Avital Ronnel, whose books are indefinable. How do you categorise *The Telephone Book*? She's been a total inspiration to us and a woman who will delve into uncomfortable areas of feminism, like technology and addiction, whose work is strongly argumentative but also poetic and experimental.

Karen: Feminism has to be about getting results, putting theory into practice as much as it is put into books.

Joan of Arc. Angela Davis. Elizabeth Tudor. Sarah Bernhardt. Martha Reeves.

Niki: Some open-course feminism should be taught in schools. It should be the law, so that women's lives don't just slip by. *Angry Women* [an American compilation of interviews with female artistes] was one of the first books that absolutely floored me.

Jo: Yeah.

Niki: So many voices and crossed boundaries . . . they talked about things a lot of feminists hadn't allowed themselves to explore. It reanimated feminism for me . . . as it should always reanimate your life.

Jo: When we were in Ireland I was recommending *Angry Women* to this girl after a show and this boy just interrupted and told us both it was rubbish and oversimplified . . . but if it's so simple, why do we keep coming back to it again and again for inspiration, validation, confusion? And if it's rubbish, why did it lead us both to loads of other feminist writings? It's been the springboard for our self-education in feminism.

SOME WRITERS WHO INSPIRED US.
Jeanette Winterson. Maya Angelou. Virginia Woolf. Julia Kristeva. Kathy Acker.

Niki: Hélène Cixous, Avital Ronnel, bell hooks and Julia Kristeva are my most important mentors. They restored my lust. They do not restrict their writing to just the economic and political realms, their scope is massive and they explore the contradictory and the unexpected. They have all undertaken the task of reanimating feminist theory so that it is exciting and powerful again and you can unite with them at various points of resistance. It is their works which have had the most dramatic impact on me. (Also, The Last Poets at the Cubiculo Theatre, New York, October 1969 has been a lasting influence. Patti Smith's records and writings are my most prized possessions.)

Niki: The hang after the show is as important as the show itself. We can always be found before and after we play, and we are sought. This opens the parameters of our show. I haven't said anything yet that I was proud of on stage. That side of me hasn't emerged yet; it might never. I felt terrible about this for a while. We were being made to feel that everything our band had to say relied solely on what we said on stage.

Jo: Our ideas weren't authentic if we didn't give speeches at shows to prove we meant them. But we're not fucking razzle-dazzle enough for that. Chris is excellent at talking on stage, but it freaks me out.

Niki: We challenged their stale-mouthed opinions on expression and articulacy. We are not showbiz. It doesn't turn me on to get hyped. We do this out of pride, out of necessity.

Karen: The best conversation I had after a show was about astronomy, which has inspired me to learn about the stars . . . Y'see we are capable of talking without it being overtly sexual or political.

Jo: I dunno who our audience are. Aliens. You start up conversations with people at shows and you realise how isolated everybody is: not just here and now and from each other, but from the past as well. We all have to learn everything for the first time because we haven't got a sense of history – as girl/women or as punk rockers. And if we're gonna make new and confusing music or say anything that sounds fresh and exciting, we've got to know what people have learnt and said before. Take it further.

Karen: When we were at school, punk and ska were being played at youth clubs and school discos. We have that sense of history because of our age, but younger kids are pretty ill-informed about British youth culture when it was at its best – raw and pioneering.

Jo: That was one inspiring thing we found in America, this feeling that a town would have, first of all a punk rock community, then fanzines that mythologised and criticised the scene and also this thing of elders – the older kids who take responsibility for shaking the scene up, running record labels to put out the music from their scene, passing down the information to the younger kids.

Karen: This is true activity, true revolution, because it recognises revolution as a continual process which needs history to stop you taking two steps forward, one step back.

Jo: In England kids who are 14, 15 and who are just starting to go to shows, have never heard of, say, the Shop Assistants, 'cause the mainstream press have written them out of history and at the moment there are no alternative circuits of information . . .

HUGGY BEAR

Chris: I don't think we're ever enough as a band – not that we don't do enough, but there's always room for more. We don't seem to be easily interpretable, and that's good in a way. That misunderstanding provokes talk, debate – ideally that's how an audience should be. Receptive, into kicks, dancing, talking, writing to us, able to see that although a lot of our subject matter or presentation is essentially dark, it reverses itself in that performance catharsis way. We are excited when an audience seems amped on seeing us, tearing up the same space. I don't think we have those false thresholds explicit in rock.

Niki: Our shows would make explicit our need and identification to point out the high female input potential at our shows. Also importantly, we absolutely wanted women to be right at the front. In the foyer with their literature. They were not peripheral to the event. We encourage this, and this should not be forgotten.

Karen: We wanted transformation. A new sense of what being at a show could be . . . making the ordinary seem strange.

Chris: To encourage the intensity in the goofy. And the goofy in the intense.

Niki: We also wanted to incite dancing, cool, cool dancing, the showing off of the latest aquatic dance moves, such as the slow fin in the crab, the lobster, the shrimp (though we realise that some would not be able to lose themselves in such a display of love and so the older pogo and the rooster were acceptable). *ANYTHING* that didn't involve hurting anyone else or touching them.

OK now, the following is equally relevant to the bigger rock spectacles and the whole scary thing of being in a crowd and the crowd mentality. There is a very real threat that you will be crushed while the opportune scumbag will squeeze you, press his dick up against you. Girls have been fingered, had their breasts elbowed, and the way you get made to feel you are drawing attention to the fact you are close to his body . . . I mean, like it has some sexual significance.

Leaflets on the subject have been handed out to encourage – OK, aggressively point out – that we as a group will not ignore (and thus condone) that Neanderthal behaviour.

Niki: We had to affect the crowd physically, totally upturn the accepted pit reality where only the strong survive. And it is *not* an exaggeration, as has been suggested. Also, the illusion that women's bodies are actually hipless, breastless and therefore not accessible or feminine, is easily played out in the pit. So you can sometimes feel like you should try to conceal yourself. You get the feeling that somehow you are drawing attention to yourself . . . and this ties up with there being a pressure, in music-making, to be one of the boys. We've implored more women to come to shows and participate and not stand on the sidelines *unhappy* about the reasons why they're standing where they are. I don't expect to have girls come to our shows and stand there like I owe them something.

Jo: Keeping the light up for more visibility helps, as does just making it known we care.

Niki: We are all responsible for making the shows safe and more conducive to kicks and excitement. And that means all the shows you play, however and whenever possible, making the promoters do something about the problem.

Jo: It doesn't only happen at Riot Grrrl shows. The Beastie Boys, for example, have taken up the challenge to eradicate this from their shows.

Karen: Someone once said we deflect tension in the manner of Tai Chi. That's cool . . .

Niki: The calling of the girls to participate more visibly was hysterically interpreted as complete exclusion of boys from our shows. As total sexual apartheid. This only furthers the point made that any improvement of women's position is seen as a threat to a lot of men and some women.

HUGGY BEAR

Chris: Like it will somehow erase their important presence.

Niki: The whole incapable misguided identity that was struck up around us served its purpose of making Huggy Bear sexually/politically undesirable, therefore curtailing its explosivity. It had us written off as fools, as hysterics totally intoxicated with the idea that we might be impostors, imitators, and of course, weak; totally out of our depth and petty tricksters. I think that when we first looked on at the festering attitudes towards our band and the ensuing advancement of women in music, we were trying to figure out exactly the critique that, when unravelled, *actually* is neither concerned with or energised by feminism or punk rock – the very two things we were reanimating in our works.

Total DEATH or RESURRECTION. We made our choice.

Is Riot Grrrl dead? Oh yes. Last year, the funeral preceded the birth. What remains of the Situationists International, the Futurists of Riot Grrrl – is it still relevant? Well, just to start, it's destructivity. It's sense of rediscovery. Don't we always focus on why such a movement failed, what was basically wrong with it?

Jo: To the point where all that was powerful, wild, effective about it is dismissed.

Niki: We always have to note its ending, its decline. Count the heads of those who were (felt) left out by it. So how do you measure its importance?

The possibilities are always evident – you just got to be smart, wise, discerning, to catch what seems far away and draw it close. The ability to win comes from within, and to lose sight of yourself – death.

Niki: So in answer to the question – true punk rock feminism will never die.

GRRRLS

Chris: I think we have set out to alienate. I'm not sure. It's a frustrating surprise.

Niki: Do we even need to purposefully alienate people? They're put off so easily – the idea of cool feminist punk might not be sexy enough.

Karen: I want to alienate people who act like they know me and I don't know them . . . They try and act like we're friends and they know my name and they ask me questions and I don't want to answer. I want to make them feel as uncomfortable as they make me feel. I don't mind talking to people, just don't come on like we go back.

Jo: I think a lot of the spite for our band within the supposed 'alternative' UK scene centres around the fact that we didn't want to go to their parties. We were reluctant to shake their hands, or accept drinks from these people when we were introduced to them. We never went to the right pubs. We never go to pubs much anyway, just to get out of the rain or use the loo. It seemed like we thought we were too good for it. And I think we are – there isn't enough time for us to indulge in pleasantries. And this attitude will never change. We never gave in . . . it wasn't just part of our act. We can be snooty. But that's just for those idiots.

Niki: Also, we insulted their heritage, their belief systems and tired philosophies. Weren't impressed by their glittering line-ups, stars and offers of fortune. We had our own future plan. What strength these feeble arms hold. We were peerless. We didn't pull back from what we found difficult, or that shocked or upset us. We didn't fear the disapproval of friends, associates or idols. *HARD*. They had to notice that we possessed things that would shine. No matter how they tried to dull the shine.

Chris: They were pissed at the fact we thought beyond them and they always have to believe like they think ahead of you. Thinking that they were smarter than the average bear.

159

Karen: We can't justify having a boy in the band and then playing to a female-only audience. You've caught us out.

Jo: I can't. It's unforgivable. It was a crime to think of starting a band together.

Niki: So feminism can only be strong when it's in a women-only environment?

Jo: And we'll all be really strong. Fuck. We don't have to justify talking about feminism, doing women-only shows – we do these things because they are important to us. Chris is no contradiction, he's fucking proof boys don't need to be bored or angered by feminism or need to spend all their time with men in order to feel their masculinity isn't under threat. Plus Chris has read more feminism than me; his interest is genuine. I trust him.

Niki: We did women-only shows to challenge the acceptance of violence against women on all levels. The woman as the centre of things. Separatist shows do not *revolve* around stopping boys coming to shows – they are a way of bringing women/girls together and actually feeling different for our pleasure.

Karen: Another measure of the distrust of women connecting up without relying on men is clear in how this has been documented.

Niki: No one has the power to marginalise us, as in control our parameters. We will reach the people we want any way that we want and, in the words of Patti Smith, 'Rock 'n' roll is not a colonial power to be exploited, told what to say and how to say it.'

Little rock star, sick and suicidal due to being driven away from the very thing that was important to them getting packed off. Wholesale. Distanced. Of course they are all greedy little fuck-heads who deserve to get sick and hurt. 'Cause we all only want to be famous and famous and utterly adored, don't we? And when you've been up close to this shit – and we've *all* read about it – we should be learning from it. It's kind of sickening and you know that you are right to want more. And to connect up with other people who want more and who are also restless and thirsty.

Chris: Who wants to create something compelling in the sense of time and space . . . to upset everything. The idea of independence is laughed at, as the idea of an underground that would be essential in our existence that would evolve rather than appear. 'Cause modern culture insists on immediacy to make your point. But things burn out overnight due to money/success/failure/excess.

Jo: An underground allows you the space and time to develop and should not be viewed as stunting your programme.

We just don't have mainstream brains in our heads.
And in the end it's you who has to live with yourself.

Niki: So this belief in independence becomes classified as elitism, you know: 'Hey kids! This excludes you!' So you've been tricked into a false appraisal of something that had good intentions but that made no attempt to sell itself to you. This line of enquiry then sets you off on the trail of exposing the real elite which surrounds you every day . . . Fuck.

Don't spend time confusing issues. It's scary to actually consider how much popular publications will totally just set you off on the wrong trails of enquiry. This is unfortunately a continuum we are all faced with.

We recognised early on that the journalist/pop star dialogue is a complex system of mythologies and identifications to do with fake hierarchies which connect preferences of desirability via the kinds of photos which are used to represent you or how much space is given to each member of a band in an interview. A leader or a scapegoat; one person is chosen. The totally evil pitting of girls in the band against each other is a science in itself. For the most part, your band's identity is out of your control (and this invention is

HUGGY BEAR

infectious – even people who should know better are seduced by it). Then the next step is that fake identity is called into question, brought to trial and overruled. They kill the monster they created themselves . . . Flippin' heck.

It seems people have to disempower you by whatever means necessary – intimidation, teasing, flattery – which is ironic, and obviously so. Then you don't feel like talking to anyone, which then becomes: 'My, isn't she snotty/elitist/self-important . . . we'll have to bring her down a peg or two.' When we're at our lowest, we forget when we ever felt good. For, like, a year, we realised we were up against a lot of ignorant, fucked-up opinions and we had to think and rethink our relationship to things, including ourselves. We turned to books and music and friendship worth everything and we beat all that shit out of us. We don't rest easy with poor relationships and dealings, whatever their stature. We're prepared to make enemies. You have to be.

Jo: Chris's position in our band confuses people, for example. So they'll ignore him, try to undermine him, or even attribute things he says to other people in the band . . . because it's easier to get a grip on an all-girl feminist band. Writers can make your voice or way of talking look dumb or cringy, maybe reveal to the reader that you stumbled.

Niki: Or hesitated over the use of a word. They construct characters, mythologise behaviour and speech. It's out of your hands.

Which is why working in this way, for this book, interviewing each other, transcribing it *ourselves*, adding monologues to the piece, working co-operatively with the editor of this book has been liberating. It's encouraged us, as the women in the band, anyway, to express ourselves, 'cause *we have final control. Maybe this is the way ahead for women's interviews* . . . maybe women will talk more, and about more difficult stuff, if they are *allowed to contribute to the editing* of *their words.*

G R R R L S

The notion that you were being melodramatic and so much the drag. This undermines the forcefulness of your original feelings.

> The Hate that cheats you as it shakes your hand.
> The Hate that leaves you poorer.
> The Hate with a pretence to liberalism and
>   radicalism that is patronising and actually
>   scared of people of colour with a voice,
>   queer kid punk rockers with big fucking
>   mouths.
> And now it's the Hate that thinks you won't
>   refuse.
> This is the Hate that you have to love.
> This is the Hate that's 'alright'.
> The Hate that finds the notion of an
>   underground infantile but still tries to bury
>   it anyway.
> This is the Hate that Hates girls again.

We will not pull back from what we find because it shocks or upsets us, because we fear the disapproval of friends, peers and idols. With their pinched and cruel mouths and rigid and corpse-like language, people apply terms/ideas/identities liberally, without care. People you didn't expect to fuck you over. You are meant to stay silent in exile . . .

Karen: But there's also the insult, the assumption that the whole group comes from middle-class backgrounds . . .

Jo: Because we're not thick. When I went to university I got told I wasn't working-class any more . . . some know-it-all boy had read a sociology book and wanted us all to know how the working-class is

HUGGY BEAR

defined by its ignorance. We know going to university makes us strangers to the people on our estates, but our backgrounds also made us strangers at university. We don't aspire to be fucking middle-class, that's disgusting, but we want and need to educate ourselves. And we're not gonna ignore our backgrounds to do it . . .

Niki: People are class conscious, whether they admit it or not.

Niki: Famous Monsters of Filmland* exists to connect a lot of random elements. It will grow.

Karen: There are independent record labels that shift low-cost singles and make profit via a network they have had to build over a few years. Rugger Bugger Discs for instance is run by Sean and Ben in their spare time and they outsell the more fashionable independent labels without having to have ads, office space and all the schmoozing. The point I'm making is that it takes time to build this kind of alternative network, if you stick with it. Also, that it isn't only for those people who have money to burn and see running a punk label as an expensive hobby. Business-wise, it can be far more effective than hobby wannabe-a-major channels. Sean's done a basic guide on how to put out a seven-inch which we can copy and send on to whoever wants it. We know that we don't need the usual entourage that hangs around a band feeding on 20 per cent here and 30 per cent there. We wanted to learn the necessary ins and outs in order to retain control over our band, our songs, our money, so that in the end we answer only to ourselves.

Niki: The idea that we would remain resolutely uncommercial has made us look ridiculous, kind of anachronistic. We appear so quaint or young and stupid because we have new values. New as in we are coming to them for the first time – an old idea reanimated.

---

*Mail-order service for records, 'zines and stuff; a record label. Run by Huggy Bear, PO Box 357, London SE19 1AD.

Chris: I don't have icons. Icons are to be worshipped, venerated utterly. I have heroes, but they change; you have to keep changing them, getting new ideas from them.

Here are just a few. Our mothers. Two Tone. Bessie Smith. Patti Smith. Germs. Last Poets.

Jo: The most effective of the many ways Riot Grrrl was undermined was to continually ask us – and other girls who were involved, or were seen to be knowledgeable on the subject because they were female musicians – where is this network? Where are the bands? Are you a riot grrrl? So even before girls had the chance to get into the idea and make efforts to approach other girls in some way – ways they weren't sure of – the whole thing became about production, proof. And if the proof wasn't there it was as if it didn't really exist. But there were thousands of girls inspired by the notion of punk rock feminism; a lot of them were young and were just learning how to express themselves, just coming to feminism. How were they going to initiate an entire network of zines and bands overnight?

Niki: Certain structures have to change. That takes a lot of commitment. So we start where we think we can actually arrive somewhere. Putting out records, connecting kids from different towns or countries, and these things take time to grow.

AND WE ONLY PUT OUT BOOKLETS, WRITINGS, RECORDS WHEN WE'VE GOT SOMETHING WE THINK IS WORTH SHARING.

Chris: Being in this band has been like giving away all your best secrets.

Niki: Strategies for survival, self-assurance, prayers, truth poems – we value oral expression – especially musical notes.

HUGGY BEAR

Jo: Music has changed my life. Architecture changes your life, graffiti changes your life. Of course music can change your life and if you combine a combustible music with lyrics that express total commitment to change, movement, love, loyalty. If you combine all that with actual radical financial management, actual autonomy, actual distribution of information, actual networking . . . how can you doubt the possibility that these things can change your life?

Niki: You have to let it change you – allow yourself to be inspired, challenged, moved. Also, in regard to Riot Grrrl, make contact with the people involved, support its efforts to radicalise the way a show is put on.

Chris: Yes, it's absolute. When feeling most lost or uninspired, deadened, threatened by fear of losing contact with what life could be, I'd write a story, a song, an idea and become somebody else. Writing was and is my freedom, my unleashing of selves. New ideas, challenging yourself, just avoiding becoming old in the way of becoming ensnared in the drag, the doom time – music is like that, to make it, hear it, love alongside it. As essential as vitamins and air.

166

Niki: Music without doubt is everything to why I'm here thinking, writing. It is totally powerful. There's a fear of *extending* the traditional way of making music . . . suddenly it becomes 'arty'. That word invalidates it straight away.

Karen: As soon as the media lay down rules of what the tradition is, however subliminally, it gives people a sound to emulate . . . rather than their punk rock coming from walking the walk.

Jo: Like that idea that three-chord punk is the only true punk.

Chris: We're an R&D band. Rhythm & Detonation.

Niki: What's important to Huggy Bear sound? Mutation of classical form, something that extends what we already know. Deviancy. We stretch ourselves with the expression of an idea and the playing of an idea. Rhythm.

Jo: I think it's really cool how much we're inside each other's way of playing our instruments because of the encouragement or criticism we've given each other. *We don't have any recognisable language to talk about music.* We've begun to develop a language of our own which is full of codes and colours, a language that we occasionally get confused.

Karen: Part of our style has come from feeling like we're on our own. Being hated and almost 'othered' has helped to liberate us from the mainstream. It's like: 'What can we do with the margins?' Any false sense of responsibility I may have felt towards an audience has disappeared. The word 'responsible' feels dirty to me, like the word 'obligation'. They require a checking of your instinct, as if we don't do that enough anyway. It's dishonest to deny the monkey in you.

Niki: When you feel like all your idols have insulted you, you start not to give a shit except for your own opinion.

Karen: You don't have a false sense of responsibility. Irresponsibility is necessary to play and play around.

Niki: So that when we get in the rehearsal room, we've broken down all ideas of logic. Insults serve only to make us strong.

Our music is made out of total collaboration, we can't identify one person who came up with a piece of music . . . or even a part. We are generous to the point of ridiculous in the way we work and express ourselves. We're mavericks with words and musical notes. We're not afraid of them. People are scared of words, sounds they're not familiar with. We want to be fucking confused by music, we're desperate to hear things we don't understand. We pay attention to detail, complexity. Don't tell us what's punk. Nixon's catchphrase was: 'Let me make myself perfectly clear.' We exist in the margins, the space alongside, in fragments, notes, between lines. The Shrine. In our practice room we've constructed a shrine with Ian Curtis, Jean Seberg as Joan of Arc, Nation of Ulysses, Vicky Anderson, Marva

HUGGY BEAR

Whitney, Betty Harris. We believe in the power of belief. We invest magic in gifts, pictures, candles . . .

Karen: Yeah, we smoke the ganga with a bongo.

---

soul. chaos. clutter. dynamism. heat. colour.
flash. disturbance. edges. grind. twisted
geometrics. fucked upness. vorticist eroticism.
angularity. perpendicularity. soul. punk.
the funk. we can never flunk the funk. and it
curves. drives. reanimate your senses. it's
in my mind it's in my spine.
this is the sound we create
and we put it out our own way. Before the Law

Chris: Our future is chaos, love, and creating out of both states. Not resting. Forever punk with whatever it takes.

Jo: I feel thick most of the time, like there is so much more stuff to learn and that's cool . . . I want to make music for ever, for punk rock and films. I'm going to learn to drum 'cause drumming just seems like the most physically extreme music you can play; well the way I want to play them it is. Fight off doom-time demons like bitterness, hate, jealousy, selfishness, boredom, apathy, and be strong and naïve enough to always be falling in love . . . with people, new ideas, places, food.

Karen: In my twenties I'll be a toy-maker, building space stations and creating monsters. In my thirties I'll be an actress putting on 30 pounds for walk-on parts saying: 'Pint for me, Sharon' at the Queen Vic. In my forties, I'll be an astronomer and an architect. I'll build a house with an observatory on top.

Niki: Karen, will you read my palm tomorrow. Or do you have a map?

Jo: What about babies?

Karen: Oh yeah, lots of them. At least five. One of each.

Famous Monsters of Filmland is our future together: we plan to demonstrate punk rockness to the fraudulent, lazy and dull.

We send ourselves up all the time and sharpen our tongues through dissing each other and we get too serious and think too much and get crazy and we beat each other up and laugh like crazy women.

Jo: When we were 17, in 1986, there were way more bands in England. There were the Shop Assistants, Talullah Gosh, the Pastels . . .

Karen: I'd just got into the Velvet Underground and was blown away by Maureen Tucker's drumming; she had her own style. And there was Bernice in the Pastels and Margarita in Jesse Garon and the Desperadoes. But especially Tucker; she branded an image in my head of me drumming very primitive Viking sounds to a wall of noise, giving it angles and shape . . . so we started to do something.

Jo: Yeah. It didn't seem so scary to pick up a guitar . . . other girls had taken the risk, there was someone to identify with.

Karen: And there were way more small venues which cultivated an audience who were receptive to anyone getting up and trying a couple of songs.

Niki: All the good punk venues have been shut down.

Karen: Regular small venues are essential for new music – it's where embryonic contacts can be made.

HUGGY BEAR

Jo: Girls in Britain seem confused at the moment about who their role models are.

Niki: It's like you're taught that one has to be more powerful and exciting than the other. You can't have a multitude of different female role models, so you end up saying the Ronettes, who sing pretty devotional love songs that are peripheral to you. Your view of what can be inspirational in your life becomes narrow and you start seeing everything as letting you down.

Jo: Mmm . . . listening to their music and criticising them for being submissive isn't a great feminist achievement. What do you gain from that? A lot of feminism has been about seeing women as subordinated in films and music books. Saying: 'This book is misogynist' or, 'This film exploits women's fear.' It's obviously fundamental to me as a feminist to be able to recognise sexism and to understand how it works. But this shit is so fucking pervasive, so obvious that I don't want to always be positioning myself as a victim in everything . . . Why add to the shit? I don't expect to see a utopia on the screen. If I can find one thing inspiring about a film, I'll think about that thing on the bus ride home. That's revolutionary, it's productive, it takes my head somewhere new.

It's the same with role models. Why say Debbie Harry was exploited by the rest of Blondie – like some imagine that we're all subordinate to Chris in Huggy Bear, that we need to be encouraged to talk more or sing more, like we didn't give up that airspace to Chris willingly, he took it away from us. The truth is we find it hard to do those things and we think Chris is an inspiration, plus we're playing the music. Don't tell us we would be stronger doing something else, something we would be doing if we had the drive. Believe, Chris Rowley couldn't stop us, wouldn't stop us, he's always encouraged us and pushed us. It's putting the men in the powerful position both times . . . Debbie Harry wasn't faking that strength or that sexual potency, she was rich.

Niki: I'm just thinking of all the ways you can lie and play the part.

Jo: Kid people you really mean it when in your everyday life you don't live it . . . which must either mean that what you talk about in your fanzines, interviews, lyrics or whatever can't be applied to everyday life or that you're just a fucking faker. And for girls to do that to other girls – to lie to them or cheat them, make them feel inadequate 'cause the image of your band is more PC, more simple, more independent or whatever than you ever lived it – that's evil.

Niki: The British accept the whole notion of American glamour. It's bullshit. Makes me wanna fucking throw up. Our cultures are so different . . . most of the time we like to think we are in America.

Jo: I saw an ad on the noticeboard in this record shop, Beanos, for a female singer, drummer and guitarist to join this boy bass player. He wanted girls who were into L7, Bikini Kill, Hole, Babes in Toyland, and I was laughing, thinking that girls from Croydon would be just like those girls. We're obviously in dire need of some British alternatives, with our own allure, our own style, or we need to start remembering those British punks from the seventies and early eighties, like the Slits, Pauline Black, Poly Styrene.

171

Certain stories become attached to bands, fucked-up stories about their sexual histories, alcohol, drugs, bad behaviour – the media will quickly turn real pain into this hot product. Rock 'n' roll and feminism, on all levels, is a powerful combination. We didn't want to buy into that: the 'Queens of noise, come and get it boys' malarkey. It's funny to us – as much as it is repugnant. Women should really talk about how they feel about being sexually provocative, whether it's through stripping, teasing and titillating men as part of your performance in a band with a feminist agenda, rather than trying to pretend it's just a political exercise. Be honest. Talk about that thrill, that power. The audience's relationship to the performer is tenuous – spurious. And feminism for many assholes is just part of the tease.

HUGGY BEAR

It would be good if we could make all the artists invisible again. There is too much attention on particular artists and if they are all invisible, as I think they have been from time to time, we would look back and we would not be able to see the stars because the stars wouldn't mean anything, they wouldn't turn out to be real stars, the real stars would be invisible. Guerrilla Girls (New York).

Niki: There is so much that I want to do and see my friends do and all the other girls and women I have in my head when I'm writing, when I'm really letting go. I want them to want to be something, to stand out, whether it be education or law or music or whatever it is that you need to do to be tough to not be told this thing that you want to do is not within you to do.

For enlightenment read: Avital Ronne; Hélène Cixous; Gertrude Stein; *Angry Women*; Angela Davis; bell hooks; Exene Cervenka; Lydia Lunch.

Actually, read the song texts the way they were written. We think then dull pre-critique will be exposed. Even if you don't give a shit, and will eternally believe we only write love songs (though obviously that is too loose an idea anyway).

I guess Riot Grrrls are extreme therefore radical. Dig it.

Tanya Donelly

tanya donelly

Belly

So he's lying on top again . . .

('Gepetto' from Star)

Poor thing, poor thing, do you have a sister?
Would you lay your body down on the tracks
    for her?
Step one tiptoe in hell for her?
Don't you have someone to die for?

('Someone To Die For' from Star)

Half-way through a meal in a Thai restaurant in a quaint New England suburb of Boston, Tanya Donelly loses it. Big time. There has been no warning; though a little wary of giving anything too personal away, she has so far been a model of politeness and charm. Then she decides, all of a sudden, that she's 'all talked out', she's had enough of talking about herself, about Belly, but most of all about being a woman. It's nothing personal, she says, it's just the way she feels these days.

Tanya is embarrassed by her outburst. We leave the restaurant to return to the studio where Belly are recording their second album, the follow-up to the barbed guitar pop of 1993's *Star*. Her car is a new, white Volvo which dwarfs her diminutive figure. 'People always expect me to be the easy, open and friendly one and Kristin to be difficult,' she begins, referring to stepsister, Kristin Hersh. 'But in fact it's the other way round. I find it incredibly hard to trust people. She can talk about anything to anyone – in fact, she gives too much away in her interviews.'

The 15-minute journey to the studio is sombre. Tanya gets tearful about Kurt Cobain's recent suicide and talks about the six years she spent living with a manic-depressive boyfriend. Her mood changes the minute we walk into the studio. She starts goofing about, showing off, letting go of the negative energy she's just built up. She dances round the kitchen, sings 'fart, fart, fart' in a ridiculous falsetto voice, sticks a feather duster in her hair, grabs a rubber stamp and prints 'ORIGINAL' on her chest. She phones up her boyfriend Dean, who plays bass with Juliana Hatfield, and laughs hysterically. Later on she spots a picture of him on a CD cover and moons, 'He's my comforter.'

Tanya Donelly met Kristin Hersh when she was about seven. Tanya's father later married Kristin's mother. The two friends formed Throwing Muses in 1982 and released four critically acclaimed albums. In the late 1980s Kristin took maternity leave and Tanya found herself writing an increasing number of songs; in 1991, after the release of *The Real Ramona*, she parted company with Kristin to form Belly. The year before, Tanya had hooked up with Kim Deal, then bass player in the Pixies, to found female indie rock supergroup the Breeders (gay slang for heterosexuals). The project has proved very successful for Kim Deal, but after the first album *Pod*, and an EP *Safari*, Tanya baled out. She had become frustrated with being marginalised when it came to songwriting, both with the Muses and with the Breeders, and Belly offered her the creative outlet she'd been looking for.

Ironically, Belly have been more successful than Throwing Muses. *Star*, one of 1993's biggest pop thrills, invited comparisons to the Go-Gos, Mary Margaret O'Hara, the Cocteau Twins and Sinead O'Connor. The album entered the charts at number two, the singles 'Feed the Tree' and 'Gepetto' were hits and Belly captured the spirit of indie going overground. Although Tanya's lyrics have a vague, fairytale quality about them, they somehow drew the attention of fans who felt she understood 'the pain of the world'. Tanya herself can't explain all her songs; while Kristin Hersh or Sinead O'Connor may write distinctly autobiographical songs, Tanya's lyrics are far more vague, although they often have a twist of the macabre. 'Dusted' is the tale of a smack addict rape victim, and 'Slow Dog' was inspired by a piece Tanya once read about how Chinese women

caught committing adultery were once made to carry a decompos-
ing dog on their backs.

The next morning at breakfast, Tanya claims she can't write pop
songs. She thinks that *Star* may have been a happy accident and
now her inspiration is gone. As she's musing, the phone rings. It's for
Tanya. It's Dean. As she talks to him, again she goes all gooey. Gary
Smith, Belly's manager and a ringer for Tom Arnold, imitates her
lovesick voice. Suddenly aware of being ridiculed, Tanya defiantly
sticks her tongue out but continues her cooing. After some persua-
sion, she puts the phone down and prepares for another day in the
studio. She's obviously dragging her heels, allowing herself to be distracted by the sight of a crowded kids' playground, and gets all
broody as she climbs into her Volvo. Whether she's in the mood or
not, it's time to start writing pop songs again.

Riot Grrrl was important because a lot of women and young girls
felt included in music in a way which they hadn't previously. I
think it actually did make a lot of girls pick up guitars. The punk
movement pretty much excluded women, it was very kind of
white, young boy oriented and it's taken a while to change that. So
in that way I think it's a very positive thing. But I don't like anything that excludes a grey area. Many of the people Riot Grrrl
attacks are other women, which I find really strange. I've been
attacked by them, P.J. Harvey has been attacked by them – in a
strange 'if you're not with us, you're against us' sort of way. It
seems a strange stance to take if you're trying to pull people into
your cause.

It's an uncomfortable world for a lot of people right now. I hate
talking about women's issues these days. I'm talked out. And a lot of
the men I know are in the same situation as the women I know; they
have a lot of the same heartfelt concerns. When I talk to my female
friends about this, they come at me with: 'You're real privileged,
'cause you've surrounded yourself with good men.' And it's true. But
I definitely understand that anger: I've been pinched in the subway,
had men comment on me physically. It happens to every single one

TANYA DONELLY

of us all the time, every single day. It's something that I have fortress-like defence mechanisms against at this point . . . I don't want to talk about this now, 'cause I'm not being lucid.

I just wish being a woman wasn't an issue, but me wishing that isn't going to make the problems go away. I don't think of myself as being specifically a woman as far as music goes. I'm very, very much a woman about how I live my life and the way I think about myself as a person. When I'm playing my guitar and singing – I don't. My vagina doesn't come into my guitar playing or my singing. As far as I know. It's something that I wish I didn't have to think about because it affects the way I do my job. It affects the way I think about my job and that's the only thing I really care about. So it makes me inarticulate and angry when I have to discuss it in terms of my gender.

I agreed to do this book so I could say that. This won't be the last book that's written about 'women in music'. Let me put it this way: I want to get to the point where women aren't treated like . . . giraffes. Like it's strange that we're interesting or whatever. It shouldn't even be interesting at this point that I'm female and do this. It shouldn't even be a point of contention. But it is. In a way, it undermines everything Chrissie Hynde and Patti Smith did, because it isn't any easier for us. It minimises them – or maybe not, because they were such individuals. They didn't represent a female movement. They were just Chrissie Hynde and Patti Smith. That's the ultimate position to be in as far as I'm concerned.

I grew up mainly in Newport, Rhode Island, which is an uncomfortable combination of tourist trade, fishermen, craftsmen and drunks. I'll always stay in New England. I like the people here and the land is beautiful. It's a really specific culture. I've tried living in other places, including London, but I was only there for a few months. I'm deeply rooted here and my family's close. I have a strong, to the point of suffocating, network of friends. So it's hard to leave.

Neil Young is my first musical memory, probably *Harvest*. That's the album which makes me feel like a kid as soon as I hear it, along with the Beatles and the Rolling Stones. With some Neil

Diamond thrown in. Both my parents were into music – my mom was into the Beatles and Joni Mitchell. My dad loved that stuff too, but he was more into the Stones, the Faces. Boys' stuff. Because music was a part of my childhood and it made my parents happy, I assumed that it was a part of everyone's life. It was something that was constantly on in our house and in the car, on the eight-track in the VW bug. My parents used to dance around – they were kids. My father's a plumber and an actor, and my mother's a legal secretary. They love what I'm doing now; my mom collects all our cuttings and they both come to our gigs, religiously. They were always very supportive. My dad used to drive Kristin and me to the shows; he'd drive us to New York and back. I had a pretty nice childhood. Yes. Atypical, but I had loving parents, very good people.

I was kind of a wreck when I was at school. Sad to the point of being pathetic. Afraid of everybody. I had had a pretty free-form and protected lifestyle and school was really my first structured environment. I think I was born shy to a certain extent, and my parents lived a very different lifestyle to most people. I guess I wasn't prepared for integration. At first I just wanted to see what school was about and figure what the hell was going on. I wasn't a rebellious kid – maybe later on in my teens to a minimal extent – but for the most part I was always a voyeuristic kid, watching and waiting to see what happened. I always felt like I was taking notes! Which it turns out I was. I should qualify this by stressing that I wasn't a quiet child at home. School was a surprise – my first exposure to unpleasant children and the longest I'd had to wear clothes. My reaction to this was not to blend in or to be actively rebellious, but just to disappear completely. Being invisible allows you to see things clearly, and I learned how to distil a situation into a few words, which is a huge benefit to me now, as far as lyrics are concerned.

I was a real puker as a kid. I threw up all through the first grade. I was eventually moved into the corner, away from the other students, who would sometimes get sick in reaction to me. These years and my later ugly adolescent years resurface whenever I start to think I'm cool. Message to the young and awkward: it's better to bloom late than to blow your best years early. It's only in the last few years that I've felt strong enough to do my own thing! Only recently have I gotten to the point where I feel socialised. It's really strange

TANYA DONELLY

'cause I always feel that, to a certain extent, I'm doing everything outside of myself. I think I'm watching myself do things, which is probably a defence mechanism in a way. When I was in the Muses, I'd throw up before each show – a strong indication that I probably wasn't comfortable with the performing aspect of my job. On the other hand, *not* doing it was never considered an option, so I must have been getting off on it on some level. Or been aware of some future potential high. Kristin and I started playing when we were about 14. My dad fiddled around with the guitar; her dad actually plays and was kind of a songwriter, just for his own personal bene-fit. He writes really good songs and is very talented. A lot of the way we initially structured things came from him. He's got this kind of Zen philosophy that you don't play music outside your room, though, so he doesn't do anything with his own music. He's really funny, he's a great person. We would play guitar with him for fun and then it got to the point where we started writing things together. The songwriting went through its awkward stages, like anything. Plus, I was always playing *with* Kristin; she was the songwriter and I wrote things that accompanied her songs.

Which is not to say that it feels better having my own band. In some ways, it's actually weirder. I enjoyed doing *Star* but, as much as I loved the songs in the end, I didn't like saying to the others: 'Now this is this and here's what you do . . .' I like having a more bare-bones form and working things up. With the second album, we're trying more of a communal approach. Tom and Gail are writ-ing as well, which is much more fun for me. Their input this time around lessens the risk of a sophomoric slump. Four heads are weirder than one.

I knew that *Star* was a pretty good record; I liked the quietness of it, the weirdness of it. We were really nervous that it was too under-produced, it sounds like we didn't pay too much attention to it. We definitely didn't expect it to do as well as it did and in some ways, as awesome as it is that it did well, it has put us in a position of fear now that we are making the follow-up. It would have been hard to write *Star II*, to write an album which was accidentally a pop album like *Star* was – that's why we haven't set out to do any-thing even similar. I find myself sitting listening to the songs and thinking: 'They're too this, they're too that. I have to go home and write *pop* songs.' If you do that to yourself you're just betraying your next stage. You won't know what you'll naturally like for the next record.

Having said that, the second album is turning into something I'm proud to be part of. The pop thing is still there and we are learning not to shy away from grand gestures. The lyrics are a mystery even to me at this point. Sometimes I have to figure out what I mean myself. These songs seem to somehow be loosely related, so maybe this album should be a rock opera.

When I write songs, they appear as loose structures. Sometimes writing lyrics comes very easily, sometimes it's difficult. I'm really hard on myself, 'cause I don't want to use words like, 'I' and 'you' and 'me'. The pronoun problem! The words that come naturally to me have 'she' and 'her' in them and I try to work them to death. It depends; it's up to my head at the time. Most of my stories have a female focus. I still tend to have the kid's lens on things – it's a good perspective for unbiased storytelling. I am learning to live with the more personal pronouns – though when I say 'I', I wonder why anyone should give a shit. So I slap a 'she' over me.

The songs on the second album are pretty personal, for the first time ever. It's exorcising some stuff that I've had lying around for a while. I didn't set out for them to be personal, I just decided it's about time I hurt some feelings. But I have obscured identities a little bit. I think a couple of people will be pissed off. I don't think I've written a real love song yet. The ones I have written are more fearful, foreboding and angry than obsessive. I wouldn't say I was an obsessive lover – I prefer the word 'focused'. I feel more confident, and not just musically. I feel protected – it might sound crazy, but I feel safe around the people I'm with right now. Yet I still get nervous when presenting them with a new song. I mumble and mumble and mumble for a long time. I chat to them first and they're very good about *not* saying: 'What's it about? Why's it like this?' They're very accepting.

Songwriting happens at weird times: if I sit down and have to be disciplined, have to write lyrics, they're usually stupid. It works out best when things happen at weird times. Sometimes I'll say

TANYA DONELLY

things, just in conversation, and the consonants and vowels sound good, sound musical, and I work things around that. I used to write short stories in college and kind of poetry – more prose. I haven't done it in a really long time, though. All my journals are wrapped in electricians' tape so I can't ever get at them. But I can't ever bring myself to throw them away, just in case.

The word 'belly' looks and sounds pretty good, and it suggests different things to different people. Some think of babies, some of beer; others think of dead fish or of sex. I think of the one black hair on my body that grows from my belly and gets to be very long sometimes.

As the Muses were pretty well known in England, there was no initial introduction necessary for Belly. I had a history and a face. But the Muses were much more underground in the States, and suddenly whole groups of young kids were discovering Belly and hearing my voice and name for the first time. It was gratifying because it was in the context of this new band – the result of a decision *I* made. All these young kids – really, really young kids – hearing my voice was strange. Suddenly we were appealing to the MTV generation. I'd never really experienced their attention before. There are lots of girls into Belly who are learning to play guitar and want to know where I get ideas from, and other unanswerable questions. I guess I'm a role model for them to a certain extent, because I'm up there doing it.

There are fans who want touch you, say 'Hi' or write to you without necessarily wanting explanations. They're babies; they're so sweet, open-faced and more excited than kids were when I was their age. That's one thing that I'm surprised by. They seem more hyper and forward than I remember being at that age. But then I wasn't a major groupie, not at all. I don't really have heroes. I have people that I admire, but not in relation to me. Frida Kahlo is the only person, the only personality, that I covet. She just seemed to be born whole, born with her schtick down. You look at childhood pictures of her and she's always had the same expression, the same composure.

I have said in the past that nobody deserves to be famous. I mean that art and artist are separate. If a song moves you, celebrate that song. Obsession with personal details is irrelevant and a waste of energy and time. Respect for someone's ideas and thoughts and sounds is one thing, but it's self-minimising to concentrate on someone you don't know. In my limited experience as a fan, finding the person behind the power always diminishes the power. I find that really good art is like a scientific discovery – already in existence and waiting for the right people to pull it out of the air. Embrace the message, not the messenger.

On-the-road anecdotes are tough because I don't document my life that well; this is too bad, because I'm having a good one so far. Once in Switzerland, Fred Abong and I picked the locks of two doors to a hotel kitchen – it was 4 a.m. and I was drunk and hungry. And once the band were in a sandstorm on a beach in front of an old, dying castle in France.

I haven't had any pressure put on me to 'be more sexy'. I draw my own lines. In the few situations when a photo shoot has come out unnaturally provocative or girl-childish, it's been due to lack of fore-sight on my part, or because for some reason I really needed to feel pretty that day and overdid it. Everything about that level of being in a band feels weird to me, so sometimes I lose objectivity. Which is not to say I don't like dressing up. A friend of ours who lives in New York does mine and Gail's make-up and hair a lot. When we did a shoot for *SPIN*, an American music magazine, he brought a whole lot of hair extensions. The pictures were great, it wasn't like anything I'd done before. I love doing stuff like that, playing 'get-up'. So image is not really something that bothers me. I love having some-body touch my face or put make-up on. I love having my hair done, I love dressing up. Those aren't things that make me uncomfortable, whereas for a lot of women they do. It is usually my idea to begin with; Gail and I both like that kind of thing. Playing, basically.

I don't often get to the point where I consider how I market myself and the effect which that could have on a potential fan base –

TANYA DONELLY

maybe I should consider it more. I don't know . . . It's a difficult thing, I go back and forth. I understand that image is an issue, but I don't want to be responsible for representing anybody but myself. That's a selfish attitude, a selfish standpoint, but I've focused on very few people in my life and very few people have focused on me personally . . . to all of a sudden be responsible for representing a gender is offensive to me. I do think about it and I have incorporated it – now, when we go to photo sessions, Gail and I definitely think about it a lot. Which is important.

It's so offensive because . . . it depends which day you catch me on. I'm also getting to the point where the older I get, the less I care about fixing myself up, the less I care about being attractive – traditionally attractive. Three or four years ago it was important for me to look pretty, to be pretty. Almost as a way of being less conspicuous; it sounds crazy but using clothes and make-up as a mask. Make-up is a shield.

I have got to the point where I'm more confident about what I'm doing, so being interesting on any level is less relevant – I don't know if that's as a result of doing well or just ageing. I am broody, but I'm not thinking babies for a while. When my mother was my age, she had an eight-year-old and a six-year-old. Which is amazing to me, 'cause I just feel completely incapable of nurturing right now. I have too much to do and I'm still selfish with my hours. I tend to be working most of the time these days, between practising and writing. I want to be able to do this for ever, as a job. Until I get tired of it, but I want it to be my only job, my only function.

It's hard to say where I envisage the band being in three years' time. I'm not specifically goal oriented. So long as the second album does as well, not necessarily better than, *Star*. As long as there's always some kind of progression, even if it's minimal. I don't think I'd be happy in a band if I wasn't singing, though I do sometimes miss playing lead [guitar] and being independent of a microphone. Eventually I may go solo, but not for a while. Maybe we've a couple more records in us. I am an advocate of change. It's a form of rebirth, to change your environment, to change your situation. It almost changes your blood, in a way. It makes things new. Saying that, my cycles are probably so much longer than most people's – I mean in terms of decades.

G R R R L S

In ten years' time, I want to be raising children and I'd like to focus my attention on something that's important to someone other than myself, and I don't know if child-rearing is going to fulfil that. I have a lot of guilt and a sense of responsibility that I inherited from my folks so I have moments of crisis – that I'm not doing what I was put here to do. That I'm just doing something that's completely self-fulfilling. To a certain extent, I guess I'm making people happy, but I think it might be limited. Yeah, there are political gigs, but it's hard to do them, 'cause most of the time it conflicts with something else.

The way male journalists flirt every time I do an interview makes me never want to talk to anybody *ever*. That is a stumbling block; the only time in my life that I ever turn into a hermit, the only time in my life that I ever run into a strange feeling about myself as a woman, is in the male journalist situation. That's the time when I most feel like a girl. A little girl. This is the angle that they use: 'She's small and looks like a child.' I don't even know what the fuck they get out of it. All I ever feel is minimised. As a person, because of my female-ness. Which is strange.

The weird thing is that if I think something went well, I'll then read the piece and it'll talk about how small my hands were, or how small and quiet my voice was. Because I haven't developed a persona when I talk with a person, it takes me as long to open up to a journalist as it would to somebody in a bar. That's what I'm like. I'm really guarded. So it's easy for people to project what they want. Or maybe there's just nothing there so they have to make something up! The shields are up! Interviews don't come naturally to me, they make me very uncomfortable. Giving good quotes isn't my forte. To be quite honest, I wouldn't be a songwriter if I were good at that. Doing interviews is the bit I hate most. It's nothing personal, it just takes me years to get used to people.

I've been listening to Ennio Morricone, Nick Drake, Mary-Margaret O'Hara, Yma Sumac, the Beatles and Otis Redding. Morricone's soundtracks are great for early morning driving. Nick Drake's *Time*

TANYA DONELLY

of No Reply is bed music. Mary-Margaret's *Miss America* (my favourite record six years' running) is a good drunk record – a weeper. Yma Sumac's stuff is hard to find, but worth it – she has a four-octave range and sings like a loon. The Beatles are humbling; Otis Redding reminds me to get my ass out of the house.

Pam Hogg

pam hogg

Doll

I'm boot leather tough and just a little cocksure
I'll be your heroine or your high-class whore.
('Boot Leather Tough')

Pam Hogg is nostalgic for a moment. 'I miss fashion all the time, but I can't afford to make a single thing, 'cause then I'd be off again. You've no idea how many collections I've designed in my head. It can be such a fantastic expression. And I've nothing to wear; it's a fucking nightmare!' She laughs, shrugs her shoulders and starts talking about music again. Until 1992, Pam was best known as one of the British fashion stars of the 1980s. She spent over seven years designing weird and wonderful outfits, from gold, silver and pale sky blue velvet fetishwear which she collectively called 'Brave New World', to her 'Recession Collection' which included a multi-coloured patchwork coat put together from every fabric she had used since she started designing.

Although she was doing music before she became a designer – including stints in DF118 and Pigface – Pam only seriously returned to it towards the end of 1993, when she got a phone call from her friends Deborah Harry and Chris Stein. They were touring the UK, hated their support and wondered if Pam could help. Pam had a week to put a band together and teach them the punky songs she'd been putting down on tape. Doll – with Rob Courtney on guitar,

Sean McClusky on drums and a new bass player every other month – survived the Deborah Harry gigs and haven't stopped since. Impressed by Pam's electrifying stage presence and her dark vocals reminiscent of Nico or Nick Cave, Dave Stewart invited her to use his recording studio and offered her a record deal.

Sitting on a sheepskin rug in the living room of her cluttered King's Cross flat and absently stroking her cats, Pam talks fast and intensely. She is skinny, skinny and fuelled by an implausible natural energy. Her Glaswegian accent is thick even though she's been living in London for a long time. Her hair is yellow today; last week it was green and the week before that orange. Tattoos decorate her hands and lower arms. She is cheeky and flirtatious, larger than life, spunky and sassy. At one point she digs out a video from the late 1980s and then leaves the room to make tea while it's playing. It shows her being interviewed on *Wogan* – the time she ended up sitting on Terry's lap, in full PVC bondage gear, and making him blush.

As she catches the end of the tape, there's a nostalgic look in Pam's eyes again, but within seconds she's sipping her tea and talking about upcoming gigs, recording in Dave Stewart's studio, signing a record deal, finding a manager. She may be short on new outfits, but Pam Hogg, boot-leather tough and just a little cocksure, is ready to rock.

The very first gig with Doll was supporting Deborah Harry. My friend Adrian said I was like a female Nick Cave; people were saying wonderful things. Chris Stein said: 'You're like the Velvet Underground. You're like a mad Nico!' Which wasn't a bad one either. Then, after another gig, Dave Stewart came up and said, 'It was great, it reminded me of the first time I saw Patti Smith.' I was nearly on my knees when he said that! Then he added, 'I want you in the studio, I want you to make a record.' The comparisons have been great, but I don't think I sound like any of them. I couldn't tell you what I'm like. It's just beginning.

At first, people wouldn't accept that I was doing music. They'd keep saying: 'But you're a fashion designer!' I'm anything I want to be. It was a compliment to be put in the same category as Gaultier, but I didn't even know how to put things together properly. I was just sticking things together and having a good time. I'm now doing the same with music.

I never really knew what I wanted to do with my life. All these passions have come out in different ways. I never intended to be in the fashion business for a start – music was always more important to me. I used to win prizes for singing when I was about six years old. I always wanted to be on the stage, but it wasn't till about 1979 when a friend asked me to front his band that I thought: 'At last!' I realised I'd been waiting for someone to ask me that for years!

It was a mad folky-punk band called Rubbish. Kent would come round with his guitar the night before a gig and go, 'OK, here are the new songs.' I never had time to learn them. I'd be up there watching his mouth, singing along with him, basically just lip-reading. Every time we went on stage there'd be a new band member he'd forgotten to mention, so there'd be a trombone in my ear or a double bass coming out of nowhere. Everybody used to play at the Pindar of Wakefield (now the Water Rats) in King's Cross. The Pogues used to play there on Thursday nights and we'd support them.

I was in another band at the same time called Rapid Eye Movement (REM – ha!) But I used to have to mumble through the lyrics because I didn't believe in them. I couldn't get up there and sing with conviction, so that was short-lived, and then Kent ran away with the drummer's wife to Spain and that was the end of it. I'd not long left the Royal College of Art where I'd studied printed textiles and I was so disillusioned with what people were doing with my designs that I started putting things together myself. I'd never cut a pattern in my life – I just threw the fabric around me and started chopping. I never intended it to be serious, it was just something I had to do. But when I showed in '84, everybody wanted it and fashion, just by chance, became my business.

It wasn't until 1986 when another friend, Angela McClusky, asked me to sing on a track that I started again. I remember this guy Darryl handing me the lyrics and me thinking, 'God, I'm not singing that!' So they gave me five minutes in which to change them, so I did. They asked me to join the band but it had the worst name – the

PAM HOGG

Occasional Project – and I said that as long as the name was changed, I'd be into it. I'd been thinking about music again and was really fired up.

I hit it off musically with one of the guys in the band – Adamski's brother, Tinley – so I gave it a shot. We changed the name to Garden of Eden and the first record we put out went to number one in the Dance Chart. Every time we did a new track, the same thing would happen; on the day of recording, I wouldn't even know what the music was going to be like, Darryl would hand me a piece of paper with these horrible lyrics and say, 'Right, you've got five minutes if you want to change them.' What I was writing wasn't great, but anything was better than that shit. In the end I said, 'This is crazy, you know I'm never going to sing your songs, give me a tape of the music in advance and I'll have a go at writing something with a bit more substance.'

When the track arrived I thought, 'Jesus, I can't write anything to this', then went out, got totally pissed, met this beautiful boy, took him home and the next day wrote my first song in ten minutes flat. They all loved it and wanted to put it out as the next single. I was so excited, but when I saw the draft for the record cover it said: '"Angel!" written by Darryl Lockhart.' I couldn't believe it. When I protested, he denied my involvement. He said: 'Singers *are* nothing, singers *get* nothing.' I'll never forget that in all my life. I realise now that it was because he wanted all the fucking money. So stupid, because I didn't give a shit about the money, I just wanted my name on my first song. It meant a lot to me, I never knew I had the capacity to write. It was like magic.

That was my first taste of the music business, but it didn't put me off. A few weeks later I met Boys Wonder in the street and they said they'd written a song for me – would I sing it with them? I couldn't believe it: I had always thought they were an excellent band, they'd modelled for me a couple of times, they had such a good look. We did a couple of things together and played once at the Borderline, but I couldn't make enough of a commitment because the fashion was full-on and all my time was swallowed up with production and business. *de*construction wanted to sign me, with the Boys doing the music, but I wasn't ready and dance wasn't really my direction. It's a shame; we would have been great together.

When I started doing major fashion shows in 1989, every second was absorbed by it. I directed the shows, produced them, did the music, cast the models, designed everything – did absolutely everything as well as run the shop and take care of the constant day-to-day production. Everything I did was really weird. I never put anything to paper, it was all designed in my head, totally unorthodox. I worked so fast in such a short space of time it was like I was tripping. Sometimes after a show I'd look at a garment and think, 'How the hell did I make that?' Most of the patterns were made afterwards – it was crazy. I work in a similar way with music. It took me over two years to stop doing fashion – it was like cutting off my right arm. I wanted so badly to do music, but every time I finished one collection, I was buzzing with a hundred ideas for the next.

Then the recession came along, so I had no money, couldn't do a show, and I thought: 'Music'. That's fate, destiny, you know . . . I could have continued doing the business but I hated it, I'm a useless businesswoman, I was there only to do the show. All the money I made from one show paid for the next. That was all I wanted out of it. So I stopped and everybody was going: 'You can't!' I was like: 'Watch me!'

I did my final show in 1992 and afterwards produced all the classics that people had been constantly buying over the last ten years. I did a big production, closed the studio and started writing. I had actually been scribbling for about two years. In 1990 I was going out with Mary Byker who at the time was in Pigface. He asked me to go on tour with them for a couple of weeks, so I joined up with them in Texas and on the seventh day I was dragged on stage to ad-lib a duet with him. It was a great song written by Lesley Rankin, ex-Silverfish: 'Hips, Tits, Lips, Power'. When I came off stage, Chris Connelly (of the Revolting Cocks) came up and said: 'You're not going home, you're part of the band now.' It was brilliant – he's such a hero. I did the last few days I was there and was hooked. That's when I knew it had to happen.

Two weeks after I quit the fashion scene I bumped into Marco Pirroni (of Adam and the Ants) and before I got a chance to tell him what I was up to, he asked if I was ever going to do any more music! Fate again . . . He knew of the very person I'd been looking for – an engineer/musician to help me get out all the stuff I'd been writing. The next day, I got a call from John Reynolds (drummer with Jah Wobble) and he asked me to come over. I put a tape together really quickly with snatches of music that I was really into – Ministry, Young Gods, Suicide and Foetus. It wasn't really the kind of music I wanted to make, but it showed him where I was coming from. I grabbed my books and went off to bare my soul to a complete stranger! Within two hours, we were well into the first track. He was great, he just started fiddling with a drum machine, and I'd be going: 'No, not like that, make it harder, faster.' I must have said 'harder' about twenty-five times. He was brilliant – never questioned anything, just kept going. Eventually we got a drum track that I felt good about. I took bits out of three unfinished songs and went for it. We put a bit of bass down and then I said, 'Right, I'm ready.' He put me out on the landing (the studio was at the top of his flat), closed the door, gave me a shout and I started.

I was so nervous that the noise that came out was horrendous. I thought, 'My God! Leave now, girl!' But it was then or never. I got Marco to play some guitar . . . It was great, he was going: 'What do you mean – "no notes"?' I just wanted the sound of pain! At the end of the day I asked Marco what he thought and he said it was the first original thing he'd been asked to play in years. I went back the next week and again the same thing – within two hours, I was out in the hall screaming, 'Who says the devil is a woman? Woman is creator, Woman is God!' When it was finished, John put his head around the door and said, 'God Pam, you need to be loved.' My songs were so bitter and sad, someone had obviously fucked me over badly 'cause I was writing all this heavy, emotional stuff. I don't even know where some of it came from. It wasn't written down, I just slipped it in between the lines as I was singing in this really tortured voice. Lines like: 'Twisted hand in soft kid glove, taunt the soul and speak of love.'

The third week I went back and I said, 'John, I want to write a happy song.' But within ten minutes I was saying, 'Forget it – give me the saddest note you ever played.' Well, the sound of that note nearly brought me to my knees. I asked him to put a kind of death march roll on top and then to leave me for about twenty minutes.

The tears were running down my face, I was terrified that he'd come back before I was ready. The song was called 'The Hunter'. It was about me splitting up with Mary and then meeting someone else when I was too vulnerable. It was about someone offering everything and then when I'd succumbed, taking it all away.

Everything I write is very personal, which is why I can go up on stage with absolute conviction. The songs are either fast and vicious, or sad. It's funny, I'm always out having a great time, and people keep asking me where the happy songs are, but I've realised that I go out when I'm happy and when I'm sad or angry, I write and just exorcise it. A friend recently said they thought they knew me until I started singing. They feel they know a lot more about me now. It's scary. I've always had to be the strong person, everybody's always come to me with their problems, I've always had to be wonderwoman. I've never really faced my own feelings before. I've always been happy just doing my work, I don't do anything by halves – that's why I couldn't put music and fashion together. I was doing the music half-heartedly because the fashion was full-on. that's why I needed to sever completely in order to give everything to it. I was turning down £40,000 orders while living in poverty. But I had to make music. I started with nothing: I've been without, so I can be there again. It doesn't bother me, I felt I'd die if I didn't explore this other side.

I'm writing constantly; sometimes I write a song immediately but there's one I've been writing for about a year. I keep changing it because it's too painful. It's about friends who have died of AIDS. It's too emotive a subject. It's killing. I've stripped it down now. It's ended up very hard and fast. I've taken the personal element out of it and it's just angry and hard-hitting. The original one just tore me apart – I'd never have been able to sing it without crying. I've lost three close friends through AIDS – when the last one went I nearly smashed up a pub. All of a sudden this rage took over me. Then when I heard about Yallé I couldn't believe it. It didn't really hit home until he never turned up to one of my gigs. He'd rung me up in the afternoon saying he felt great and was definitely going to make it to this one. His friend Monica arrived on her own again and

PAM HOGG

I knew by her face just how bad he was. I couldn't get it out of my head. I got totally plastered, came home, woke up at seven o'clock the next morning and wrote this song from beginning to end. I cried the whole day. Writing it down was the only way I could come to terms with it. I'd accepted it. I had to . . . He has.

The song's called 'Yallé's Got the Fever'. It's about all the things I love about him and all the anger AIDS makes me feel. It's like a Romanian punk song. I heard the whole thing in my head, I was thinking: 'I want Yallé to know how much I love him by telling him I've written this song.' But some of the lines are too sad, it would be too upsetting. There's lines like: 'Can't bear to see you wither, like a flower in the dust/Your shining light will linger/On forever in this godforsaken world of ours that's cursed.' How can I sing him that? We've talked about his illness and he's shown me the worst areas of his body. It's been difficult not to cry.

It's not until something really serious happens that you realise that your time is limited. We were talking about how vulnerable we are and I wanted to tell him about the song, but I'm going to change some of the words because I want to record it, actually give him this thing – because what else can I give him? I can't give him his life back. At some point I'll be strong enough to show him it, it'll be a time when he can cope with it. Actually, he's probably the strongest person I know – he's so positive and determined to beat this bastard of a disease that it would make you ashamed not to live every inch of your life to the full.

After my accident, I wrote a lot because I was meant to stay in and be good! I can laugh about it now – I had just dyed my hair fluorescent orange, I was head to toe in silver, and I'm lying under this car with the driver going, 'Sorry love, I didn't see you.' I wrote twenty songs in just over two months. An old friend, Rob Courtney (who used to front One Million Fuzztone Guitars), had been asking for about five years to work with me but I'd kept putting him off. I didn't want him to end up frustrated because I knew I had a total vision. I left my last band, DF118, because I was writing the lyrics but holding back or fighting over the direction of the music. That's why I wanted my own band – I don't want to be stepping on anybody's toes, and I thought it would be difficult telling someone what to do when they're not used to it. But Rob hadn't played for about six years and was really happy to sit back and help me realise my vision.

We'd been working for about three months on a four-track, just getting my ideas down, when Chris Stein came to stay for a couple of days before the Deborah Harry tour. He heard the tape I'd been working on and then half-way through the tour he called up saying, 'We hate our support band, what can you do?' They wanted someone to liven up the audience, so I said I could arrange a band for Glasgow which was two days off, and if they liked them, I was sure they'd do the rest of the tour. Then I thought, 'Jesus, I'm giving away the gig of a lifetime.' I said: 'If I get a band together, could we do the last two dates?'

Debbie knew what I was like, she'd seen my last band, and Chris had heard the new stuff on the tape, so we just went for it. Sean McClusky had been asking to play drums for ages, so I got him, and Mary loaned me his bass player, Karl Leiker. I chose six songs and we rehearsed for less than a week. You can imagine how mad it was. When I got on stage it was like alien music, I was conducting the band with all these arm movements to let them know which bit they were at. It was like I was doing semaphore! I expected everyone to start walking out, but the reaction was fantastic. People were coming up to the bar later asking when the next gig was and did we have a record out? The band were great, they were all hugging me, 'cause we'd had a bit of a bad time getting it together and I thought they'd desert me after it.

I'm not a 'musician' in the orthodox sense, but I hear it all in my head and know exactly what I want. We had five days, so it was literally: 'This is how I want you to play it.' It wasn't a case of maybe this, maybe that, it was: 'This is it!' Sean's got this other band Speedway, and when I went to see them the guitarist came up to me laughing and said, 'I hear you really crack the whip!' I was going, 'You're damn right I do!' The first song in our set is called 'Boot Leather Tough'; it's wonderfully appropriate.

I've never let this gender thing interfere with what I'm doing. People used to say to me, 'Don't you find it really difficult being a woman in the fashion industry?' I'm a person, whether male or female, and

PAM HOGG

I've never allowed anyone to put on me their view of how a woman is or is not meant to be. I think the best thing I gave to fashion was the liberating of women who wanted to be sensual in their dressing without being hammered by other women who couldn't get past thinking that being sexy was only for men. I made clothes that were really sexy but so strong that you were wearing your steel-toecapped Docs with them. I had girls who had never put a frock on coming up and buying one in every colour because it was the first time they'd found something they felt great in.

I used to get lots of fan mail, some of the most beautiful letters and some of the weirdest. People said that I'd encouraged them, given them hope, probably because I just spoke my mind in the interviews I did. I was very upfront about what I felt. I was your original Riot Grrrl without the name tag. I got this phone call from this girl in LA saying, 'I think you're wonderful, I'm getting my friend to paint your picture on the back of my leather jacket.' This is what happens to pop stars, but I was getting this when I was doing fashion!

The music business is really fucked up with this gender thing too. I went to a gig one night and a record company guy came up to me and said, 'I saw you with DF118 and it was OK but you hadn't quite got it together.' And I said, 'That's why I'm doing my own stuff now. It's my own band, I'm writing it and directing it all.' His response was, 'Oh yeah, a real power bitch.' He wouldn't have said it if I was a guy, he'd have got smacked in the fucking face if it was a guy. Why put someone down for having a vision? I wanted a band where I didn't have to answer to anybody, where I could do what I want to do, make decisions for myself and go for it without people holding me back. In other bands I was always apologising for being known, feeling embarrassed that I was always the one people would write about. Now that it's my own band, I can enjoy that attention. I am the spokesperson for the band, I write all the songs, I know why they are as they are. I've got excellent musicians who know the score and who don't have an ego problem. They're not stupid; they wouldn't fucking well be there if they didn't believe in it.

It's so difficult sometimes, there's always some stupid barrier that you're constantly having to tear down, like the boxes people desperately want to put you in. Sometimes people can't understand how you can have more than one talent – everybody has as many talents as they are willing to give their time to. If you have a passion and desire to do something, why shouldn't you do it? I've recognised my desires and have the energy, drive and determination to see them through. People go around talking about things – I put my ideas into action. There are things I dream about but the reality is when your passion is so strong that you are willing to put yourself through hell to achieve it. Ideas are ten a penny. People can sit around and go: 'Oh, I thought about that.' Yes – but how many went out and did it? Dreams are wonderful too, especially if they happen. Can you imagine if I knew twenty years ago that not only would I become one of Debbie Harry's friends but that I'd also be on stage singing a duet with her . . . When in my wildest dreams did I think that would happen? Never.

199

Kristin Hersh

kristin hersh

Oh no don't you put me in that box
You know what you can do with those locks
Bet your life I'll come crawling out again
You'll have to deal with me then . . .

('Houdini Blues' from *Hips and Makers*)

11 a.m. Sunday, in a west London hotel. Kristin Hersh answers her bedroom door clutching a white towel in front of her naked body. Her black hair is a wild mess. She smiles sheepishly, rubs her eyes, apologises for oversleeping and promises she'll come downstairs 'in a sec'. Ten minutes later Kristin stumbles into the empty hotel dining room, wearing ripped faded blue jeans and a floppy jumper which envelopes her fragile frame. She is still bleary-eyed; she and husband-cum-manager Billy O'Connell were up late drinking tequila and champagne. Her energy is low, but each anecdote she tells is accompanied by sound effects and visuals; as she talks about the bat which flew into her room when she was a child, she shouts and squawks, arms flailing through the air. The waitress brings tea and frowns at us sideways.

Kristin Hersh was brought up in the deep South; in the 1960s her family moved to Providence, Rhode Island, where they lived in a commune. Since the age of 14, Kristin has been visited by what she calls 'forces'. These are powers which once scared her, gave her seizures and made her hallucinate. She heard voices in her head. Her brain felt as though a live wire was slowly burning inside it. She lived with the confusion for years – the only way to control the internal poltergeists was to translate them into songs, using the discipline as exorcism. As a kid, she hung out with Tanya Donelly – who also grew up in a commune – and the two started to make music together while barely into their teens.

As a joke, they formed the Muses with a third friend in 1982. It was an acoustic all-girl outfit – they swore not to let any men join. But the only drummer they knew was male, so they had to break the rules and David Narcizo joined. They bought electric guitars, Kristin became the main singer-songwriter and their name developed into Throwing Muses. They were the first American band to get a deal with London-based indie record label 4AD. Gary Smith, who manages Throwing Muses (alongside Tanya Donelly's own band Belly) has a slightly blurred photo pinned up in his Boston office. It's a close-up of Kristin and Tanya aged about 14, grinning madly, all innocent eyes and puppy-fat cheeks.

Throwing Muses released their first, self-titled album in 1986. Kristin and Tanya were both 19; Kristin was pregnant with her first son, Dylan. Whilst with child, she mentally divided herself into 'Good Kristin' and 'Bad Kristin' to protect the baby. 'My voice felt so big and dangerous,' she later explained. 'I was horrified to think that this *voice* was in there with the baby.' The album, which was dominated by Kristin's wild, screaming vocals, was critically acclaimed in the UK but largely overlooked in the States.

With their blend of angry and submissive, vulnerable and precarious, beauty and the beast songs and blazing guitars, Throwing Muses captivated British indie fans, releasing an album a year from 1986 to 1991, with the exception of 1990. For Kristin, the first year of the caring, sharing nineties was like one of her hallucinations becoming a reality. Tanya Donelly was moonlighting with Kim Deal's 'indie supergroup', the Breeders. Kristin's former lover and the father of four-year-old Dylan was suing for custody. Her former manager was suing. The court was not impressed by Kristin's rock star mom status; she was not deemed capable of being a full-time mother, and her ex won custody (at one point, Kristin could only see Dylan when she was in Rhode Island; now things are more relaxed).

Two weeks before Christmas 1990, the voices in her head were becoming increasingly insistent and Kristin checked into hospital, hoping to stay a short while and be calmed down. Instead, she was diagnosed as 'bi-polar' (schizophrenic) and kept in. Talking about her condition for the first time in *Melody Maker* in January 1991, Kristin explained: '[The doctors were] afraid that you might hurt yourself or other people. I told them these voices have had a job for a long time, they're not telling me to pour oil on my kid or anything. But they just don't know what to do but keep you safe for a while.'

One thing saved her life: she met Billy O'Connell. Billy could count her down and talk to 'Evil Kristin'. He offered her marriage – she often talks of the importance of playing the 'good housewife' role in keeping her perspective on the record industry in context – and stability. He also fathered her second son, Ryder. In 1991, in the wake of Kristin's 'bi-polar' diagnosis and her marriage, Throwing Muses released *The Real Ramona*, an album less intense than their last, *Hunkpapa*, which suffered from being Kristin's emotional dumping ground. In the same year, Tanya Donelly, a frustrated song-writer anxious to form her own band, handed in her notice. Kristin considered changing the band's name, then decided against it. With Kirstin and David Narcizo as the core members, the sixth Muses album, the soft, melodic *Red Heaven*, came out in 1992. The band toured until Kristin was eight months pregnant, when her bulging stomach made it impossible for her to play guitar.

Despite the strength of their indie fan base, Throwing Muses had few forays into the mainstream. Their deeply personal guitar songs were filed under 'difficult' and given limited radio airplay. Then Tanya Donelly danced into the spotlight with Belly and Kristin decided to take on a solo project between Muses records. When *Hips and Makers* was released in January 1994, its delicately frac-tured acoustic songs, with occasional stabs of cello, started a never-ending press frenzy and gave Kristin her first recognition in the mainstream press. It was also the first time she had any real impact in America.

Hips and Makers was born out of a blinding physical necessity to write – Kristin says she can hardly remember making it – but it is an accessible, coming-of-age record. Produced by Lenny Kaye (who has also worked with Patti Smith and Suzanne Vega), the album is jerky, painful, honest and feminine, Kristin's voice sometimes serene and almost in control, her confessional songwriting fitting the

203

acoustic genre better than it does guitar-driven indie rock. 'The Letter', a 'verbal vomiting' which Kristin wrote ten years ago, is delicate and croaky with pain:

> I'm turning in circles
> And I'm spinning on my knuckles
> Don't forget that these are circles left undone and very close to
>   me
> Forgive me
> Comfort me
> I'm crawling on the floor . . . I'm gonna cry
> You look for me
> Love Kristin.

'Your Ghost' is a tender torch song, its subtle melodies cut with crooked vocals from REM's Michael Stipe.

As Kristin pushes away a cup of tepid grey-coloured tea in the hotel dining room and laughs about her hangover, she lays her arms on the table and turns them palms up. There are white scars zigzagging across her lower arms, faded and almost invisible. I want to reach out and touch them but stop myself. There is a song on Throwing Muses' first album called 'Delicate Cutters' which was inspired by people who cut themselves superficially, occasionally carving words into their flesh, as an act of humiliation or simple confusion. Kristin Hersh slowly lifts her hands off the table and puts them in her lap. She is still laughing, her small body shaking with convulsions. *Hips and Makers* may have been sweetened with serenity and innocence, but its scars are still showing.

I was born in Georgia. My family come from the Tennessee mountains, so all the music I heard as a kid was mountain songs – almost Celtic. It's real whiny and minor key, with bad grammar. It was dreamlike, but I could never figure out if that was simply because it was music or because my family were drunk or religious or starving. There's this weird kind of misty confusion about my childhood – yet at the same time it was very down to earth, with my parents always talking about how much they wanted a car or another drink.

But the music . . . it wasn't the blues, it was more Celtic than that. My dad used to play these songs to me every time I took a bath, which I guess was every day. He'd sit there for an hour and play through all these Great Depression-era mountain songs. I have fond memories of him doing that. I never kicked him out the bathroom. 'Cuckoo', a song from *Hips and Makers*, is one of those songs – it was always my favourite. It was my nickname from the day I was born because I sneezed and then cooed. But no one ever told me the cuckoo is a crazy bird. And my father, my whole life, has called me 'Cuckoo' or 'Bird'. He's never mentioned the name 'Kristin' to me. Just calls me 'Bird'.

When I was still very young, we moved into a commune with a bunch of other people. I guess we all lived in a barn; because I was really little, it seemed massive to me, like an airplane hangar. There was a parachute covering the ceiling – hippies are really into para- chutes 'cause it's cheap wall covering. This heavy-duty stoner called Matt wanted to write 'Be together' on the barn roof, but he came up with 'Be a tog eater' instead. Dad still signs all his letters to me: 'Be a tog eater, love Dad.' The people in the commune were all on acid all the time, so they saw all these great things that I used to think older people got to see. I really wanted to see these incredible things too. This woman Carol used to see ostriches with their heads in the sand, along the banks of the river . . . Unless they were all just lying to me, they were always seeing these beautiful things. Once a bat flew into my room – they gave me a room 'cause I was a kid and everybody else slept downstairs together – a bat flew in the window and I'm actually shaking, shouting: 'There's a bat in my room! Get it out!' They were going: 'Wow, that's beautiful, that's really like you, Kristin.' My father finally came up to get the bat out of my room and it stuck in his hair – he's got big Doctor Who hair.

I guess most kids are happy; I think I was happy. I was *con- fused*, but I was happy. I have endless memories from my teenage years of warm beer and cold surf – just going out to the cliffs and drinking. Then the cops would come and bust it up and take your beer away and drink it themselves. But I could never smoke pot. When I was younger, I had a little dog and we would go out to the

KRISTIN HERSH

woods around the commune and hunt bears all the time. There were really bears out there and I used to think: 'Great, I'll find one.' Because everyone was so kooky about everything being beautiful, nobody mentioned that bears could kill you! My mother would say: 'I never want to see you feeding the rats. I know Carol feeds the rats, I know Matt feeds the rats . . .'

Dad started teaching me guitar when I was nine. He's a philosophy professor, he teaches all the weirdy courses: Zen Buddhism, Native American symbolism. He only knew the chords that were in the song books, like E minor . . . I started to get frustrated, trying to describe to him how the songs should go next, I was driving him crazy. I'd yell: 'It should get more, more *bent* here, and then it should sound happier.' And he would just play E minor again. 'No! It shouldn't sound that way!' And I would try to sing it – but you can't sing a chord – and he was like: 'Here, you do it!' So I started making up my own chords. I eventually learned what they were. But some of them I never learned, some of them still don't make any sense at all! I always drive my bass players crazy – I play chords which I think are beautiful 'cause they bounce all over the spectrum but there's no root, so the bass player doesn't know where to go.

I learned to play all the songs that were in the music books around the house and at first it was hard on my fingers – changing chords was really hard. I had little, tiny nine-year-old hands, and my father's guitar was this nylon-stringed Yamaha, which has a big fretboard. So I'd be sliding my hands up against the strings. That's probably why I started making up my own chords. I've always liked playing leads, so the first few songs I wrote all sounded Indian. They were terrible, terrible songs. Someone asked me the other day if I thought I was a prodigy because I started writing songs when I was nine and I burst out laughing: if you could ever hear the songs that I wrote – so sad! It's incredible anyone ever wanted to be in a band with me.

When it came to school, I was really smart. So I wasn't particularly into it. It just was not interesting. I was fine. I was normal and fine, people liked me and I was a cute little blonde kid. Then when I was about 14, everything came crashing down, rock music just fell right on my head, and it became ugly and crazy and obsessed – I couldn't stop playing music. I stopped going to school so I could play guitar all day. I used to drive a car before I was old enough, and carry the guitar around, just because it was easier to run away and play the guitar anywhere it was quiet, where I could be alone. The songs I was writing, I was afraid of, because they were saying real crazy things and they didn't seem to be following any rules that I knew as far as writing songs went. So I wouldn't let them say everything, I would only put the pretty things down, or the things that made sense, and I would make them conform to pop structures. Then the other bits of the songs would get stuck in my body and they would haunt me. I literally had wolves jumping out of the walls at me, or jumping in front of my car – I'd screech to a halt and they'd be staring at me in the dark. Just yellow eyes, peeking around bushes at me, until I would write their song and finish it and let it say all the fucked-up things it wanted to say; they would haunt me, you know . . .

I didn't sleep very much, I don't really remember sleeping at the time. I had a burning that never let go. I literally had fever. I walked through the blizzard of 1978 for twelve hours without feeling a thing. I was just trying to kill the burning, it never went, there was nothing that could make it go away. I would cut myself, hoping that some of the fever would come out in my blood. I'm just scars all over, I'm a mess. It helped a little to feel some pain on the outside instead of on the inside. At least it was pain I could understand, but it was hurting my body, which was another thing I had to live with. So I just got darker and darker. Then I thought: 'Fuck you! These stupid songs are just attacking me, using me for what I'm worth and then I'm gonna die and they're going to go somewhere else. This is what I grew up to do?'

The other picture was that I was schizophrenic. So I was put on a lot of medication. I was really, really skinny 'cause I was awake all the time and I couldn't eat or the medication would make me really sick. It was a bad time for many years. So I just started frantically making demos of all the songs with the Muses, playing every night just trying to make sure the songs got out. When I was 18, I got pregnant and it all slowly cooled down. I did become afraid of the songs again because I felt they'd hurt the baby, but it was such a positive physical experience. It was fascinating. As soon as I knew I was pregnant, I went to the beach. I was the only person who knew I was pregnant . . . I don't really have any words for the way I felt. I remember sitting on the wall at the beach, looking out at the ocean and it seemed like a little light after all that darkness was stuck in my stomach, and that made me decide to keep the baby. I had a boyfriend, and though we'd just broken up, we got back together to have the baby and make a home round him. There's never been a question about whether or not I was going to live through the pregnancy; whether it's schizophrenia or bi-polar or just songwriting, you just don't die on your children. Dylan just answered that question.

Having Dylan was a crazy, crazy thing. It's such a good lesson to learn about what we're here for. You're not here for yourself. It didn't make sense of everything, but turning to the physical has been my answer, I guess. My body loves my children and it would never hurt anyone or anything. It would never hurt itself now. I have had to deal with some lousy chemicals in my time, but given the opportunity, I'd give them all to the songs now. I don't mean I exorcise my demons. I hate that. I'm done with all that, which has made me a real songwriter. But if the songs have living chemicals, if they wanna take a piece of my brain for a while, I'll keep them in their piece of my brain and I'll do without that part. But the rest of me is owned by my family. The songs can say whatever the hell they want and they're much more beautiful for that. But they can't walk in my front door any more.

My bones still shake when I sing; I was at the BBC yesterday doing a string quartet session and when I sing the really loud notes I'm one of the loudest singers around. I can't seem to sing quietly. When I hit a note it gets really loud and the microphones distort and I have to stand ten feet away from them. And all my bones rattle. I think that's why it sounds like it does when I sing. It feels good when it comes out, but when it's stuck it's . . . I wish I didn't have it. I don't like to live that way. It makes me very sick. I still have seizures if I can't write a song. A seizure's a violent, violent thing and I know it's taken years off my life. It's an epileptic seizure; my brother has them too, but he's never written any songs, he just took drugs instead. It means that I can't stop writing. The songs would get stuck again. I could write songs and not publish them . . . I recorded *Hips and Makers* myself 'cause I didn't think anyone would release it, but I don't have any capital to keep recording music without record companies. I also have a contract with 4AD, so I'd get sued. People shouldn't be calling me as crazy as they do. I didn't tell them that I had any kind of psychological or mental illness for years and they were calling me crazy just because of the music – just because I was screaming in the music, and because the lyrics didn't make literal sense. But they're songs – people have been screaming in music for ever. They shouldn't have been calling me loopy.

I never wanted to be centre of attention at all. I got most of the attention in the Muses, but Tanya was the cute one. We don't see each other all that much now, not as much as we did when we were in the same band. I never understood what people meant when they thought we would no longer get along, like: 'You're in a different band now, fuck you!' We know too much about the music business. But anyway, it was great having somebody who'd be the focal point of photos. I'm bad at the whole photographs thing. I hate the whole idea of it. I hate fashion, and to combine music and fashion seems so *evil*. I don't know what to do about that. I wish we thought it was attractive to show people with real faces, real bodies. I do. I think I can tell what somebody's like by looking at them, but the idea that we can tell what someone's like by judging whether or not their face is following the rules is such a weird idea and I just wanna remove myself from it.

209

I don't mind nudity at all; I did a photo shoot for the music press recently and I posed topless, arms across my chest. Nudity's great, that's real. I'm naked at least once a day. But I would never wear one of those fucking trendy teen outfits they try and make you wear the rest of the time. That's lying. People are so screwed up about sexuality, they're so adolescent about it, so it's good to say, 'Well naked is sexy. Go with that!' If you want to make something sexy, at least make it nudity. I just wish you could publish music without putting forth some kind of image. If you're not a babe in a short skirt, you have to look grungy *on purpose*. I used to get so much shit in France for looking like a slob. Their response to me and Billy was like: 'What is this indie fashion statement you are making? You are looking like a couple of tourists.' 'Well, we are a couple of

KRISTIN HERSH

tourists.' Then grunge happened and they fell all over themselves. 'Oh, like grunge – you still look like a slob! Yes! We love it!'

My hair colour . . . Yeah, I'm blonde naturally. Dyeing it was kind of a mistake. I did it because *Melody Maker* wanted to do a feature on the most recognisable members of a selection of 4AD bands and I'd been through this long housewife stint . . . it's so easy to lose that 'people are looking at me' thing. I had to look OK 'cause people were going to start taking my picture any minute. But at home, nobody's out with a camera and I can look like a normal person. I didn't wanna be recognisable, so I dyed my hair the opposite colour, only to find out you can't really dye it back. So it may go on for ever. It was a long time ago. It doesn't bother me, although people seem to read a lot into it.

When I was on tour in the spring/summer of 1988, the left side of my head shut down and I couldn't sing right or see right. It was just like half my head was gone, just blacked out. I thought: 'Hmmm, interesting.' When I got home I went to a specialist doctor who X-rayed my head and discovered a tumour on the brain the size of a small fruit. I was like: 'What's small fruit? What's big fruit? Grapefruit or watermelon?' It was about the size of a plum, which made me feel gross. Why do they have to compare it to *fruit*? What is their hang-up with fruit? The doctor said he didn't know what would happen if I didn't get it operated on, but at that time I had the tour bus parked in my driveway and everybody was sleeping over at my apartment, ready to leave on tour early the next morning. So I kind of blew it off for a little. I figured that if I ignored it then it might go away.

I got kinda used to it; nothing happened on tour and I had surgery when I got back. When I was lying there with all the tubes hanging out of me, the anaesthetist comes up to me and says: 'I see from your chart that you're a musician: you're not a singer, are you? I can't guarantee your voice is going to be anywhere near its normal range after this operation.' That was when I had all those squeally, high sounds. He said he'd be very careful . . . Those songs are out of my range now, but that's more to do with smoking and screaming than anaesthetists. It was the only time I'd been on MTV during the day – they tried to get me to say over the phone that I was going to die. I still don't know how they found out. They tried to make me say that my life was in danger – that would have been a much better story, and much better for my career.

I did a lot of coke in high school, and they used cocaine as the anaesthetic without telling me; I woke up coming down from coke, which is why I quit in the first place – that crazed feeling, like jumping out of my skin . . . I woke up and there were tubes everywhere, I didn't know what was going on, so I pulled all the tubes out. 'Waagh!' Blood started pouring out every orifice. I was throwing up blood, it was pouring out of my ears, so gross! My boyfriend was sitting in the chair watching it happen, and the nurse came running over and pulled the curtain around me so that none of the other patients could see me. It was funny.

You know, I didn't even expect 4AD to release *Hips and Makers*, much less convince anybody to listen to it, 'cause it's so raw. I thought it was personal, a record for me and Billy. I thought people liked big, glossy, hot records, which I think is pretty sucky and I would never do. So far *Hips and Makers* has outsold everything the Muses ever did. Everywhere: England, America . . . It finally implies that people out there are listening, but I don't really see it continuing. There was hype built around it, and hype is usually what determines success for a record. I don't know why it happened; I guess 'cause it was the first time I'd gone out on my own. Next record we'll see.

Making and promoting *Hips and Makers* was the first time that I've really thought sexism exists in the record industry. I thought I could bypass it by not being a bimbo, by making either gender-free music or music that's real, instead of dip-shitty music that they usually pass off as feminine; by being three-dimensional or at least confusing enough to not be lumped in with a bunch of women who are not really musicians. But if you do that, I think they disappear you; they really cannot market three-dimensional women. That's where the confusion comes from, the fact that famous women are supposed to be one-dimensional. Whether it's art poet or bimbo or jock, they have to be easily understood. That could go for men too, but I think we're used to seeing men more. They're everywhere and

KRISTIN HERSH

they talk more, we've heard a lot of things from them. They don't confuse us as easily as women. People like Exene Cervenka [singer with X] and Mary Margaret O'Hara should have been the role models for all young women as far as music goes, but they were disappeared and so people, at least young girls, don't really know who they are. Which is odd, because they're just real. Which is what's confusing about them.

Ever since I've started making records, every time I talk to the press they ask, 'So what do you think about this new women-in-rock thing?' That's when I slap 'em. It's not new. When women shout, they end up making it – when they're angry, serious or depressed. Which is really offensive; it cheats the music. We let men roll around and writhe and scream and yell, and go all post-feminist quiet, and say that they're in the throes of rock 'n' roll ecstasy. Meanwhile, women are pissed off and depressed. It's like saying that all women suffer from PMS. I don't know how to tell them that in real people humour is everywhere and happiness is everywhere – that's what music is. But I'm not going to say that love has a punchline or that my happy feelings are goofy. They're not, they're *high*, and they deserve a gravity of expression – that is the only way to serve them.

I'm not gonna change my music 'cause people are confused. I have thought about not including songs on records for that reason. Like 'The Letter' on *Hips and Makers* – I thought it was too confusing for people to hear something that harsh. It's not even a very good song. It's honest, it never lies. So it's worthwhile as a piece, it's true expression. But I don't really believe in expressing yourself in music, I believe that music has too much to say. When you're that low you can't write a real song, you're too self-involved, so it's a real piece but not a great song. I thought people would hear me as tortured if I included 'The Letter'. The title song of the album came along and said you're supposed to take a ride up and down, over here and over there, and if you don't take it, it'll take you, which is all right. That's what we're here for, to ride the waves; you don't see how high the highs are if you don't go down to the limit.

I won't perform 'The Letter' live 'cause it makes me puke and I don't even want to hear it. If they play the record in the store I leave by the time 'The Letter' comes on, but I don't want to change the piece: the record wrote itself and it's not my right to step in and second-guess other people's reactions. I just sit in front of them and say, 'There's humour and joy all over everything. Stop not seeing it.'

I tried to figure out why it was OK to publish songs on *Hips and Makers* which were about *me*, because I'd never done that before. It felt like the songs were very, very external and very, very internal. They just bypassed my personality entirely, they were Kristin's photo album. That's why I just wanted it for me and Billy. That's why I didn't want anybody to release it, but they seemed so pretty anyway. The songs didn't seem to have suffered for my pictures being on them. I couldn't figure out what the balance was. I thought, 'I'm old and I suck. All I do is talk about myself, like fucking Rod Stewart.' Then I thought – these are my life pictures, but why wouldn't they be anybody else's? It's evident that I have a dorky little life and so does everybody else, so they can relate to it. But they also have certain chemicals that my biochemistry has to match, or I don't qualify as their singer.

Sometimes my songs feel like drugs, they feel like injections. Depending on the song, sometimes they're like adrenalin, sometimes they make my bones shake, sometimes they're like a sedative. It's like hypos shooting different colours into my bloodstream. That's exactly what it feels like. And if my life experience hasn't given me the right chemicals, I can't sing those songs. I don't know how to bring it out of my own biochemistry. They used to all come from my left shin; I didn't realise it until people started taking footage of the Muses on stage and panning down to my foot. My foot would get all sweaty and twist up and shake and twitch and keep time, but really maniacally, and the rest of me would be stock still. All the chemicals were stuck in my foot and it's the only part of my body that's ever been seriously injured. My foot was cut off in a car accident, smashed under my leg, and I had to pick it up and put it back on. All these pieces keep falling off everywhere! It was a bad accident, my face was just like meat, it wasn't there any more. I was in a wheelchair for a long time. My foot had simply busted off; and it's the only place where all these chemicals would come from. It's extra strong now, because of the healing. If you touch my foot I feel it up on my shin.

I was on tour and I hadn't seen Ryder for two months and I watched this video . . . I was completely emotionally unprepared for this

213

slo-mo shot of him running to me, his hair blowing in the wind. I burst into tears. I talked to him on the phone that night and he said, 'Hi Mom, how y'doin'?' I told him, 'Well I saw that movie of you and it made me sad and I miss you so much that I cried, but I'm OK now 'cause I'm talking to you.' He yelled, 'BIG FAT DOG BUTT!' It's his favourite joke, the funniest thing he could ever say. I just burst out laughing, and he asked, 'Did I make you laugh? You're sad and then you're happy, you're sad and then you're happy!' Zen baby!

We try and talk every day, but sometimes it's very expensive to call, and if he doesn't feel like talking, Billy and I get all depressed. And if he does, the bill goes up and up. I don't talk to Dylan as much because I have to call his father's family. It's OK, but it's harder to do. I send him postcards. I've sent him postcards ever since he was three and he stopped coming on tour with me, but there's only so much you can write on a postcard to someone who doesn't read. I have to draw a different picture every day: salt shakers, spoons . . . he's collected them all. My stepfather sent me a picture of Dylan holding this huge stack of postcards I'd sent from LA and he was making everyone read them all. He's a really smart little boy, a freak of a kid; I don't know what the other kids think of him, the poor thing. He's beautiful, he looks like Bambi, but he has this weird look on his face all the time. I guess it's a mad scientist look.

Whatever's going on on Planet Dylan is his deal, it's what he's looking at. You can look at him and go: 'Dylan. Dylan! *Dylan*!' and sometimes he's just not there. He's not in the outside world. Him and Ryder were sitting having breakfast a couple of weeks ago, giving that kid-talk thing that's really hard to follow and I realised that Ryder was yelling 'Big Fat Dog Butt!' and Dylan was going, 'My brain is a television and it's flicking through the channels.' It's like, remind me never to listen to what they're saying again. The other day, Ryder said he had music in his head. I looked straight at Bill – it was like getting slugged in the stomach. He said it a few more times, but he was just amused. I wanted to slap him: 'No! Dirty! Bad!'

I'm missing my boys growing up. Soon that's going to be over and I'll have spent my time on the road. Right now I'm working a little too hard and growing a little too old to go without food and sleep for months at a time. So I'm trying to work a real life in. I have no great plans for the future. But my career in music is not something I'll ever quit; I love being a housewife, but I'm not a very good one. My kids are more important than the music *business*, so I might quit the *business* for them. But music is my religion, I guess, that's where it can shove me down hard and lift me up high. It's the closest I come to religion, so it serves the kids as much as they serve it.

I've spent a lot of time with my kids – more time than most nine-to-five working mothers have – but it's short bursts of intense time. When a record does really well and you have to be gone months and months . . . Because I don't have custody of Dylan, I don't have the option of taking him out for more than a week with me, so I have to find a way to work it – it's hard to know if I'll ever get custody of him again. People still don't have a good attitude towards working mothers, they think it makes you less of a mother. Even when I feed and clothe Dylan with the money I make, it is not being a good mother as far as the authorities are concerned. And for that job, to be working in a rock band is a hundred times worse. That, and the legal fees alone, in addition to all the child support I already pay – I don't see how it could be possible to regain custody. He can testify in court when he's nine, but I don't think I would ever do that to him. I know how awful court is.

It's OK when I'm at home, I get to see him three nights and four days a week. It's just that I'm rarely home. He's cool about it. He's actually proud of me now. For the first time this year he got really embarrassed, which I thought was great! I thought: 'Well, I'm a real mom now, I embarrass my son!' I caught him taking one of my CDs to school with him. He said, 'You have a lot of these, can I have one?' He slipped it into his coat and he took it to school, so that when I came to pick him up all the kids asked, 'Are you Dylan's mom? Are you the one on the CD?' And he's trying to sneak the CD into his jacket again.

One of the kids' fathers is in jail and Dylan said, 'I don't know what he did but he lives in jail.' So I told him: 'Some parents are in jail, it's very sad but . . .' He interrupted: 'I know somebody's dad who works on brains, he fixes brains for his job.' I thought he was just making stuff up. 'You mean he's a doctor?' 'Yeah, he's a brain doctor.' Dylan had this cartoon image of a hammer and chisel and a brain . . . I said, 'Parents do lots of different jobs, everybody does

KRISTIN HERSH

something so we can make money to feed our kids.' 'Yeah, but nobody but me has a mom who's a rock star.' The most time we spend together is in the car. When I'm home, I put both boys in the back seat of the car and just run errands for hours. Because they're stoned by the car, they just get on and start talking; that's the time when I get to hear what's really in their brains. They had a big argument over whether or not I was 'spicy'. Ryder asked, 'Do you think Mom's spicy?' Dylan retorted, 'People can't be spicy.' 'But Mom's spicy.' 'No she's not!' 'Yes she is!' Eventually Billy just said, 'Don't say your mother is spicy!' Everybody on the last tour called me 'Miss Spicy'. My band members used to call me 'Miss Sporty' 'cause I used to wake up very early in the morning and just disappear. I used to swim a couple of miles a day and I had lipstick that was called 'Miss Sporty . . . Now they call me 'Miss Spicy' instead.

Liz Phair

liz phair

> I met him at a party, and he told me how to
> drive him home
> He said he liked to do it backwards and I said
> that's just fine with me
> That way we can fuck and watch TV.
>
> ('Chopsticks' from *Whip-Smart*)

<T>alking about Liz Phair's first album, *Exile in Guyville*, the
Raincoats' Gina Birch recently gushed:

> All those bloody records I'd listened to for years and years with
> the boys – The Rolling Stones' *Exile on Main Street* and Bob
> Dylan's 'Lay Lady Lay' – I was having a good time, but I always
> wondered where I fitted into it as a woman. Suddenly, four or
> five tracks into *Exile in Guyville*, I knew Liz Phair's songs were
> on my side, that they were twisted to my viewpoint, my advan-
> tage. Lots of women have written like that, but to me it had the
> edge.

1993's *Exile in Guyville* is a song-by-song response to the Stones'
1972 album and a wry take on the world of boy rock. With lyrics
like 'I wanna fuck you like a dog . . . I wanna be your blow job
queen' (on 'Flower') and track titles ranging from 'Fuck and Run' to
'Girls! Girls! Girls!', Liz presented herself as a sassy songwriter going
some way to challenge and subvert women's traditionally submissive sexual roles in music. The album, filled with bold folk melodies,

won widespread critical acclaim in the US – although it sold only 20,000 copies on indie label Matador in the US, it was voted album of the year by *Village Voice* and *Spin*, while *Rolling Stone* named Phair best, new female artist.

Because of her sexually uncompromising lyrics and don't-fuck-with-me attitude, Liz has been called the 'indie Madonna' by more than one American journalist. The label doesn't irritate so much as it bemuses her and although she's been quoted as saying 'I hope I can handle myself better than she does', Liz told *Details* that 'Madonna kicked a huge rough-hewn patch through the jungle and we're all tiptoeing behind her saying: "Look at all the pretty flowers." Madonna made it possible for me to be interpreted properly.' In Ms Ciccone's wake, Liz talks ruthlessly about wanting to exploit herself better than anyone else could and is not afraid to admit that she has 'just bought a manager'.

She has been slammed for such an approach – taking on an aggressive male persona – and for her direct sexuality. A white female folk-rock singer writing sexually overt lyrics has elicited responses similar to Madonna's dalliance with the virgin/whore imagery – including 'a sex-kitten sell-out' and 'whorish ball-buster psychobitch'. American feminist rock critic Ann Powers takes a more positive view:

There's something unprecedented about what women like Liz Phair or Polly Harvey are doing. In the early 70s, even with singers like Joni Mitchell, it was more about having a romantic vision that was saying 'I want to be independent' but not necessarily 'I am oppressed'. It's hard to imagine a song like 'Fuck and Run', with its blatant message, appearing at any earlier time and being accepted.

Liz is hardly 'oppressed' – she was born in Cincinnati, moved with her parents and brother to an affluent Chicago suburb in 1976, and later majored in visual art at the liberal Oberlin college – but she rails against role-playing and sexism. At the start of 1991 a friend convinced her to record some of the songs she had been secretly writing. Under the moniker Girly Sound she made a tape using her voice and electric guitar, made a few copies and discovered that East

220

G R R R L S

Coast musicians and critics were duplicating the songs for each other. In spring 1992 Matador signed her and *Guyville* appeared the following year.

The likes of Chrissie Hynde and Winona Ryder declared themselves fans and Liz was (star) struck by paranoia. She could hardly bring herself to do live shows: a winter '93 London gig was chaotic and no testament to *Guyville*. Six months on and she was so bolshie on stage in New York that it was hard to believe she was ever self-conscious. When it came to making album number two though, the paranoia returned until exile in recording studios in the Bahamas stoked up her creativity. Between swimming and rum-drinking sessions, *Whip-Smart* came together. The themes are familiar – sex, love, relationships, emancipation and rock – and although it is as honest, cheeky and knowing as its predecessor, it is also a stronger, funkier and altogether more accessible album. 'Chopsticks' is slow and sultry compared to the tough pop rock of 'Super Nova', the title track addresses an imaginary son and boldly steals the chorus to Malcolm McLaren's 'Double Dutch' while 'Jealousy' wonders at her lover's past: 'I can't believe you had a life before me.'

Liz Phair is all about balancing the tension between freedom (to fuck and run) with her own take on feminism and her flirtations with image control – she considered but turned down *Playboy*, 'because there's no way to be subversive about it, even if I take the pictures'. As Liz Phair herself said in an interview in the September 1994 issue of *Harper's Bazaar*: 'When people were exclaiming over my album [*Guyville*], I thought, you've got to be kidding. If this was the greatest thing that ever happened to a female, where *is* everybody? It's like showing up at a party and wondering where everyone is who said they'd be there.'

I was always into rock, even when I was very little. I really liked the beat and the speed, the toughness. I picked up my first guitar in seventh grade – I'd been playing the piano for a long time. I was in various musical classes and there were always instruments around.

LIZ PHAIR

I felt like people were trying to expose me to lots of different creative outlets – so it wasn't weird to pick up a guitar. I don't think it really snapped into place and I hated reading music, but I could imitate my teacher because I had a great ear. My teachers would always let me get away with playing from memory instead of actually reading music.

I remember growing up and listening to a lot of Bob Dylan, Joni Mitchell, the Beatles, Peter and the Wolf, *Jesus Christ Superstar*. My parents were into a lot of different music, but this was just the stuff that I would actually waddle out and pay attention to. I was definitely excited by music at an early age. My mother used to sing me to sleep every night when I was very young; there was always a ritual where we'd be in bed and she'd sing cultural things like 'Down the Valley'. That must have clearly gotten into my subconscious. I'd sing along with her and I learned all these pretty classic structures, the 'little ditty'. I sung around when I went to camp and I was in a choir for a while.

When we were on car trips, we'd always be singing. It sounds like we were the Von Trapp family! We weren't . . . I am just scrunching it all together. I always felt like there was room for me in music; that was definitely where I felt at home. But you know what? I never really had that great 'I discovered this kind of music'. It was always there. My babysitters in Cincinnati used to give me all their old singles. I was listening to the Kinks when I was about five. My brother – who's two years older than me – had a huge collection of singles. He would get them all 'cause he had the record table. You know what's odd? I just realised that in junior high I would leave the radio on to get to sleep.

It was hard to go to shows from where we lived; it was too suburban. I never felt I was missing out, I didn't really care. It wasn't until I got to college that music was even something I wanted to do, and then I think it was more of a social direction. It was more like I wanted to be in that scene. I went from an extremely preppy conservative high school to a relatively radical, middle-class liberal, but very defiant, school. I became a rebel, but not in a really colourful way. I enjoyed being messy and obnoxious and sexual – at least superficially – because I guess my social life was split off from the rest of my friends from high school. Suddenly I found this new, more dramatic, more exciting social scene which was connected to music.

My first gig was just terrifying. I didn't throw up at all; I'm not a vomiter. For a week beforehand I went through every scenario in my mind. I could picture *everything*. I could picture humiliation and people talking about me afterwards. I could picture the whole audience just standing there judging . . . You know, when I watch a performance which is awkward, *I* cringe. I remember being little and going skating at the Ice-capades and someone would fall over. I'd be like: 'Oh God!' It would kill me. I projected this on to everyone watching my show. I imagined an audience to be so much more attentive than clearly they would ever be. They're wondering about the girl standing next to them, they're about to go get another beer, whatever. They may be watching, but it isn't that severe. Of course I was convinced otherwise. During my first gig I felt really awkward and my voice cracked a bunch of times, but I got through it. It was fine. It really wasn't the kind of thing where I thought: 'No way, never again. What a dumb idea!' Clearly, the ball got rolling.

Now I've had lots of practice. Doing it again and again and a-fucking-gain. And I don't even tour that much. I figured that I wouldn't be lousy at it if I could just get through the fright. You know what it is? I grew up being the manipulator. Being the person behind the camera. I grew up an academic; I was never, ever, a performer. I never did recitals, never acted in plays, even though everyone always said I should. I really hated the idea of having that kind of attention without being able to control it. To me, you're really naked on stage. Now that I've got some tools in my vocabulary to get me through, I can finally get into places that have space – mental space, where I can get above myself, my appearance and everyone's judgement of me. And simply be in the music. But I waited a good fucking year and a half for that. There was no watershed that broke me through. It was literally step by little step. I imagine it'll continue like that 'cause it isn't something that came naturally to me. It was real interesting to watch myself do it.

It's still weird seeing images of myself. I can see myself and I think it's kinda cute. 'Aw, there she is, all scared.' I've seen so many photos that nowadays I don't get that upset, I don't read into them so much. I see the pound of make-up and the clothes, I see the shot that they took and I see what they were trying to show me as. You know, *why* they took it from that angle. I still am so much behind the camera; my brain is still back there with the photographer and stylist. I'm not letting myself be totally in front, which is good, I guess, because a lot of people end up winging out into the world of cheese if they get too into being the one in front. The funny thing is, if I were styling myself, I would make myself just as sexy. I would exploit myself, only I think I'd do it better. What I find is most detrimental is the fact that they're trying to mould me into something but it's never what would have been the best mould for me. They're not looking at how I dress normally and trying to enhance or dramatise that, they're almost trying to shove me – to take a circle and shove it into a square. You can see where it's not fitting. I almost always see that in photographs.

I usually tend to analyse myself in terms of socio-economic and cultural upbringing. The kind of people that I may have tried to style myself after were never celebrities, it was always the beautiful prep. I just saw *Wolf* and the way Michelle Pfeiffer was styled was great. Or Audrey Hepburn. That sort of stylish chic. Yet . . . worldly. I thought about it every once in a while – every month or so. 'Damn, I got to get some rock 'n' roll clothes. I gotta get something like . . . silver!' But I don't have a face that looks prettier for having exotic clothes on. I tend to look better in something that's traditional and, at best, elegant. So it's funny, 'cause you have my music – which is kind of tough girl with the soft side – and it doesn't really mesh with my appearance. There's a resonant disparity between what I look like, where I come from and how I choose to express myself. I can't really change it.

There's *tons* I wouldn't do to sell my product. There's a shitload I wouldn't do to sell a record. I was recently talking about what the bad or awkward words are now. Which are a mark of where feminism is at. Lately, I came up with 'slut'. Who would you call a slut? Trying to get women to say that about other women is really hard just now. I was thinking about this 'cause I was in a hotel room in LA and I turned on the porno channel. I got really upset about this one woman's performance and I was calling her a 'slut, mumble, mumble'. And I was thinking: 'What does that mean? Why am I thinking that? What is it about her?' And I kept trying to explain it – my boyfriend and I got into long discussions.

It isn't really that I wouldn't use sex to sell a record, 'cause I would. My songs have sex in them so I would definitely include sex in the visuals. It's subtle and possibly a funny distinction to the mainstream, but I think how your sexuality is used is really important. It can be worlds apart within one category. There's a certain type of portrayal using my sexuality which I would never, ever do. I toyed with the idea of doing *Playboy* because everyone does. I thought: 'Can I really be subversive in the ultimate men's magazine?' And you really can't. It's that desire to show that you vote *for* sex and yet *against* sexism. How do you get away with this kind of thing?

I had a whole bunch of times with *Whip-Smart* where I was trying to keep control. 'Cause I didn't really want to share my emotions any more. Every time I tried to write a song, I found the discipline was no longer my outlet; it was a product that I knew was going to end up being used in some way and it really fucked up my songwriting for a while. I kept coming up with catchy chord progressions which I really didn't want to share. It's so ironic. I call my mom every once in a while, and she'll be like: 'Honey, you're a private person.' That is what's going wrong here. As much as I feel like an exhibitionist – I like to make a bold statement when I make one – I only like to make it when *I* want to, under controlled circumstances. All of a sudden I didn't have the time to be monitoring that and I didn't have the leisure to mull over what I did want to say.

I haven't listened to *Exile in Guyville* in eighteen months. I don't tend to go back and analyse too hard. But I do think I set up a paradigm, I set up a structure around myself that I found really hard to work within once it had been set up. I found myself working within limitations. It's tough for anyone who goes from anonymity to being watched. The songs' expressions were so intimate, it was almost ironic to go public. In my case, the private/public is so extreme – as was the difference between the kind of intimacy I

LIZ PHAIR

foster on *Guyville* and the kind of publicity it generated. I was totally surprised at the response. Wasn't everybody? This has become my little soundbite, but I thought about 1,300 people would listen to it and I'd sell about 1,300 copies – which was exciting, 'cause in the indie market that gives them a reason to re-press. And I needed it to be heard by people that were within a mile radius of my apartment. That was what I was picturing. I freaked out when I found out that people like Chrissie Hynde liked it.

Writing the follow up to *Guyville* took longer as a result. I fell in love when *Guyville* was coming out and I've been with the same person, living with him for a year now, and we have a very close relationship. So all that longing and loneliness has changed, 'cause I've *never* been in love like this before. It's like what I hoped and pictured and yet, it's never exactly like what you picture. It's *better*. It's just so funny, it's really weird . . . This next album [*Whip-Smart*], you know what? I really like it now. I can honestly say: I think it rules. It went through a lot of stages of: 'Well, I don't think it's there . . .' Then we'd add a different song, change it a little bit; it took for ever to get the order 'cause the sequence wasn't right. I just went through it last night again, and it sounds great.

There's probably not the same intimacy as on *Guyville*, but there's just as much *me*. It's really, truly me. Instead of reaching out and longing, as I was on *Guyville*, I'm sharing – in a weird way. It's still very opinionated and there's a bunch of songs that are pretty poignant and personal. But at the same time, it's almost like I sound a little cured. I hope not at the expense of being mainstream. I don't think it is, because when I play it to people, they say, 'You know when you hear a Liz song.' To me, the difference between the two albums may be really huge, but to other people it's probably going to seem like a logical extension. I think I got the sophomoric slump or something, but we'll see.

I guess the lyrics are just as dissatisfied, but in a different way. But they're not so much: 'I'm needy!' They're more like: 'This is how I see it.' I'm standing up for myself on this one. I'm calling it as I see it. And I'm still musing back and forth; there's all that contradiction stuff that there was before, that's just my personality. I think there's a certain amount of strength and, I wouldn't say it's happy, but it's definitely more kinda . . . If *Guyville* felt like there was a big hole somebody needed to fill, then this one sounds like the hole got filled. Only I'm still complaining! That's the art of the songwriter: you always write about what isn't fixed in your day-to-day life. That's the forum for those parts of you that feel like: 'Hey, wait a minute . . .'

I wrote songs that are better than I could have written before, and I didn't use a ton of them. I found that I wrote a billion songs about me and the industry. Like: 'Oh it's so hard for me/Oh it's so tough . . .' No one wants to hear that sort of shit. That made it difficult, it made it gruelling to find enough songs. I think that the toughest thing about the sophomore album is to come up with fourteen more songs that are going to last over time.

In some of my new songs, I swapped a bunch of gender roles. In a weird way, I'm refuting the traditional love object. My lyrics tend to be putting myself back and forth from female to male shoes. In 'Whip-Smart', the song begins: 'I'm going to lock my son up in a tower till I write my life story on the back of his big, brown eyes.' And in the second verse: 'I'm going to lock my son up in a tower till he learns to let his hair down far enough to climb outside.' There you've got a locked-in Rapunzel and it's all over jealousy. I take on the man's role, see it through his eyes: 'I can't believe you had a life before me, I can't believe they let you run around free, just putting your body wherever it seemed like a good idea.' In 'X-Ray Man', I'm calling the man a girl: 'As far as I know, baby/As far as I know, Funky lady.' And literally, in the last song, I call him 'May Queen' and I treat him like he's an attention-grabbing, sexually manipulating woman. It's all over the place and I don't know what it is, but it's almost like it transcends gender roles.

When Juliana Hatfield says women aren't biologically equipped to play the guitar, I understand what she's saying and I think she's *wrong*. I'm the kind of person that tends to bring out things like that. I wouldn't say *that*, but I have said things like: 'There are biological differences between men and women which determine some behaviour.' I'm always willing to say something that sounds too overarching, too generalised to possibly be true. Just like I was talking about 'what is a slut?' because it's very telling. That's my college education coming out there, the provocative statement which we all have to acknowledge the truth of it – but at the same time you *know* it can't be true. I think it's really neat Juliana Hatfield said that because she's gonna get pounded for it – she should get pounded for it – but clearly she can take it if she said it.

In a certain way, why don't women do guitar solos? I know everyone wanted me to do a solo on *Whip-Smart* and I didn't do one. It was going to be this big thing: 'And this will be her first solo!' I said: 'Nah . . .' 'cause it isn't in my stomach to do a solo. But then again you've got Lousie Post in Veruca Salt who's pulling a solo every single song. So it can be done, clearly. I have just always been attracted to the sing-song melody because, like I said, we grew up with camp songs. With mom songs and Girl Scout songs and car trip songs, fire songs . . . And think about all the women that are on the radio, what are they doing? Ballads.

I totally agree with the idea that women don't *have* to be guitar performers. I think we're all exploring our gender differences 'cause suddenly they're thrown up in front of us in a way they never really were before. I think it's really cool. I got really upset about a movie we were watching the other night and then I got even more upset because my boyfriend didn't invalidate it and his 15-year-old son is sitting there. It was some dumb fucking sci-fi thing – this life force where a woman travels naked throughout the film, kissing men and sucking the life out of them. And I'm like: 'Aagh!' These idiotic stereotypes should hopefully be replaced by discussions about things like whether girls can play guitar solos or not. I much prefer to get everyone's hair raised by talking about what women can and can't do in terms of what they are actually *doing*. I feel that now I've got a lot more room to be doing things that people can then analyse – instead of having things done to us that *we* have to analyse.

Being a female musician gets easier year to year and then it falls back for a while. I think everything in life is like that – your health is like that, weather is like that and I think it shouldn't ever be taken for granted. I know every woman in the world has those days where they just sit and shudder because they know power can be taken away. If it can be taken away from a country, it can be taken away from a gender, and I think it's really important never to take it for granted. Never to get numb to it, never to get blasé and think: 'Well, hell – we've got money . . .' There's so many things left to be done and America's so far ahead of so many countries. In a weird way it's really creepy.

I get frustrated with the way male journalists treat me . . . not daily, but weekly. I don't spend so much time now trying to find out whether it's because I'm a woman or it's because I'm a person with certain strengths and weaknesses. Or it's because I'm a commodity to their business. I am always aware of power and the interplay between those that have it and those that have less. As a woman, people still get away with stuff on me that I don't even know they are getting away with – they wouldn't treat a male band this way. But I wouldn't really know; I've never been a guy in rock 'n' roll. I do know when I smell condescension and that's what pisses me off.

I tend to surround myself with a better world than the average, just by whom I associate with. Whether it's my record label, my band mates, my booking agent, or my new manager – I try to pick people that I just sense will treat me with a certain amount of respect and equality. I pick people to be friends with, people who can greet me as who I am as a person rather than as a woman. It doesn't always work, but that's what I try to do. So I don't think in any way, shape or form, I'm living in the average slice of America any more. I think one of the biggest privileges of being singled out like this has given me the ability to do that – to isolate myself in a type of human environment. Reading badly put together interviews drives me *crazy*. Drives me utterly crazy. It's such a drag to be manipulated into this personality that comes across on the page. It's retarded: it's guy-retarded. And it's so clearly people who are unwilling to allow my overactive will to cohabit with my feminine, almost girlish, demeanour. They just see one or the other – they either want the doe or they want the lion. Not even a lion . . . let's say the rhino. That pisses me off, I really hate when my personality's so tightly boxed.

To me, feminism means that I believe in women, in their potential, their words and their value. And I am disgusted by people that don't share my opinion. In that sense, feminism is, to me, the 'of course' clause. 'Should we be paid the same amount?' 'Of course.' 'Should we have control over our bodies?' 'Of course.' To me, it's shockingly logical. Last year, I was asking people whether they think women could be geniuses which, to me is, 'Of course!' I have met them many times! And you would be so surprised how many men who run in the indie music circle, who run around with women who are clearly in control of their lives, literally do not believe that women can be geniuses. They think it's the province of men. They think it's literally a type of brain that men possess. Maybe, one in a million women comes along who actually has these capabilities, but clearly is very male-like.

Sometimes, I get a shuddering . . . Sometimes I get downright frightened by the fact that I'm walking around taking it all for granted – 'Yes, I can do this. Yes, I can do that' – when there's so little precedent to say that I can. I think that people who break ground don't think about it, they just go do it. It's like the warrior mentality, which we still need to possess. Isn't that funny? The results of some study showed that most women who achieve on par financially and in corporate status with men were tomboys. That women would have to be, still today, half-male to be able to achieve. It's so telling. It's so grotesque.

I think this fear of feminists comes from the fact that a lot of women are in love with the image of women, and to some extent that is created by traditional views. Delicacy or guile, whatever . . . I figure that the more women are up and out there, the more it will naturally diversify. Right now, the main aim is to get women everywhere in relatively equal percentages. Certainly I believe – 'cause I believe biology matters – that areas will equate to one gender or another. Men may prefer one thing because of their inclinations and women may prefer another. But if we can see, as a culture, that these things shift and flux and that men and women can participate in the world equally – then GNP [gross national product] would be a product of both genders.

I think we're at a very early stage of women's liberation – we're talking *maybe* a century of some kind of enlightenment. Women will naturally gravitate towards certain things and become relied upon in society for things other than domestic. Because life is cyclical, the struggle is, in a weird way, ongoing. The best thing you can do is to literally do *something*. Be *visible* doing something. And if you have to be a tomboy at this point, maybe in fifty years' time you won't. I don't think we're going to get it like we want it for a long time. It's the *worst* fucking feeling when you think everything's going OK and suddenly you realise it's not. Nothing makes me burst spontaneously into tears like that sudden feeling that I'm a woman and this is a man's world. That scares the living shit outta me.

Sometimes there are drunken guys at my shows – what do they think they're doing there? That's the thing I said about isolating myself. They're such an anomaly to me. I occasionally run into them in a bar and I think: 'What fucking stone did you crawl out of?' The arrogance to fucking take up my stage time with their bullshit. I remember once in Manchester – that was the grossest. Totally being harassed backstage by the band that played before me – really evil, ugly stuff. Like, do I pay my band mates with sex? There were about thirty-five of them sitting backstage, all of them hostile as shit – trying to see if they could make me cry, run, whatever. I don't know if they're just dumb, and they think that this is how bands behave at shows – maybe they go to lots of other kinds of rock shows where the dudes are all drunk and that's what you do. It's really hard to know what the hell that is.

I usually try and hear a couple of them out – in the same way you respond to men on the street. You try and field one comment to see if you can quiet them by acknowledging them. 'Cause sometimes, if you don't say anything and clearly they know you can hear them, they get way louder. They start shrieking and they get a little more hostile – it's almost like terrorism defusion, trying to defuse the situation before it gets really bad. I try and hear a couple of things and maybe I can snap back at them in a witty manner. Then they just start yelling again, so I really ignore them and try and do my job. My big fear is having things thrown at me on stage – when it starts getting physical. I've seen that a couple of times and heard about it a bunch. That's a nightmare. In some ways, by behaving in that aggressive manner they're getting what they want – they're getting my attention and they're making me uneasy. That, I resent. Strongly.

I'm sort of misanthropic and I believe that crowds turn violent and ugly and bring out the worst in people. I do not like being on stage in front of a huge amount of people. I'm always aware of the

231

LIZ PHAIR

potential for things to get out of hand. I think it *is* a guy-to-girl thing. They don't throw that bullshit at men. I think partially they feel uncomfortable standing in front of their little 'schoolteacher'. If there's a female teacher, they want to see if they can make her cry. I feel that these are the guys who only know about a few words from a song – 'I wanna be your blow-job queen' – because it was mentioned in some article they saw. I don't think they have the album, any of those guys. But they paid to get in, ha ha!

I'm a wife and mother in my daily life. I live with my boyfriend and his 15-year-old son. I've probably never been more girlie. Yet at the same time here in my music I'm writing these lyrics. It kind of amused me, it was really neat that there was this bizarre theme. My boyfriend doesn't listen to lyrics that much, although he fixed part of the order. He's a musician too. He really likes *Whip-Smart*, but we don't talk about each other's work. In a weird way, we leave it separate. Some of the songs are older than our relationship, some of them are just about people – I can write retroactively or just imaginatively. Some of them are about him, but he doesn't tend to analyse my lyrics simply because he realises it wouldn't be a wise idea. And I don't analyse his work, although it's not the same thing. Our relationship's separate; the rock thing doesn't really encroach. When he goes to a show, he's always just shocked and weirded out.

Do I have groupies? Not those who want after-show sex. They don't do *that*! They blush and they shake and they say, 'Your album's just the most amazing thing! Thank you Liz, for making it.' They freak out. You just want to remind them that you could have been in Social Studies with them! This could be *you*! You could be up here! And I could be there. Most of the time I think I get relatively respectful groupies.

There's a boy/girl balance, honest to God. People always ask me this, but I'm not lying. The girls tend to freak out while the boys are a little more sheepish and they're not all dweebs – some of them are very good-looking, thank you. I'm pretty happy with my audience as it stands right now. That's something that I'd have to worry about – if you look at the audience and you don't like the people you see, there's something wrong. This record could totally blow that theory to hell but thus far, people have been pretty cool. They're recognisable to me as people I could hang out with. Younger, but they seem really nice – all excited and freaked out – but they don't do anything. Occasionally, there's a real fucked-up guy, drunk or something, who's a little scary, but that doesn't happen so often.

I get tons of letters, but they usually go to Matador [the record company] or my parents' house – they keep bringing me balefuls and I just put 'em in a closet. I don't even write to my grandmother. That's my failing. There's many people close to me that are waiting for me to become a decent correspondent. Generally speaking my fans are really cool. There's nothing weird about my career. And anyway, I told Matador to watch out for repeat writers that might be psychotic.

Bibliography

Books

Amburn, Ellis, *Pearl: The Obsessions and Passions of Janis Joplin*, Warner Books, 1994

Des Barres, Pamela, *I'm with the Band: Confessions of a Groupie*, Jove, 1988

Faludi, Susan, *Backlash: The Undeclared War Against Women*, Vintage, 1992

Gaar, Gillian G., *She's a Rebel: The History of Women in Rock & Roll*, Blandford, 1992

hooks, bell, *Black Looks: Race and Representation*, Turnaround, 1992

Landau, Deborah, *Janis Joplin: Her Life and Times*, Paperback Library, 1971

Leonard, Linda Schierse, *Meeting the Madwoman*, Bantam Books, 1994

Paglia, Camille, *Sex, Art and American Culture*, Penguin, 1992

Palmer, Myles, *Small Talk, Big Names: 40 Years of Rock Quotes*, Mainstream Publishing, 1993

Roberts, Chris, *Idle Worship*, HarperCollins, 1994

Stewart, Sue & Garratt, Sheryl, *Signed, Sealed, & Delivered*, Serpent's Tail, 1994

Wolf, Naomi, *The Beauty Myth*, Chatto & Windus, 1990

Magazines, newspapers and fanzines

The FACE; the *Guardian*; *i-D*; *Leeds & Bradford Riot Grrrls*; *Melody Maker*; *New Musical Express* (*NME*); *New York Times*; *Select*; *SKY Magazine*; *The Sunday Times*; *Vox*; *Q*.